# THE MINNESOTA LIBRARY ON STUDENT PERSONNEL WORK

## EDITED BY E. G. WILLIAMSON

---

1.* *Trends in Student Personnel Work*, edited by E. G. Williamson

2.* *Student Counseling in Japan: A Two-Nation Project in Higher Education*, by Wesley P. Lloyd

3.* *After High School — What?* by Ralph F. Berdie, Wilbur L. Layton, and Ben Willerman

4.* *Vocational Interests Eighteen Years after College*, by Edward K. Strong, Jr.

5.* *Vocational Interest Measurement: Theory and Practice*, by John G. Darley and Theda Hagenah (out of print)

6.* *Origins of Personnel Services in American Higher Education*, by Eugenie Andruss Leonard

7. *Toward a Philosophy of Organized Student Activities*, by Herbert Stroup

8. *The Outcomes of Counseling and Psychotherapy: Theory and Research*, by Theodore Volsky, Jr., Thomas M. Magoon, Warren T. Norman, and Donald P. Hoyt

* Published before titles were assigned numbers.

# THE OUTCOMES OF COUNSELING AND PSYCHOTHERAPY

*Theory and Research*

THEODORE VOLSKY, Jr., THOMAS M. MAGOON
WARREN T. NORMAN, DONALD P. HOYT

*UNIVERSITY OF MINNESOTA PRESS, MINNEAPOLIS*

*Library of Congress Catalog Number: 65-63028*

# *Foreword*

---

How does my counseling or casework influence my counselees and clients?" This persistent question is asked by every thoughtful counselor and caseworker every time he rationally plans his procedures and whenever he attempts to justify his role in society. Psychologists, psychiatrists, and social workers, along with their clients and patients, assume that counseling and casework affect future behavior. The community insofar as it supports these professions accepts this assumption. The crucial questions remain, however. How is future behavior affected? What changes result from discussions and how great are these changes? To what extent do previous experiences of the person and his current status influence the outcomes of these conversations? Most importantly, what does a psychologist, psychiatrist, or social worker *do* that determines the outcome of his efforts?

This volume deals with these questions and is primarily concerned with the effort to learn about changes that occur in an individual's behavior during, and resulting from, counseling interviews with professionally trained psychologists.

The evaluation of counseling has been of concern at the University of Minnesota since the establishment of the University Testing Bureau on October 26, 1932. Six months after the establishment of the bureau Dr. E. G. Williamson, its first director, wrote in a letter to President L. D. Coffman:

There are several ways of validating the services which the Bureau is rendering. In the first place, there is the technical validation of the instrument.

v

On this point the Bureau has been particular to select only those tests which are as reliable and valid as can be had. Another way of validating these services is by the method of indirect evidence, as for instance, in case histories, or again in the number of students who, having once been tested and interviewed, returned to the Bureau for additional help on new problems. In the neighborhood of one-third of the cases already tested have come back for further advice. Again, the number of referrals to the Bureau, particularly if these referrals show a definite and systematic increment, should indicate the degree of validation consonant with such increase. Previous reports have shown that such increases have taken place and in a measure beyond even our most sanguine anticipation. It may be pointed out, moreover, that colleges and agencies not heretofore interested in using the Bureau's services are now referring cases in increasing numbers, e.g. Home Economics, Colleges of Education, Chemistry, and Engineering, the Graduate School, probation advisers and high school principals and counselors. These last have committed themselves favorably on the point that such services as the Bureau offers are most helpful in bridging the gap between high school and the University. Further methods of validation involve much time and a larger staff, namely to set up a critical experiment involving the use of controlled cases in counseling by the Bureau and, after a year or two, to make an exhaustive analysis of the total adjustment of both groups to problems of vocational orientation and scholastic achievement. Such an investigation is being formulated and will be presented later.

Since the early days of counseling at Minnesota, many studies have attempted to determine the effectiveness of counseling, in a research program that has extended over thirty years. The initiators of these efforts were Dean J. B. Johnston, Professor Donald G. Paterson, Dean E. G. Williamson, Professor John G. Darley, and Professor Edward Bordin. These persons, with the help of many graduate students and assistants, have formulated the need for counseling evaluation, developed evaluation methods, and applied methods of research in psychology and the social sciences to this problem. The authors of the present report have added recent thoughts about the rationale and philosophy of science, current methods of statistics and experimental design, and applications of contemporary counseling theory and practices. The viability of the research program is demonstrated by the continuing research and developments that have occurred even since the manuscript for the report presented here was prepared in its final form.

When work on the project reported in this volume began, a decade ago, we recognized that effective assessment must be based firmly on a sound theoretical foundation. Theories of counseling, personality, and psychotherapy were available, but none of these led directly to a research program such as we had in mind. The first steps in the program were the development of a theoretical structure that would lead directly to hypotheses that could be tested and the discovery of means for testing these hypotheses.

The ideas on which the research is based can be ascribed to no one person or small group, for almost all of these ideas have been entertained for many years by persons in many different professions. Many of the ideas have been published in books and articles; many have been discussed by counselors and others at professional meetings, staff conferences, and in the course of daily work. The synthesis of these ideas, however, into the theoretical structure which governed the research was mainly the joint product of two of the principal investigators, Dr. Donald Hoyt and Dr. Thomas Magoon. Although they will be among the first to admit the debt they owe to their fellow counselors, to them certainly belongs the credit for defining testable concepts of counseling effectiveness.

After these concepts were evolved and it was agreed that counselors could reasonably hope that their efforts resulted in increased ability to solve personal problems, decreased anxiety, and decreased defensiveness on the part of their counselees, it was possible to search for means of assessing these behavioral changes and, when such means were not available, to develop appropriate instruments. The imagination of the investigators in developing new instruments and adapting previously existing instruments is to be commended. As far as I know no other systematic and comprehensive attempt to assess the outcomes of counseling has made use almost exclusively of instruments optimally designed to measure the hoped-for effects. The imagination and energy needed to develop these instruments is truly impressive.

The experiment reported in Chapter 8 is unique. It tests hypotheses derived from careful analysis of counseling and casework. It makes use of instruments explicitly designed for this purpose. It is an efficient and, to use a term included in the report, an elegant experiment design that leaves little to be criticized by either the laboratory scientist or the expert statistician. The experiment is the only one in counseling and casework that makes use of a control group beyond reproach. Relevant concepts, careful measurement, and skillful use of randomization are perhaps the three most appropriate phrases to use in describing the program.

When one reads the results of the experiment and finds that the systematic behavioral changes proposed in the main hypotheses cannot be observed, that test and retest differences were not statistically significant, one might well be tempted to ask whether the project itself was worthwhile.

There is but one answer. Never before have we had such a strong indication that the evaluation of counseling is an extremely difficult and complex matter. If basic behavioral changes do result from counseling, and the results of the follow-up study reported in Chapter 9 indicate they do, these changes are likely to be detected only by instruments much more precise than those we now have and designed for the purpose of detecting subtle changes.

The results reported in Chapters 8 and 9 raise another, equally important question. When psychologists, psychiatrists, and social workers have relatively brief contacts with people, averaging three or four one-hour interviews, are they justified in assuming that their counseling does more than help the person solve his *immediate* problems? Perhaps counseling helps a person solve a problem that is blocking efficient behavior and making him unable to develop skills and habits conducive to adjustment or productivity. The counselor may help his client free himself of these disabilities, and yet not alter basic personality patterns, directly change anxiety levels, or remove long-established defense mechanisms.

The results of the follow-up study bear on this question. The differential graduation rates reported in Chapter 9 are not only statistically but also socially and educationally significant. The study shows that counseling does have an effect, and it clarifies some of the problems of identifying the relevant mechanisms, while at the same time raising the question of the ultimate specificity or generality of counseling outcomes. Perhaps intensive psychotherapy may be found to have more generalized effects than student counseling. Perhaps the techniques of the social caseworker have different effects on behavior than the techniques of the counseling psychologist.

Because it raises such basic questions, this program of research, although conducted in a student counseling center by counseling psychologists, has equal relevance for all counselors, psychologists, psychiatrists, and social workers. Insofar as their general aims and purposes are similar to the ones defined here, they may also find the evaluative instruments useful. Workers in many fields should be interested in the ideas expressed here, the methods used, and the results obtained.

The testing instruments and scales, forms, and procedures developed by the authors in their study (and identified in the books as Schedule A, B, etc.) have been multilithed, and copies are available to interested readers from the Student Counseling Bureau, University of Minnesota.

Although many persons contributed directly or indirectly to this research program, the four authors should be given special acknowledgment. Dr. Magoon and Dr. Hoyt served as the two initial principal investigators. Their imaginations gave rise to the project, their initiative and persistence found a way to conduct the project, and their careful planning, perseverance, and professional competence saw the research through to near completion. Dr. Volsky, who worked with the project several years and who during the terminal stage served as principal investigator, carried on in admirable fashion when the first two investigators moved to other institutions. Throughout the middle years of the investigation Dr. Norman provided the knowledge of statistics and experimental design that was so needed, proving to be a tireless and excellent scientist. The final report was written by Dr. Volsky and Dr. Norman in careful consultation with the other authors.

Finally, all concerned with the project acknowledge a great debt to the Louis W. and Maud Hill Family Foundation and to Mr. A. A. Heckman, the Foundation's director, who has shown so much understanding of our effort. We hope sincerely that the results as presented here will at least in part serve as a reward for both the great material support and the sympathetic interest received from the Hill Family Fund.

RALPH F. BERDIE

*Director, Student Counseling Bureau*

*July 1, 1964*
*University of Minnesota*
*Minneapolis*

# Acknowledgments

O UR sincere gratitude is due to the University of Minnesota Student Counseling Bureau, Office of the Dean of Students, and to the Louis W. and Maud Hill Family Foundation for the encouragement and financial support received from the outset of the research project that forms the core of this book. Special thanks are due to E. G. Williamson, Dean of Students, and Ralph F. Berdie, Director of the Student Counseling Bureau, for their continued support and counsel; also to John G. Darley, C. Knight Aldrich, and Werner Boehm, who with Dr. Williamson and Dr. Berdie served as consultants for the research project; and to A. A. Heckman, Executive Director of the Hill Family Foundation for his personal interest and suggestions. In addition, we owe a great debt to all members of the Student Counseling Bureau staff who so willingly accepted a part of the burden in performing the research.

Special acknowledgment must be made of the work on the final manuscript done by Lorraine H. Volsky. She undertook to edit (and for some portions to rewrite substantially) the material prepared by each of the authors according to his own personal ideas of prose style. If the several chapters sound as if they belong in the same book, the credit goes to her not inconsiderable effort to that end.

The financial support of the Hill Family Foundation made it possible — the moral support and encouragement of those mentioned above and countless others made it imperative that this book see print.

# Table of Contents

# THE OUTCOMES OF COUNSELING
# AND PSYCHOTHERAPY

# 1

## Problems of Clinical Research

COUNSELING, casework, and psychotherapy occur in many forms and settings, with different clienteles and under the sponsorship of a wide variety of agencies. The specific objectives of such practice vary: the counselor's purpose may be to increase the client's information about himself or his environment, to produce insight into emotional conflicts, or to effect certain alterations in behavior. Nevertheless, explicitly or implicitly, the final goal of counseling is to bring about some attitudinal or behavioral change in the client.

Research efforts to date have provided relatively little unequivocal evidence about the efficiency of various counseling practices. This is not surprising in view of the complexities involved in behavioral research. Pepinsky, for example, cited several limitations on research designed to evaluate the effects of counseling, such as "(a) uncontrollable stimuli which impinge upon the client outside the counseling situation, (b) difficulty in establishing controls for the many possible factors in the counseling situation which may be related to changes in client behavior, and which may or may not be responsible for changes attributed to counseling, (c) lack of adequately tested, systematized knowledge requisite to setting up meaningful criteria of change, and (d) lack of adequate criterion measures." (Pepinsky, 1951, p. 329.)

Williamson and Bordin (1941), in their critique of counseling evaluation methodology, stressed the importance of specifying the criteria to be employed, and of recognizing the assumptions underlying them. They also pointed out that all too frequently impeding attitudes are present among counseling personnel. The most prominent of these attitudes are

3

based on belief that the effectiveness of counseling is self-evident, and that counseling is not accessible to evaluation because the process is so personal that evaluation would be disruptive. Frequently associated with this latter view are assertions that certain attitudinal and behavioral events are known to occur during, or as a result of, counseling, but are too intangible to be subjected to measurement. An excellent example of the effect of such attitudes on a well-designed counseling experiment is the study reported by Ashby, Ford, Guerney, and Guerney (1957), in which counselors refused to conform to the treatment techniques designated by the research design because of their precommitment to assumed effects of other treatment methods. Such attitudes have done little to increase the quality of counseling research.

Assessing the outcomes of counseling requires serious thought about just what the objectives of counseling are. Williamson and Bordin, as well as Travers, some time ago stressed the importance of specifying the outcomes, or goals, of counseling and operationally defining such concepts. Williamson and Bordin stated: "Counseling can be evaluated only if certain outcomes or criteria of effectiveness are assumed to result from the counseling process," and "these assumptions must be formulated as hypotheses to be 'tested' by experimental and statistical analyses." (Williamson and Bordin, 1941, p. 8.) Travers said that "adjustment is worthy enough as a goal of guidance but useless as a concept unless it is operationally defined in great detail." (Travers, 1949, p. 214.) More recently Dressel reiterated this point in his discussion of different approaches to research in counseling, stating: "It seems, then, that it is not particularly significant to study various phases of the therapeutic process or to compare processes until we have some reasonable hypotheses as to the results of therapy and are able to compare processes in terms of outcomes." (Dressel, 1953, p. 285.) Although many outcomes of the counseling process have been mentioned by different writers in the counseling field, they are usually not rigorously defined and often overlap in meaning.

Another difficulty observed in research on counseling outcomes has to do with the criteria and criterion measures employed. As Dressel has noted, "the more obvious aspects of counseling may actually have less significance than the subtle aspects which are difficult to isolate." (Dressel, 1953, p. 285.) Various psychological tests are readily available as criterion measures; so are grade records and client testimonials to the counseling service. A dangerous common practice has been to seek objectives for which there are readily available criterion measures (although they probably were not intended or constructed for this use). Such criteria may bear little relationship to the client's characteristic manner of feeling and behaving in his extra-clinical environment, which is, after all, the primary concern of the counseling psychologist. The client comes from and returns to this environment. He seeks assistance with regard to his adjustment in this environment. The counseling relationship is of brief duration in the life of the client, and changes brought about in his attitudes and actions are of questionable significance unless they extend beyond the confines of the counseling relationship.

A third factor inhibiting research on counseling outcomes stems from the generally vague formulations of counselors' interview behavior. Few experimental investigations have been able to shed any light on what counseling techniques (and conditions) will produce what types of results with what types of clients. The lack of clarity about counseling methods is probably a function of ambiguity about therapeutic objectives as well as of the complexities involved in attempting to order counselor behaviors in any meaningful way. Once the objectives of the counseling process have been identified and defined, it should then be possible to define, at least roughly, the therapeutic process associated with such objectives.

Thus, there is a lack of any comprehensive framework within which to judge the outcomes assumed to result from counseling. Still we are confronted with the assumption that a counseling experience produces changes along certain dimensions of client attitude and behavior. Our problem, then, may be stated as follows: (1) to define goals or outcomes of counseling operationally, and to determine to what extent such goals or outcomes are realized; (2) to develop, as measures of these goals, criterion instruments which will accurately assess clients' extra-clinical behavior; and (3) to define as clearly as possible the nature of the counseling process employed to achieve the defined objectives.

In the chapters ahead we will discuss these problems, both in a general review of methodological considerations in outcome research and in an analysis of an extensive research program, conducted in the Student Counseling Bureau at the University of Minnesota. This program committed itself to an examination of psychological interviews in terms of their outcomes or effects on subsequent client behavior rather than to the alternative approach of studying the counseling processes in which it is assumed that desirable results are being achieved.

The study to be described must be viewed as one segment of an ongoing effort in counseling and psychotherapy interview research. The most immediate experimental antecedents of the program were the experiences of three investigators as they attempted to glean from the literature, both speculative and experimental, a clearer picture of expected or assumed outcomes of the counseling process. There was from the start much doubt about how many hypothesized outcomes could be specifically defined. In a coordinated series of investigations, Hoyt (1954), Jesness (1955), and Magoon (1954) tried to define and measure such outcome concepts as problem-solving, acceptance of self and others, planfulness, defensiveness, and self-other-ideal discrepancies, which came from exponents of quite different theoretical orientations. These concepts were ambiguous, and existing instruments measuring such variables needed much more demonstrable validity before they could be used as outcome criterion measures. Furthermore, because of the diversity of sources, the outcome concepts seemed to be expressing similar ideas in quite different theoretical and semantic garb. In brief, the three investigators took such concepts as existed and set about, through a study with a control-group design, to determine the degree to which counseled individuals manifested changes on these variables.

The shortcomings of these investigations led two of the investigators to pursue further their interest in developing an ordered conceptual framework with hypothesized interrelationships of counseling outcomes. From the outset, they believed that a broad conceptualization of the counseling process would be equally appropriate for social work, counseling, and psychotherapy. The most direct means of developing such a framework appeared to be to identify their concepts in terms of the commonly held objectives of the counseling or therapeutic relationship. These objectives are frequently stated in implicit, rather than explicit, ways, as evidenced by the host of outcome or evaluation studies employing such criteria as rated improvement, changes in client satisfaction, changes in academic achievement, decrease in symptomatology or severity of problems, congruence of self-ideal and others' perceptions, self-understanding, and accuracy of prediction of one's future behavior. The reports on counseling and psychotherapy in the *Annual Review of Psychology* record these studies in faithful fashion. Many of these investigations will be reviewed in our discussion of methodology.

Several beliefs guided the approach to concepts, their measurement, and their application to the counseling process reflected in this book. One of these was that concepts of client change could be formulated best on the basis of operationally defined behavior. As a result, the investigators limited the variables they were to identify. They did not assume that defensiveness, for example, was being conceptualized or measured in all its meanings. Rather, the variable was defined in terms of certain commonly observable behavioral manifestations. The measurement of client status was in terms of selected behaviors which individuals in close and continuing contact with others would notice and associate with them. This approach was taken primarily because of interest in criterion behaviors external to the interview interactions of client and practitioner. Identifying what treatment effects should occur is certainly a basic point from which to consider questions regarding the kinds of clients, practitioners, techniques, and interactions associated with achievement of expected goals.

In similar fashion, therapeutic goals were viewed by the investigators as changes in client status over the course of the counseling experience. The term "success" as it has been used in evaluation is ambiguous; it implies a universal standard to be established. "Change," on the other hand, does not, although it is clearly linked to specified therapeutic objectives, and suggests eventually the directions in which changes should occur.

Many writers have expressed the view that therapeutic outcomes are far too multifaceted to be encompassed within a single index. We, the authors, agree, and consequently we have attempted to develop a multivariable framework within which client status and change may be viewed, interrelationships among the variables studied, and differential hypotheses advanced and tested. It remains a moot question whether the objectives of change in client status on the variables employed in the investigation we will describe are generalized sufficiently to be considered appropriate for all clients even when stated as directional changes rather than as some standard status.

Certainly a synthesis of the variously phrased statements of what the practitioner is attempting to accomplish with a client is not an easy task. One approach to such identification of treatment goals has been reported by Mensh and Watson (1950). To specify client characteristics which might be amenable to change or regarded as treatment goals, they condensed the list of nearly 18,000 trait names published by Allport and Odbert (1936) to 70. Groups of first-year and second-year residents in psychiatry and a group of experienced practicing psychiatrists then indicated the degree to which they believed treatment would bring about change on each of these characteristics and also identified the variables which appeared so significant to them as to constitute treatment goals. The authors found substantial agreement among all groups on characteristics expected to change, although there was less agreement about those characteristics in which change would constitute a desirable goal of treatment. Among the staff psychiatrists, however, there was at least 80 per cent agreement that the following characteristics should be regarded as the subjects of treatment goals: the states of being emotionally inhibited, discontented, passive, unassertive, melancholic, uncommunicative, insecure, discouraged, guilty, and indecisive. It would appear that focusing upon goal variables reduces the number of characteristics on which some common agreement may be reached. The data also indicate that a group of experienced therapists will hold more goals in common than will a less experienced group. It should be noted, however, that agreement on goals was still quite limited. Of course, specific trait labels represent rather limited, and possibly intractable, material on which to conceptualize therapeutic objectives.

The rapid developments in psychological science have led to the emergence of many new concepts as well as new definitions of old concepts. As a result, many terms have become ambiguous, and it is imperative that writers specify as exactly as possible the sense in which they use them. Maslow (1945) has suggested the need for subscripts as cues to clarify such meanings. Thus the identification and use of such concepts as manifest anxiety, defensiveness, and problem-solving have many limitations, particularly when one tries to extend them beyond operational definition of the measures used to estimate their magnitude. Each of these terms has been defined in many different ways by writers attempting to describe dispositional concepts that affect observable behavior, and it is doubtful that any two devices purporting to measure one of these concepts, such as anxiety, in reality estimate the same behavior. In the interest of minimizing confusion and ambiguity, it might have been wise to delimit our framework labels to numerical or alphabetical symbols. We did not do so, however, and the reader is therefore cautioned to use only the definitions specified when interpreting the experimental results reported.

Chapters 2 through 5 review general methodological topics related to outcome research in counseling and psychotherapy. This presentation is by no means complete. We selected topics whose importance was most often overlooked in previous counseling research, or which had received inadequate coverage in the current literature. Systematic theory formation, design, techniques in analysis, and some related technical and procedural problems all are discussed as they relate specifically to outcome research.

Chapter 6 describes the development of the theoretical framework guiding our research program, along with specification and definition of the key variables which we examined. It will be noted that only a *framework* is presented. Too often in the field of psychotherapy a theory is extended so far in its initial inception, before hypotheses deduced from that framework are tested, that when experimental findings dictate a change in the basic framework, it becomes easier to throw out the theory than to undertake a complete revision. This conclusion is attested to by the infrequency with which previously offered theories in the field of counseling or psychotherapy have been revised on the basis of experimental findings and subsequently subjected to additional empirical investigation.

Chapter 7 details the development and validation of the criterion measures and classification instruments used in the evaluation study. Chapter 8 outlines the design and analysis as well as the results of an evaluation of specifically stated and defined outcomes attributable to counseling services. Chapter 9 provides additional descriptive information from other studies on the subjects and instruments of the experimental study in the course of summarizing and discussing both the results and the theoretical framework underlying this project. The final chapter of this book summarizes the conclusions and implications of the research program as they relate to further research.

In presenting this material, we hope to make some contribution to two areas: first, to the development of research techniques in future outcome research in counseling, casework, and psychotherapy; and, second, to an extension of theoretical work concerned with a neo-behavioral approach to counseling or psychotherapy. Admittedly, this extension is primarily a simplification of current theories amenable to an experimental approach. However, to maximize the utility of the framework for further research,

9

we would advise careful and judicious introduction of additional variables only as they are demanded by the data. We have attempted, then, to develop a framework which will contribute some knowledge about variations in client behavior attributable to treatment, rather than to evolve a total behavioral theory which will account for *all* treatment effects or *all* client behavior.

# 2

## *Methodological Considerations in Outcome Research*

For the experimental scientist the term "methodological considerations" covers a wide range of topics extending from the problems of epistemology and philosophy of science, through the mathematical niceties of statistics and experimental design, to the more specific technical concerns of treatment administration and data collection.

In the most general sense, the experimentalist is bent on the discovery of truth, or as G. A. Kelly (1958) would have it, on its "invention." But whether the scientist sees as his task the discovery of natural phenomena and their regularities, or the construction of elegant linguistic systems for predicting and explaining natural events, he is faced with the same perplexities that have concerned logicians of science for many years. Fortunately, many useful suggestions for building and testing theories have resulted from debates among the logician-philosophers, especially since the late 1920s. The problems are not all solved by any means, and the probability of continued controversy and disagreement is very great (as is the prospect for further contributions). But much of value is already available and the experimentalist who proceeds in ignorance of modern philosophy of science walks a needlessly hazardous path and does himself and his field a genuine disservice.

To be specific to the subject at hand, present-day attempts at systematic formulation of the changes in human behavior that result from counseling and psychotherapy not only must be ingenious but must be able to withstand a penetrating analysis of their logical structure and empirical basis.

11

The bright ideas, the intuitive hunches, and the creative insights which characterized so much psychological theorizing in the past still have an important place in the development of useful and constructive theories; but more is required. To be convincing, the theorist must justify his assertions. He must relate his theoretical concepts to an acceptable set of observable events, and he must show in rigorous detail that the consequences of, or predictions derived from, his theory are nontrivial in a logical sense and can be confirmed by carefully collected data. Thoughtful reading of the recent literature on theory construction and confirmation will contribute a great deal to improving the quality of psychological research and theoretical efforts. In Chapter 6, we will give a brief account of one theoretical framework which we feel holds considerable promise for clarifying the status of current theories and provides, by implication, precepts for the conduct of fruitful research and theory development.

To many, the term "methodological considerations" in research means the choice and use of statistical methods for analyzing data. Those who are more sophisticated will be aware that the *design* of the study from which the data were obtained also is an integral and crucial part of methodology. The development of statistical theories of sampling, experimental design, and data analysis during the first half of this century has been truly dramatic, and their impact upon psychological research has been substantial. However, the gap between what is available in the statistical literature and what is employed in current research still is too great.

Too often reports of studies representing commendable research effort leave one with the impression that insufficient thought was given to possible analyses of the results *before* the data were collected. Perhaps the author's statistical training did not extend far enough for him to recognize that consultation with a trained statistician at a preliminary stage would increase the value of his work manyfold without adding unduly to his expenditure of effort. Such studies often are described as "exploratory" and the implication seems to be that the resulting observations somehow can be made to yield the stuff of science. Nothing could be further from the truth. If anything, greater care than usual is needed in designing exploratory investigations, where knowledge of the area is apt to be slight and where the effects of many variables are unknown.

In the field we are concerned with here, the list of possibly relevant variables and their effects is very long since little is known as yet about the effects of counseling or psychotherapy, the influence of client and counselor characteristics, and the role of social factors in the process or outcomes of such treatments. This means that investigations must be well designed and carefully controlled to permit simultaneous comparisons among the several possibly relevant factors under consideration. Only in this way is it possible to isolate variables whose simple or joint effects merit further study in less complex investigations. As investigators we can better afford to be "simple-minded," once we know the nature and degree of the complexity in which we work. Until that time, there is no reasonable course but to acknowledge the extent of our ignorance and the magnitude of our problems and to attack both with the most powerful tools at hand.

Fortunately, much of what researchers require by way of advanced statistical methods is already available. The problems of evaluating therapeutic outcomes are many and complex, but so are those of research in genetics and animal husbandry. It is highly probable that by a conscientious application of the mathematical and statistical methods found to be so effective in the latter areas, researchers can make important advances in the former. The social environment of a counselee is certainly difficult to control, but so is the amount of rain that falls on a field of corn. Giving therapy or counseling to a client is not exactly the same as spreading manure on plots of ground, but it is entirely possible that the effectiveness of both kinds of treatment can be evaluated by similar procedures of analysis applied to appropriate criterion measures.

Many counselors believe that successful treatment depends jointly on the particular pattern of client and counselor characteristics and on the counseling method used. Some reliable evidence supports this belief. However, the tone in which this proposition is sometimes expressed leaves little doubt that the speaker considers this interdependence unique to his particular calling and therefore regards attempts to apply rigorous statistical methods to the study and analysis of therapeutic outcomes as doomed to failure. One is reminded of Meehl's statement in a similar context: "the only possible inference a listener could draw was that they had never heard of the interaction term of the analysis of variance!" (Meehl, 1954, p. 132.)

The serious researcher in this and other areas of behavioral science can ill afford to be oblivious to, or dilettante about, the mathematical and applied statistics generated during the past half-century. Efficient methods have been developed to handle just the kinds of involved problems that so often confront the research psychologist. Failure to recognize and use them only needlessly postpones the day when answers to some of these pressing problems will be forthcoming.

The final set of methodological considerations to be discussed here has more to do with the implementation and conduct of research than with its philosophical structure. This class of considerations encompasses the techniques of data collection and observation, the variety of treatments to be employed and the manner in which they are to be administered, the development and calibration of apparatus and measuring devices, and the many administrative details that are always involved in the conduct of complex research studies.

In a certain sense, effective solutions to the methodological problems in this category are the most difficult to achieve in studies of counseling outcomes. The experimental subjects (or clients, or patients) are human beings. Usually they are not under institutional care, and only the loosest sort of experimental control can be exercised over their conduct. Typically, their participation in the research project is voluntary and seldom is there any adequate guarantee that those with whom the study begins will see it through to completion.

What has been said concerning clients applies also to therapists and counselors, as was outlined in the technically excellent study of Ashby, Ford, Guerney, and Guerney (1957). Despite the fact that most therapists and counselors have been trained in academic settings where the ideals of research and advancement of knowledge are generally held in high esteem, few have any real enthusiasm for participating in research themselves. This is especially true when the study entails any appreciable changes in their preferred methods of operation, or any time and effort beyond that required in coping with what is usually an already burdensome caseload.

From the experimenter's point of view, the knottiest set of problems within this class pertains to the assessment of *effects* (or outcomes) of treatments. More past failures to determine, unequivocally, the effects of therapy can be traced to the lack of agreement on desired outcomes than to any other cause. This problem has its roots at a more general methodological level. Unless the intended objectives of treatment are made explicit and the counselors at least conditionally accept these objectives, there is little point in doing an outcome study at all.

Even if the objectives are clearly formulated and counselor agreement is obtained, the major part of the problem still remains — how does one

14

determine a person's status on an outcome variable? What constitutes adequate evidence that the client has changed in the desired manner? Can one trust the client's verbal report or the considered judgment of the counselor? Are there available, or can one hope to develop, assessment devices which yield data clearly relevant to the stated outcomes? Can such instruments also be made to meet the criteria required of any scientific measurement procedure, i.e., objectivity, reliability, sensitivity, and freedom from personal bias and other contaminants?

Devices or methods of assessment which meet all these requirements can rarely be found ready-made. One reason is that the construction, standardization, and validation of adequate assessment devices is an extremely costly and laborious process. Discouraging as this may be to the experimenter who is eager to begin his study of the effects of counseling, there is no justifiable alternative to the expenditure of time, effort, and money required to provide the tools needed to do the job. Avoiding or ignoring these technological necessities can lead only to confusion or, what is worse, to the statement of conclusions for which no basis exists in fact. In Chapter 4, we will describe in more detail some of the shortcomings of the assessment methods frequently used in studies of counseling outcomes and point out why we believe they are inadequate for their intended purpose. Further, we will indicate what we consider should be done about this problem in future studies.

With this overview as background, let us now take a closer look at each of these classes of methodological considerations. The pertinence of each topic to the conduct and evaluation of research studies of counseling or psychotherapeutic outcomes has been touched on briefly. In subsequent chapters we will attempt to show in greater detail how careful attention to each is necessary for the successful conduct of outcome research, and how disregard for any one of these matters can minimize the value of a study.

# 3

# The Relevance of Philosophy of Science

THROUGHOUT this book we shall direct specific attention to the question of what happens to the psychological attributes and behaviors of clients as a result of counseling. We are concerned with the development of a theory within which these outcomes, and the functions of the treatment in producing them, can be described. The goal is to construct a theoretical system from which meaningful experimental hypotheses can be derived — meaningful in the sense that they can be subjected to test by appropriate research methods. A theory must be so constructed that the outcomes of subsequent investigations have an impact on its status, either confirming or disconfirming, as the data indicate. A "theoretical system" which leads to no testable propositions or which is insensitive to relevant experimental findings is really no theory at all, but merely a statement of faith or a point of view.

This general orientation to theory and research is basic to all modern empirical science. We would not reiterate this point were it not for the fact that so much of what passes for theory and research in psychology in general, and in the area of counseling and psychotherapy in particular, seems not to fit into this framework. There has been an abundance of "theories" which, because of the way they were stated, turned out to be "proof against disproof." If we are to move forward at a reasonable rate toward understanding the effects of counseling or psychotherapy, we will have to give more rigorous attention to conceptual schemes and kinds of research.

It is in this area of concern that the philosopher of science has something valuable to contribute. Scientific theories are miniature, specialized

16

languages composed of a vocabulary (the theoretical concepts), a grammar or syntax (the rules by which functional relations are formed among the theoretical terms), and a system of semantics (rules for relating terms of the theory to phenomena in the real world). The modern philosophers of science are specialists in the analysis of just such theoretical languages. They have taken as their task the logical analysis of scientific theories and the explication of the role of experimental research in testing and refining those theories. As an outgrowth of thirty or more years of this kind of study in numerous areas of empirical science, a generally accepted set of criteria has evolved for the analysis and evaluation of both established and newly proposed theoretical systems.

It should be clear that the role which the modern philosopher-logician can play in the development of empirical science is different from the "philosophizing" about science that was characteristic of earlier philosophers. Psychology, following the lead of physics and the other natural sciences, has won its deserved freedom from armchair pronouncements about matters of "fact" in the areas of human and animal behavior — for almost a hundred years the proper appeal in such matters has been to data rather than to authority. In scientific psychology the divorce is now final, and to persist in an emotional aversion to all of philosophy because of an unhappy earlier marriage would certainly be maladaptive behavior, especially when an amicable relationship is to the advantage of the psychological theorist-researcher. In view of the statements of faith which still guide many of the practices in counseling and psychotherapy today, one might even question how far psychologists have actually progressed on their own.

Assuming, in any case, that a consideration of the "new philosophy" is relevant to our present purposes, we will try to give a brief and simplified description of one conceptual scheme for the development of theoretical systems (a metatheory) which has evolved since about 1930 and attempt to identify its implications for counseling theory and research. We will look at the work of logical empiricists in general and that of Rudolf Carnap in particular. An excellent statement (Carnap, 1956) of the position of these scholars together with a discussion of its relevance to psychological concepts and theory is contained in Volume I of the *Minnesota Studies in the Philosophy of Science,* edited by Feigl and Scriven (1956). Many psychologists may be more familiar with an earlier paper by Cronbach and Meehl (1955) which dealt with construct

17

validation of psychological tests from a similar point of view and which is also reprinted in Volume I of the *Minnesota Studies.*

Briefly what is proposed is ". . . to divide the language of science into two parts, the observation language [$L_O$] and the theoretical language [$L_T$]. The observation language uses terms designating observable properties and relations for the description of observable things or events. The theoretical language, on the other hand, contains terms which may refer to unobservable events, [or] unobservable aspects or features of events . . ." (Carnap, 1956, p. 38.)

Each of these languages contains its own vocabulary, designated $V_O$ and $V_T$ respectively, a set of logical constants, and a set of rules which governs the formation of admissible sentences within that language. The two languages are linked by means of a set of "correspondence rules," C, whereby sentences in $L_O$ may be connected with certain sentences in $L_T$. Let us now take a closer look at the characteristics of these two languages and the means by which they are joined to form an understandable scientific theory.

The terms of $V_O$ are the descriptive constants of the observation language used to designate observable properties of events or things. When joined or modified by means of the logical constants of $L_O$ to form sentences, these statements are completely understandable to all members of the language community. Examples of such sentences within the present context might include "X marked item 236 of the MMPI 'true,'" "Y reported 30 minutes late for his second counseling interview," or "Z scored 2.8 sigmas above the mean of the 1956 Minnesota norm group on the Taylor Anxiety Scale." There is no question about the meaning of these statements since no appeal is required to any debatable or any theoretical connotations in order to understand what is being expressed. This is the salient feature of the observation or data language: it is atheoretical with respect to the meaning of its terms and the meaning of admissible sentences which may be formed. In addition to the primitive descriptive terms of $L_O$, other terms may be introduced by means of explicit definitions. Strict equivalences of this sort add nothing essentially new to the language, of course, and if necessary one can always explicate the meaning of any new term so introduced by recourse to the terms used in its definition, all of which are ultimately primitive constants of $L_O$.

Carnap (1956) gives a more detailed account of the requirements for an acceptable observation language, but perhaps enough has been said

18

here to indicate the general nature of this part of a theoretical system. Its role in the interpretation of theoretical terms and propositions is to provide an atheoretical, completely understandable basis for the meanings of theoretical concepts and assertions. We will shortly introduce an additional type of term and discuss the means of connecting certain parts of the theoretical language to the observation language. But first let us examine the characteristics of the theoretical language, $L_T$.

The primitives of $L_T$ are also divided into logical and descriptive subsets. The theoretical terms (or hypothetical constructs) constitute the vocabulary, $V_T$, or descriptive primitives of $L_T$. A "theory" in the abstract sense consists of a set of postulates expressed in terms of $V_T$ and the logical primitives of $L_T$. At this stage the "theory" is devoid of empirical meaning — it is an abstract calculus within which internally consistent derivations may be performed but which, as yet, says nothing about the real world.

It should be emphasized that the primitive terms of $V_T$ are *not* introduced by explicit definitions based on the terms of the observation language, $L_O$. If this were the case, there would be no point in maintaining the distinction between $L_T$ and $L_O$. However, this distinction is very useful, indeed absolutely necessary, in analyzing many accepted theoretical systems in psychology — theories which do, in fact, provide effective and fruitful means for the prediction and explanation of behavioral phenomena.

This is not the place to go into detail about the strengths or weaknesses of a strict operational ($L_O$) approach to the introduction and use of theoretical concepts. Those who are interested in the original statement of the operationalist's standpoint are referred to Bridgman's excellent book (1927). Within psychology there are still those who subscribe to essentially this same point of view (Bergmann, 1943; Skinner, 1938, 1950, 1953; Spiker and McCandless, 1954). To find criticisms of strict operationalism as an adequate basis for theory construction, we can do no better than refer the reader again to papers by the logical empiricists, notably Carnap (1936–37, 1939, 1956), Hempel (1950, 1952, 1954), and Feigl (1945). Also relevant are the previously mentioned paper by Cronbach and Meehl (1955), an earlier statement by MacCorquodale and Meehl (1948), and a more recent treatment by Rozeboom (1956).

No one questions the fact that the operationalists' emphasis on the importance of observable phenomena in specifying the meaning of theoreti-

19

cal concepts has had a salutary effect, providing scientists with a tool for culling meaningless notions from the body of physical and psychological theory. But the proposal may have been too sweeping: many concepts that served effectively to mediate predictions and explanations of physical and psychological phenomena were found wanting when examined against this stringent criterion. The advocacy of this position had the effect, as Feigl pointed out, of throwing out the baby with the dirty bath water.

Clearly a criterion for the meaningfulness of theoretical concepts must be rigorous enough to prohibit the introduction of purely metaphysical notions into scientific theories, but at the same time it must permit the introduction and use of theoretical terms whose empirical meaning is not *completely* stipulated in terms of any specified set of observables. A proposal for such a criterion has been advanced by Carnap (1956). The clear presentation of this proposal first requires a discussion of the manner in which the "free-floating" theory, composed of postulates expressed in the theoretical language, $L_T$, gets connected to its observational basis, $L_O$.

This is accomplished by introducing a set of "correspondence rules," C, which might be formulated as rules of inference, or as additional postulates in either universal or statistical form. They connect sentences of $L_O$ with *certain* sentences of $L_T$. Ordinarily, it is neither possible nor desirable to link every term in $V_T$ to $L_O$ by means of a C-rule, but as long as certain theoretical terms are connected by C-rules to $L_O$ and to the other terms of the theory by means of the postulates, then, to quote Carnap: ". . . these other terms thereby also acquire observational significance. This fact shows that the specification, not only of the rules $C$, but also of the postulates $T$, is essential for the problem of meaningfulness. The definition of meaningfulness must be relative to a theory $T$, because the same term may be meaningful with respect to one theory but meaningless with respect to another." (Carnap, 1956, p. 48.)

With this statement of the importance of both the correspondence rules and the theoretical postulates in determining the observational significance (or empirical meaningfulness) of theoretical terms, the divergence from a strictly operationalistic meaning-criterion is brought into focus. The meaningfulness of any given term in $V_T$ in general cannot be ascertained without reference to the theory in which it is embedded.

A term M of $V_T$ is *empirically meaningful* if a certain assumption in-

20

volving M makes a difference in the prediction of an observable event. Ordinarily such a prediction cannot be derived solely from the elements of $L_0$ and the single theoretical term M; other theoretical terms and a set of C-rules are required. Hence, the meaningfulness of M depends on the status of a subset of other theoretical terms as well as on the outcome of the empirical test of the prediction.

Essentially, Carnap proposes that the meaningfulness of terms in a theory be established by using the smallest possible set of untested terms in the examination of each term as it arises. Clearly under such a program no single experimental result will be sufficient, of itself, to establish the significance of a given theoretical concept, much less of an entire theoretical system. The notion of a crucial experiment for testing the adequacy of any but the most elementary theories is, therefore, unjustified.

One virtue of this approach is that it gives a fairly accurate description of the way in which many productive scientists do proceed. A well-conceived theory is not come by easily and a single negative experimental result ordinarily is not considered a sufficient basis for scrapping the entire structure, or even a major postulate. Assuming no fault can be found with the experimental procedure, the experimenter ordinarily seeks to modify the system in some minor way that will take account of the finding. He then proceeds, and this is crucial, to *further experimental tests* until confirmations of truly predictive deductions are obtained. If it becomes apparent that no amount of local modification will do the job, then more sweeping revisions must be made or a completely new approach must be taken. The final appeal is *always* to the results of empirical investigations. As long as that is borne in mind there can be no danger, as some have suggested, of opening the floodgates to muddle-headery and irresponsible thinking in the guise of scientific theorizing.

The effort to construct simple and elegant theories is a worthy one, and much to be encouraged. However, too much stress upon conceptual simplicity derived from a naive metatheoretical viewpoint is less likely in the long run to produce the desired result than is a more realistic approach to the constructing, testing, and progressive refining of theories. There is no sacrifice of logical rigor entailed in advocating this latter approach. If anything, greater logical sophistication and experimental know-how are required to evolve and progressively refine a theoretical system as described above than would be demanded under a more rigid, operationalistic approach.

Our summary thus far has dealt with the observation language $L_O$, the theoretical language $L_T$, the correspondence rules C for connecting the two, and a proposed criterion for establishing empirical meaningfulness of theoretical concepts and propositions. We would be remiss if we failed to discuss one additional notion which fits into neither of these languages as described thus far. We refer to what MacCorquodale and Meehl (1948) identify as an "intervening variable" and what Carnap (1956) calls a "pure disposition concept." We quote again from Carnap: "The extended observation language $L'_O$ is constructed from the original observation language $L_O$ by the addition of new terms in a way now to be described. Suppose that there is a general regularity in the behavior of a given thing of such a kind that, whenever the condition S holds for the thing or its environment, the event R occurs at the thing. In this case we shall say that the thing has the disposition to react to S by R, or for short, that it has the property $D_{SR}$. . . . When both S and R are specified, then the disposition concept $D_{SR}$ is thereby completely characterized in its meaning." (Carnap, 1956, p. 63.)

Both S and R must be expressible in $L_O$ for the introduction of the first disposition term but others may be subsequently introduced by reference to $D_{SR}$'s already contained in the extended data language $L'_O$. An illustration of a disposition concept in the present context might be "John becomes defensive when his counselor asks about his relations with his mother." This illustrates a disposition concept, "defensive," if we choose to mean by this term only that when certain stimuli or conditions are present (the counselor asking about relations to mother) a specifiable set of responses, completely describable in data language, occurs in the client. If anything more than this is meant, or if the term "defensive" is used in other theoretical statements where its meaning is not so restricted, then it is better viewed as a theoretical concept and belongs in the vocabulary of theory, $L_T$.

There are those, best illustrated by Skinner, who contend that the only admissible "theoretical concept" is of this form. However, Scriven (1956) has pointed out that the sense in which supposed disposition concepts are *used* even in Skinner's "radical behaviorism" actually implies meanings which cannot adequately be handled solely within the observation language. It is doubtful that any significant theoretical attempt in psychology or other sciences can get by exclusively with concepts of this type for the same reasons as were given earlier in the discussion of the shortcomings of strict operational definitions as criteria for the meaningfulness of scientific concepts.

What are the implications of the outlined metatheoretical viewpoint for theory construction and research on the outcomes of counseling and psychotherapy? Many should be obvious. First, a theory is not a loosely formulated notion that flashes to mind while seeing a client or while having martinis at an APA meeting. Such a notion eventually may achieve status as a component of a theory in the more rigorous sense, or as a hypothesis deducible from some more carefully and soberly worked-out system. This will happen only if the terms and the grammatical form in which the ideas can be expressed are compatible with some more adequately conceived theoretical framework.

One who wished to do so could call such conjectures "theories" — usage is, after all, conventional. But this is the sort of freewheeling, unsystematic conjecture that has long characterized our field and its replacement by a more adequate set of conventions (such as those outlined above) is to be desired.

For those who are serious about the task of constructing a well-formulated theory of counseling and carrying out a research program to refine and confirm that theory, there is the problem of how to conceptualize the major components (e.g., characteristics of the clients and counselors, specification of the treatment methods, definition of the outcome variables) and the functional relations among them. We think the most fruitful and justifiable approach is to represent these elements by terms and postulates in a theoretical language. To provide an interpretation for this abstract theory, one would link at least some of these postulates (presumably those at the "input" and "output" ends) to a set of observation terms in an acceptable data language. A partial interpretation of the terms and sentences formulated in the theory then becomes possible and this interpretation serves as a basis for setting up relevant hypotheses to be tested. When the results of studies conducted to test these derivations become available, linkages between the observation language (in which the experimental results are expressed) and the theoretical language (in which the theory is formulated) provide the means of confirming or disconfirming the relevant parts of the proposed theory.

For instance, in the conceptual framework proposed in Chapter 6, the major client attributes of anxiety, defensiveness, and ability to solve personal problems, and interactions among these variables, together with

23

the function of counseling in changing a client's status on these variables, are best viewed at the level of the theoretical language. These variables, in conjunction with the other client characteristics — perception of counseling and motivation to change — constitute the major descriptive terms of the theoretical language used in the research program to be described. In that program each of the major client-characteristic variables was partially defined as specific kinds of observable behavior. These observations of manifest behavior led to the development of indicator variables (measuring instruments) that would assess the degree to which a person could be characterized by each of these attributes. These test scores then were used to specify values or magnitudes for their theoretical counterparts (more correctly, a band of values within which the client's "true" value on the attribute lay, since the C-rules in this instance are best formulated in probabilistic form). Once these magnitudes were specified for the theoretical client-characteristic terms and the structure of the theory was given, we could proceed within the postulate system of the theory to derive predictions for the effects of counseling upon each of the experimental and control subjects.

Even though for each client characteristic (e.g., anxiety level) an attempt was made to list as many manifest behavioral indicators as possible, nothing like an exhaustive, explicit definition of any of these concepts (in terms of the observation language) was, or could easily be, given. Clearly there are aspects or connotations for the term "anxiety," even as formulated and utilized within this context, that were not part of the specifications used in constructing the indicator variables employed in the experimental study. Clearly it is no more satisfactory for our purposes to define "anxiety" as that which our self-report anxiety inventory measures than it was in the 1920s and 1930s to define "intelligence" as that which the Stanford Binet or Army Alpha measured. This type of definitional practice, though operationally clean, is too tightly circular to be theoretically interesting or experimentally fruitful.

These, then, are our views on general metatheory and its implications for theory construction and research on the outcomes of counseling and psychotherapeutic treatment. Let us turn now to a consideration of the problems of experimental design and methods for the analysis of research data in counseling.

24

# 4

## The Design and Analysis of Outcome Studies

---

THE preceding chapter stressed the importance of a carefully formulated theory of counseling or psychotherapy as a basis for research. This is not to imply that the theory initially must provide a complete and exhaustive account adequate to predict and explain all experimental findings. That would be an unrealistic requirement, especially in a field where little is known. Rather, it is important that whatever theoretical notions are held must be made explicit from the beginning of the research program. In most situations the effort required to do this will reward us at once by giving indications of logical inconsistencies, if any, by focusing attention on parts of the system that need additional thought or data, and by suggesting aspects of the system where experimentation would be most profitable.

A theory, especially in the early stages of development, is a means for generating research. It is a working model, subject to change and elaboration, if accumulated research data so indicate. The occasional happy accident or serendipitous discovery that contributes mightily to the clarification of a field of study is by no means ruled out. However, without an explicit notion of what one is looking for, it is hard to imagine how one would recognize this sort of finding should it occur. The major virtue of this approach is that it tends to focus research effort and thought on those aspects of the problem where such attention is most likely to yield advances. Hence, not only does the theory serve as a statement of what we know or believe at a given moment, but what is more important, it serves as the basis from which further work can reasonably and fruitfully proceed. In this sense, it is the mechanism of its own destruction. Any theory should, by including in its explicit formulation the points where supporting data are meager or absent, lead to experimental studies whose outcomes provide the basis for modifying the system. It is in this manner that the experimentalist regards and uses a theory.

## Process vs. Outcome Studies

Before proceeding to a more detailed discussion of *how* a theory may be used as the basis for designing, conducting, and interpreting research investigations, we should pause to consider a distinction that is receiving much attention in the field of counseling and psychotherapy, that is, the distinction between "process" and "outcome" research. This distinction has served as a basis for organizing part of the presentations in a number of *Annual Review* chapters on psychotherapy and counseling (Berdie, 1959; Luborsky, 1959; Shaw, 1957; Snyder, 1958; Tyler, 1958; and Winder, 1957), and much of the discussion at the Washington conference on therapy research sponsored by Division 12 of the American Psychological Association (Rubinstein and Parloff, 1959) was concerned with this topic.

In past years many published studies have attempted to deal with the effectiveness of counseling or psychotherapy in producing certain outcomes. By and large they have been poorly designed and executed. More often than not, they have suffered from the absence of appropriate experimental controls, the use of unstandardized data collection methods (often on irrelevant or oversimplified outcome dimensions), and inadequate specification of the treatment method and the characteristics of counselors and clients employed in the study.

Perhaps experimenters are averse to being identified with this mass of poor research or perhaps they are genuinely interested in another facet of the problem. Whatever the reason, the current emphasis is more on the processes than on the outcomes of counseling or psychotherapy. The assumption seems to be either (1) if only we can learn more about what happens during the course of therapy, we will then be able to predict and explain whatever the outcomes might be; or (2) since we know that we are helping and producing changes in our clients, the proper focus of study is on the process of achieving these effects. The first of these views has some merit but the second must at the present time be based more on a commitment of faith than on available, trustworthy evidence.

Whatever their motivation, increasing numbers of investigators are choosing to transcribe and categorize responses during counseling, to record autonomic reactions by therapists and clients, and, in general, to concern themselves primarily with the process of client-counselor interaction during the interview. A number of systems have been developed for categorizing protocol material, and in a few instances experimental interventions have been attempted during the interview to examine the resultant differences in the nature and flow of the material produced.

In general, process studies have not been designed in such a way that the data gathered lend themselves to easy analysis or unambiguous interpretation. Attempts to analyze the mass of material that results from this kind of study are likely to be frustrating as well as tedious. Unless a researcher has a clear idea of what he is looking for and a means for extracting it from the seemingly endless protocols, he is almost certain to become lost in the search. If some regularity or consistency in the process appears, it is difficult to determine the confidence one should place in the finding. Can the finding be verified? What has been ignored in the selection of material? How much has been inferred in the interpretations made of the recorded data? Answers to questions of this sort require more rigorous designs for data collection and analysis than are possible when one simply wades into the sea of material hoping to find something interesting and valuable. Although much of the data collection and analysis in process studies has been unsystematic, it need not be. Process studies conducted in this manner can contribute no more than can so-called outcome research which also proceeds unsystematically and *post factum* in search of "interesting" phenomena.

If the experimenter gives careful attention to questions of the design and interpretability of his research, are there any methodological points on which these two kinds of study essentially differ? Well-conducted process research requires objective, experimentally independent means for assessing movement or changes in client status on pre-defined, theoretically relevant variables, just as does outcome research. In order to analyze the data from a process study, it is usually necessary to quantify in some manner the continuous flow of the material (by hours or minutes or responses). One might think of the evaluations from such segments of the process analysis as the results of a series of short-term outcome studies. In studies of both process and outcome, the method of analysis employed must be made explicit and the characteristics of clients and therapists must be carefully specified or assessed if the findings are to be adequately interpreted and generalized. In both kinds of studies care must be taken to provide the controls needed to avoid contamination of the data by artifacts that might otherwise arise in the conduct of the investigation. Aside from these common or analogous features of the two approaches, some important differences do exist.

First, the dependent variables of a process study are almost always derived solely from the verbal behavior of the client. To be sure, a number of studies, many of which have been reviewed by Lacey (1959), have focused on other response modalities, for instance, galvanic skin response and heart rate. However, the verbal productions of the client — including pauses, tones, inflections, and higher order inferences the experimenter makes about the content or "meanings" of statements — are the greatest part of the criterion data.

Many outcome studies also utilize verbal responses as the basis of evaluation (the major study to be reported later in this book does so almost exclusively); however, they are not necessarily restricted to this form of behavior. Other kinds of objective data about the client's post-treatment behavior, his work and social relationships, the remission of his symptoms or problems, often can be obtained when the study focuses on the outcomes of treatment rather than on the process. Even when essentially verbal material is used for assessment of outcomes, it usually can be more highly standardized than when the responses must be taken as they arise *in situ*. This facilitates analysis of the data, and moreover it permits prior validation and standardization of the assessment instruments themselves as measures of status on the criterion dimensions. We will turn our attention to this matter in some detail in the chapter to follow.

Second, it seems to be almost a matter of common sense that one ought to know *what* (if anything) happens to clients with various characteristics as a result of getting one or another kind of treatment from this or that sort of counselor, before one gets overly concerned with the questions of *how* these changes take place. It must be granted, however, that much of the available outcome research is of little use in showing where process studies might profitably be undertaken. When no differentiation is made among different kinds of clients, counselors, or therapeutic treatments, or when the only outcome assessed is a general measure of the change in client (or counselor) "comfort" (socially important as such effects may be), there is little theoretical basis for proceeding to finer-grained analyses of how these effects were accomplished. But when data on a number of specific and theoretically pertinent outcome variables are obtained, then an adequate foundation exists for subsequent investigations of the process during which these specific outcome-client-counselor effects occurred.

This suggests that a reciprocal relationship between outcome and process research might well be the most efficient and fruitful basis for investigation. Well-conducted outcome studies based on a carefully formulated theory of counseling or psychotherapy and for which complete transcripts of the interviews are also obtained can be used to guide the selection of material and analyses to be performed on the protocol material. The results of process analyses, in turn, can be used to suggest new hypotheses to test in further outcome studies, and also to indicate desirable modifications in the theoretical system. Though an investigator can focus his attention and proceed, perhaps profitably, with a program of research involving only one or the other of these two types of study, we believe there is much to be gained by taking a broader, more integrated view of the research problem.

Because we also believe that a great deal more needs to be known about just what effects do arise from counseling treatment, our emphasis has been more in the area of outcome research. We have left the question of "How?" until we learn a little bit about "What?" The rest of this chapter and the one to follow will focus primarily on the design, analysis, and conduct of outcome research studies, though much that will be said will also be pertinent to process studies.

## Basic Principles of Design

*Stating the question.* Well-designed research begins with explicitly stated questions. It would be hard to overemphasize the importance of this step in the design of research; this is the link between the theoretical system and the collection of data. The statement of the experimental hypotheses, the selection of a sampling scheme, the choice of test statistics, and the interpretation of the results from the data collected, all ultimately hinge upon the questions asked and their relevance to the underlying theory.

Often when a question is explicitly formulated, the method for answering it grows clear. In some instances, what appear to be real and important problems turn out on closer examination to be pseudoproblems on which there is no need whatever to collect data. But when real and important problems do exist, their explicit formulation as questions to be answered by appropriately collected data is crucial to the design of any investigation or series of studies. The statistical hypotheses that are subjected to test and the admissible set of alternatives are directly obtained from the set of questions asked. The logic of experimental inference based on fallible observations (containing random error components, as all data do) requires that for any outcome some specifiable decision can be made.

Explicit formulation of questions to be tested by research studies also serves another function. Often questions asked concerning "relationships" between two (or more) variables are seen to be asymmetric when put in more specific form. That is, the functional form of the association involves changes in one variable as *effects* of changes in the other, but not the converse. Hence, distinctions between independent and dependent variables which are crucial in designing a research study frequently can be clarified by the process of explicitly stating the questions for which answers are desired. Related issues of limitations on the generality of the answers — limitations pertaining to subject populations, environmental conditions, and treatment methods — frequently will become apparent (in the form of conditional clauses) when sufficient care is taken at this stage of research planning.

The importance of clearly stated hypotheses for the design, conduct, and analysis of research studies has been stressed repeatedly by textbook writers and teachers of research methods and statistics. R. A. Fisher first published his classic on experimental design in 1935, and ten years before that he discussed these matters at length in his book on statistical methods (1925). Since then there have emerged numerous other texts (e.g., Cochran and Cox, 1957; Winer, 1962) which deal in detail with these basic considerations in research design, analysis, and interpretation. With the development of a consistent and powerful statistical methodology, the critical role that explicit statement of the experimental hypotheses plays in the presentation and interpretation of results from research studies has become more and more apparent. Despite the great advances in recent years which have provided analysis schemes for an increasingly wide variety of experimental plans, there is still no appropriate way to analyze just any set of data that is conveniently available.

If the reader gets the impression from this discussion that the major part of any research effort is necessarily done before the first datum is recorded, he has grasped a valuable truth. The conduct of the study, the collection and analysis of data, are fraught with their own difficulties and are not to be undertaken casually. In a real sense, however, these aspects of research are largely mechanical and consequential in nature, once an adequate job has been done of casting the problem into an explicit and testable hypothesis, specifying independent, dependent, and control variables, and stipulating alternative interpretations for any outcome that may result. To proceed with data collection before adequate attention has been given to each of these matters of design is to run the risk of unnecessary disappointment later on. Rarely can statistical manipulation of the data compensate or correct for mistakes made at this stage of the process.

*Specifying the variables.* What we have said thus far about experimental design has been general and equally relevant to any content area. Let us now become more specific about these matters as they relate to the design of studies on the outcomes of counseling and psychotherapy. The importance of explicitly stated hypotheses concerning the effects of counseling upon measurable attributes of the clients should need little additional discussion. At least implicit in such hypotheses must be a specification of the kinds of clients to whom the hypothesis applies, the relevant professional and personal characteristics of the counselors, and the nature of the treatment to be administered during counseling or psychotherapy.

In most outcome studies, the distinctions among dependent, independent, and control variables will be fairly easy to make. The specification of independent and control variables will no doubt differ from one research program to another depending on particular emphases. They could differ from time to time within a single program as different aspects of the theory come under experimental test. Almost always, however, the dependent variables or criterion dimensions will reflect the status (or changes in status) of the clients on some psychological attribute or set of attributes. Whether it is a single, global characteristic such as "general adjustment" or a complex of more specific attributes, the objective of treatment typically will be expressed as changes of some specified sort effected in the client.

Indicator variables or measures used to assess such changes may differ widely, however. In some cases self-report inventories may be used; in others, ratings of change or judgmental evaluations of movement by observers other than the client may be employed. Pre- and post-treatment projective test performances, Q-sorts, behavior tests, or subsequent social history data could conceivably be used to assess changes in the clients as a function of treatment. Not all of these indicators are equally adequate in all situations; much depends on the nature of the theory and the client characteristics on which attempts to effect changes are based. But whatever specific devices are used to assess the dependent variables in counseling outcome studies, the variables themselves refer to changes taking place in the client — usually changes in some set of his personality attributes or changes in the organization of these attributes.

In most outcome studies, the principal independent variable will likewise be easy to identify. It will be some therapeutic treatment or counseling given to the client. But this is a deceptively simple specification. Not all counseling or therapy involves similar behaviors by the counselor or therapist, similar durations of time, similar settings or surroundings, or similarities in any number of other aspects of the process. To avoid confusion in the interpretation of results, the salient characteristic of the treatment must be clearly specified. The qualifications and characteristics of the counselors, the attitudes and behaviors they display, and the techniques and devices they employ in the process of treating the clients are all important in an adequate definition of the independent variable.

Often one sees reports of studies in which the only mention made of the treatment variable is that it was "client-centered" or "psychoanalytic" or "eclectic." Except for the grossest inferences and comparisons, such description is clearly insufficient. If the effects of treatment are to be understood and experimental results are to be used to refine a theory of counseling or psychotherapy, the description of treatment must be made as complete and accurate as possible. Only by so doing can the experimenter delimit the scope of his inferences to the class of independent variables to which they properly apply. Extensions and generalizations of the results to other kinds of treatments are fitting conjectures which might well form the basis for further experimental study. However, without a detailed specification of the treatment actually administered in a given investigation, there is danger of unwarranted generalizations of the results by both the researcher and his audience.

The same definitional specificity is required when attention is turned to other possible independent and controlled variables in the study. The nature of the populations from which clients are drawn and the individual characteristics of the particular persons treated are sometimes primary foci of the research and sometimes only tangential to the principal questions under study. But whether explicit hypotheses are tested concerning the effects of these characteristics on the criterion variables, or the subjects are merely classified on them to increase the precision of the analysis, the clients used must be clearly described. In many kinds of counseling or psychotherapy it makes a difference whether the client is male or female, whether the person is a self-referral or is committed by someone else, whether he or she comes from an upper, middle, or lower class home, is bright or dull, young or old, and so on. When such considerations are important to the method of treatment employed and to the interpretation of the outcomes of treatment, detailed specifications are obviously needed.

The kinds and numbers of clients employed in outcome studies have additional implications for the design of research beyond those just discussed. On this topic there come to a focus all three major aspects of research design: local control, replication, and randomization. Let us consider these as they apply to counseling outcome studies.

*Local control.* By local control is meant the introduction of experimental procedures either (1) to rule out factors whose effects on the dependent variable are viewed as contaminating, or (2) systematically to incorporate into the design factors whose effects are known or assumed to be appreciable. An example of the first kind might be the restriction of the client population to males rather than a mixture of both sexes, when reactions of males and females on the outcome variables are believed to be different but not of major concern in a specific study. An illustration of the second kind of control procedure ("controlling in" rather than "controlling out") might be the grouping of clients by the complaints presented. In this case, the effects on the dependent variable could be examined and compared for complaint categories, separately within each category, or in terms of specific combinations of treatment and presented complaint taken jointly.

The effects of control procedures are two. First, by eliminating un-

33

wanted sources of variability or by homogeneous grouping of experimental subjects, one reduces the magnitude of error variance. This accordingly raises the precision of the comparisons in which one is most interested and permits an easier identification of effects of counseling which might otherwise be obscured. Second, when a "controlling in" procedure is employed, it becomes possible to estimate the magnitude of the effects of side conditions on the outcome variables. Clinicians and counselors talk repeatedly of the importance of client characteristics for the course and outcomes of treatment and of the importance of interactions of these kinds of variables with the treatment. When controls of this sort are built *into* the design of a study, a means is available for detecting and precisely estimating the magnitude of such main effects and interactions. We will have more to say later about the difficulties that arise in the use of complex or multidimensional designs in studies of counseling outcomes, but these are some of the major virtues in such procedures.

Many still think of control procedures only in the first sense, recalling the stereotype of the laboratory experiment in which effects of all but one factor are, insofar as possible, eliminated. To be sure, some kinds of contaminating influences properly ought to be "controlled out" in studies of counseling outcomes, but at the same time, the unifactor Galilean model of research, which has proved valuable in many research areas, is inappropriate for most investigations in this field. (It is possible that greater progress could have been made in other areas had current methods for the design and analysis of complex studies been available earlier. In fact, in many so-called laboratory sciences the use of these later methods is increasing and with considerable success.) In studies of counseling and psychotherapy, where factors other than just the treatment given are critical in the interpretation of the results, the only reasonable course is to incorporate these other factors into the design of the study as major controls.

Other special features of the general topic of controls deserve additional comment. The first has to do with the use of control groups in counseling outcome studies. In terms of the general discussion above, this practice amounts to the addition of one or more categories on the principal independent (treatment) variable. The rationale for including such groups of control subjects is to provide a basis for comparing the effects of counseling with the effects of simple time-lapse on the outcome variables. Without such a mechanism one could not be sure that the effects observed in the counseled subjects were not due to something other than the treatment they received.

Some persons working in this area have argued that the use of control groups is always difficult, really not crucial, and sometimes even misleading. When therapy for the treated clients takes an extended period of time, it becomes very difficult to maintain a truly comparable control group, similarly motivated for treatment. In practice what often happens is that those so motivated will seek and get treatment elsewhere, often without the investigator's knowledge. The fact that such persons fail to get the treatment they desire until after an extended period of time can in itself have marked effects on certain kinds of important outcome variables. The use of such control groups may introduce more sources of confusion into the results than it eliminates. (An additional problem involves the ethics of withholding treatment from persons, even temporarily, when they want and perhaps need it. We recognize this as a serious problem, but one which would require a more extended discussion than is possible here and one which would certainly get us out of the sphere of purely methodological considerations in outcome research.)

Some critics assert that the use of control groups is unnecessary or irrelevant because the questions to which this procedure provides answers are not the questions that really interest us. In a sense, studies of the effects of counseling or psychotherapy are concerned with changes that occur *within* treated clients. That is, the critical issue is whether a client is different in certain specified ways after treatment than he was before.

Sometimes suggested as an alternative to the use of control groups is a design calling for pre-treatment and post-treatment assessment of the clients. The difference between these two measures then represents an estimate of the effects of treatment. Both the criticism of a control group approach and the proposed alternative seem at first blush logically compelling, but difficulties exist in each.

We must agree to some extent with the criticism that different questions are being answered by the two procedures. These questions, however, are not completely unrelated — both approach somewhat different aspects of the general question of the effectiveness of counseling or psychotherapeutic treatments. Since they are different questions, ob-

35

taining answers to both might be important. However, it is crucial to note that using only the pre-treatment assessment (or "own control") offers no assurance that differences observed are in fact due to the treatments given! Changes may be observed simply because subjects went through the mechanics of seeking help, or because they took part in the experimental testing, or for some other completely independent set of causes in their extra-therapy experiences.

Suppose, for example, that one of the objectives of a certain treatment was to reduce anxiety, and accordingly a measure of manifest anxiety was administered to a group of self-referral college students before and after counseling. Suppose, in addition, that the study began shortly before the middle of the term (just prior to midterm exams) and that each client was seen only for a few weeks (though possibly several times per week during that period) as is not unusual in many college counseling centers. If the results indicate an appreciable reduction in anxiety for these clients between the two assessments, the implication to be drawn from the logic of the pretest–post-test design is that counseling reduces anxiety. We submit that there is a more parsimonious alternative explanation for this result. What is more crucial: there is no way within the framework of such a design to determine which alternative (if either) is correct.

Both methods of control can be incorporated into a single design and thereby permit a distinction to be made between those effects due to counseling alone and those attributable to all other causes. Let us assume that the difficulties mentioned earlier in connection with control group studies can be adequately overcome. (Not all kinds of treatment extend over long periods of time and in some institutional settings, including many college campuses, the possibility of alternative sources of professional care can often be precluded.) Then if control subjects comparable in all relevant respects to those receiving treatment as experimental subjects are also given an initial as well as a "terminal" assessment, any observed difference between the net effects for the two groups can be attributed to the intervening treatment received by the experimentals. Without *both* of these design features incorporated into the study, interpretations can only be equivocal and needlessly ambiguous.

It is, of course, imperative that the controls be strictly comparable to the experimentals at the outset in all relevant respects. One frequent misuse of the control group principle occurs when the experimentals

36

are drawn from among applicants for counseling but the controls are drawn from some other population. Motivation on the part of applicants to seek help, and insight into one's problems sufficient to recognize the need for help, are undoubtedly relevant and important aspects of comparability. When the control group method is used properly, comparability is not only useful but necessary if the aim is to identify the effects that are clearly attributable to the treatment given.

One final matter deserves some attention in connection with the topic of controls before we turn our attention to replication. Arising more from statistical considerations than from general logical concerns, this is the question of how degree of change on the outcome variable is determined. Even our best measuring devices for assessing an individual's status on a given psychological attribute contain an appreciable amount of error. This is especially true for measures of personality characteristics that are the most likely candidates for outcome variables in evaluation studies. The problem can be stated this way: When a considerable amount of the variance in a set of measures is due to error, one can expect that persons who score at the extremes on a given administration of the device will tend to score closer to the mean on a second testing *even though no actual change in their "true" status occurs.* This is simply the well-known regression phenomenon.

If we had virtually errorless measures of our dependent variables, then simple difference scores between pre-treatment and post-treatment assessments would be completely adequate to describe the changes that occur. When we must use measures of the sort now available, and when we employ complex multiple classification designs of the sort we have previously recommended, this simple difference between pre- and post-treatment scores will not be appropriate. In the first place, difference scores have relatively large standard errors when, as is usually the case, the two assessments are correlated. However, this is a minor matter compared to other problems.

In many studies the pretest scores (or scores on classification variables highly related to them) are used to group the experimental subjects into homogeneous subsets. In some cases, only subjects with extreme scores on the pretest are kept in the study while some proportion of those scoring in the middle range are dropped from further consideration. (Usually this is done without realizing the effect on inferences which can justifiably be drawn, but let us bypass that matter for now.)

37

In either case, persons grouped into extreme categories on the basis of such fallible measures will, more likely than not, be somewhat less extreme when assessed on a similarly fallible device on a second occasion. A simple differencing of scores for *these subgroups* will give the illusion of movement (quite often to an average or "normal" score in the case of personality instruments) apparently due to intervening treatment when in fact it is attributable (at least to some degree) to an artifact. As long as average differences are based on the entire range of scores (i.e., as long as there is no partitioning of the group on the basis of the pretest or classification measures highly correlated with it), then these random regression effects will cancel each other and no major problem will arise.

When grouping of subjects is employed (and this is often highly desirable), then simple difference scores definitely are not appropriate to measure changes. However, a statistical method is available which takes regression effects into account, and it should be used in such situations. This is the analysis of covariance. By a properly conducted covariance analysis of the post-treatment scores, adjusted according to their relation to the initial scores, effects due solely to intervening treatments can be isolated. Most advanced texts in statistical analysis and experimental design discuss the assumptions involved in the use of covariance analysis and provide formulas and procedural outlines.

*Replication.* Let us turn now to another major facet of research design, that of replication — the taking of multiple observations on a criterion variable under the same set of experimental conditions. Sometimes this involves several measures on the same experimental unit (or subject). Sometimes, however, only a single assessment is made of each unit but the same assessment is made of several similarly treated or similarly classified subjects.

Most persons feel, justifiably, that the larger the number of cases on which a conclusion is based, the greater is the confidence one can place in it. The technical justification for this belief, of course, is the fact that the sampling distributions for certain statistics (e.g., means and mean differences) become much more "tightly packed" about the true values as the number of cases increases. This same relationship holds for more complex functions of statistics such as the $t$ and $F$ ratios which are often used to test experimental hypotheses. Hence, the larger the number of cases, the easier it is to detect real differences and relationships that exist and the more precise are the estimates of the magnitude of such effects, differences, or relationships.

One of the functions of local control — increasing the precision of results — can also be accomplished by replication, but in quite a different way. Under local control, sources of variance that would otherwise contribute to error are excluded, either from the study as a whole or at least from the error estimate, by introducing a "blocking" or classification dimension into the design. When replication is used to increase precision no contaminating sources of error are eliminated, but the precision is increased by having greater numbers of observations for the estimation of the effects being studied.

Both of these approaches are valuable, and their combination provides a powerful way to improve research on the problems we face. By building into our research designs factors which are believed to be the major contributors to variability on our outcome measures and thereby eliminating some sources of error, we also obtain increased precision due to a sort of "hidden replication." As an illustration, consider a study done to compare the effects of two counseling methods. Suppose we are also interested in comparing high- and low-ability persons on these outcome measures. Let us assume that because of the nature of our measures and the magnitude of the errors involved we have decided that we would need at least twenty subjects in each category for each of the two studies, or a total of eighty cases to get the desired precision.

Instead of running the two studies separately, we can combine them by treating separate subgroups of high- and low-ability persons by each of the two counseling methods. We discover that we can make the two comparisons using the same subjects if the matrix to be analyzed is balanced, that is, if the same proportion of high- and low-ability persons receive counseling treatment A as receive counseling treatment B. Actually, we can get the desired degree of precision for both of these comparisons with only slightly more than half the total number of subjects required if the comparisons were made in separate studies. In addition — and this is no small matter — we can obtain information on the interactions of the different treatments on the two kinds of persons, information which would have been lost under the other arrangement.

As more factors are built into the design, the effect on precision of this "hidden replication" becomes even more pronounced. At the same time, the control aspect also leads to increased precision through the elimination of what would otherwise be components of error. Hence, there is a compelling set of reasons for using designs of the factorial or multiple-classification sort in counseling research. In no other way can complex interactions of causal factors on the dependent variables be detected or their magnitudes estimated. In no other way can one have a marked increase in the precision of results at no additional cost in terms of number of subjects required. The total number of cases needed is greatly reduced compared to what would be required to assure the given degree of precision (and then only for some of these comparisons) if the studies were done separately.

Some problems arise in both the conduct and the analysis of complex studies of the sort just described, but they in no way offset the virtues of so proceeding. Certainly there is no good reason for not using designs considerably more complex than those ordinarily employed. This is especially true when the cost of research (in terms of time, subjects, and facilities) is considered.

*Randomization.* We have thus far sketched the nature of two of the three major facets of research design and some of the implications of each for the design of evaluation studies in counseling and psychotherapy. Let us turn now to randomization and its role in research.

Local control and replication procedures have their principal effects upon the *precision* of the experimental results, whereas the function of randomization is to ensure their *validity*. No matter how much care is taken to control sources of variation other than those due to treatments, it is never possible to eliminate all possible side influences. Some irreducible amount of variability in the observations will always exist owing to factors other than those under test or otherwise controlled. The use of randomization in the choice of subjects and in their assignment to categories is the mechanism whereby uncontrolled sources of variation are taken into account in the analysis and interpretation of the results.

Most modern statistical textbooks treat the rationale and method of randomization and these will not be discussed here. However, some specific points might well be emphasized in connection with the use of randomization in outcome studies.

Often the tendency to "improve" on arrangements produced by a random procedure is almost irresistible. We have discussed above the use of controlled variables as an appropriate way of taking into account side effects related to counseling outcomes. Once *these* control dimensions have been built into (or, in some cases, out of) the design, all other sources of variability must be distributed in a random fashion. Problems arise when, having used a random procedure to select and assign subjects to treatment categories of the design, the researcher notices that by changing one or a few such assignments some other factor becomes "better balanced."

For instance, suppose that in the study discussed in the section on replication, a random procedure was used to assign subjects within each ability level to one of the two treatment methods. Upon examining the assignments, one might observe that in the high-ability group six men and four women were assigned to treatment 1, while three men and seven women were assigned to treatment 2. It might be reasoned that by interchanging one man from treatment 1 with one woman from treatment 2, a better balance would be achieved on the sex distribution.

This procedure would, in fact, obtain a more even balance on the sex distribution, but would produce an invalid error estimate. Let us see why. Remember that sex was not one of the variables on which control was exercised in the original design of the study. If it had been, then a different assignment procedure would have been appropriate — one which would have preserved an exact balance on both ability and sex while randomizing all other factors over the two treatments. By "adjusting" the assignments after randomization to achieve better balance in the sex distribution (assuming that sex has an effect on the outcome variable), the researcher would partially remove this effect from the treatments but not from the estimate of error. The result is that the treatment differences will be harder to detect (i.e., there is increased probability of a "Type II" error: accepting the null hypothesis when it ought to be rejected).

Modifying the random arrangement will not always affect the results in the manner just described. Suppose that instead of balancing sex within each treatment an effort was made to have each treatment group as homogeneous as possible with respect to sex: e.g., the high-ability group receiving treatment 1 would be all male and the group receiving treatment 2 would be all female. To the extent that this is possible, the treatment differences are confounded with those due to sex, and the sex variable no longer contributes as a component of error. As a result, no separation of the effects due to treatments and those due to sex differences is possible.

When alterations are made in otherwise appropriate randomizations, many other kinds of invalidating effects are possible. What's more, it is

41

usually impossible to determine the nature or the extent of these effects either from the data or from the knowledge of what changes were made; in this sense, the two illustrations given above are exceptional.

The point to be stressed is that if a variable is known or believed to have an appreciable effect on the outcome measure, it should be incorporated explicitly into the design of the study *before* the random selection or assignment is made. Any modification of the random arrangement after the fact can serve only to invalidate the results. The derivation and use of statistical test procedures and their interpretation are dependent on the use of an appropriate randomization process. If an investigator feels that he could "improve" on the results of the randomization by an adjustment here or there, he should ask himself whether he has used an appropriate design in the first place. If the basis on which he plans to adjust the assignments is not important enough to incorporate into the design as a controlled variable, then he is well advised to leave things as they are.

Additional aspects of the design problem related to randomization theory and procedures are pertinent to our discussion. We have mentioned only two — the sampling of subjects from a population about which inferences are to be made and the assignment of subjects to categories of the design. Randomization procedures are also relevant to the choice of categories of a controlled variable and to the form of the analysis to be employed. We will indicate briefly the kind of situation in which such applications of randomization arise.

Suppose that in a large counseling center or clinic there are two groups of counselors. Those in one group, let us say, profess to be nondirective or "client-centered" in their methods. The other group, differently trained but equally competent, takes a more psychoanalytic approach to treatment. (For the sake of simplicity in our example we will bypass the question of what kinds of behavior each counselor actually exhibits during treatment, though such considerations would be of utmost importance in any real study of this sort.) Now suppose that we want to compare the effectiveness of these two kinds of treatment on some specific outcome in which we are interested and which both groups profess to accomplish. The inferences we will be able to draw from such a study and their generality will depend not only on the manner in which subjects are selected and assigned to counselors but also on whether all the counselors are used or only some of them, and if the latter, how they are selected.

If all the available counselors are employed in the study, then inferences can be couched in terms of this entire population of "treatments." The analysis is appropriate for a so-called fixed-effect model and one may legitimately generalize to "these two methods as practiced in this clinic." If, on the other hand, only a subset of each group of counselors is used, then the scope of the generalizations depends entirely on how the participating counselors are chosen. If the counselors are selected at random from each group, then under a random effects or components-of-variance model the inferences may still be drawn in terms of the total population of counselors in the clinic. But if any other system of selection is used, then the only course available is to limit inferences to just those counselors used rather than the populations from which they were selected.

In this illustration we have indicated the manner in which randomization is important in the choice of treatments to be used in a study. What has been said about the treatment variable applies also to the constitution of control variables. When the categories of a control variable are not exhaustive (as, for instance, when only the top and bottom thirds of the distribution are used to "maximize the effect"), then the form of the appropriate analysis also changes and the inferences that can be made are modified accordingly — usually becoming more restricted.

These illustrations indicate in a general way the considerations to be given the independent and control variables in selecting an appropriate analysis and method of interpretation. The problem of what "error term" is appropriate in the analysis of data from multiple classification or factorial designs hinges primarily upon this matter of how the independent and control variables are defined and sampled in the study. Winer (1962) presents an excellent discussion of this issue.

## Data Analysis

We have by no means exhausted the topic of experimental design in relation to counseling and psychotherapy outcome studies, but we have attempted to outline some of the major considerations in the planning of research in this area. Until now, we have almost completely ignored the topic of data analysis and accompanying questions about the nature of the dependent variables in the study. Such questions are important parts of the general design problem. Clearly a different analysis scheme would be chosen if the outcome variables were expressed in terms of "measures" on the clients than if they were expressed as frequencies in some set of qualitative categories. It is also important to know something of the distribution of the dependent variables in the population of subjects and something about the psychometric properties of these variables (e.g., internal consistency, or stability over time, not to mention the several kinds of validity that may be relevant). We will dwell at greater length in the next chapter on the construction of measures of outcome variables and their standardization for experimental use.

The point to be emphasized here is that analysis procedures are *derived*. The derivation depends upon how the populations of subjects, the independent and control variables, and the dependent variables are defined. Analysis procedures will depend also upon how the populations are sampled and in what numbers, and how subjects are assigned to treatments. When the assumptions underlying the use of the particular statistic are met by the experimenter in the conduct of his study, then the analysis and interpretation of results are relatively simple. The full power of the data can be brought to bear on the questions under study, and inferences can be drawn in a rigorous and meaningful fashion.

Because of the essentially derived character of the analysis method, we have chosen to stress the design aspect of research. In an important sense, if the experimenter gives sufficient care and attention to the design of his investigation, the question of how to analyze the data often will be answered almost automatically. Powerful statistical techniques for the processing of data from well-designed and carefully conducted studies are well known and readily available. This is not to say that powerful statistical tools are available to meet any contingency, but rather that their availability is a function of advance planning.

A few items connected with the procedures of data analysis deserve brief consideration. The first has to do with a pair of assumptions on which certain kinds of analysis techniques depend. We refer to the assumptions of normality and homogeneity of variance required to derive test procedures in the analysis of variance. While these assumptions are strictly necessary for the derivation of the usual analysis formulas, there is an increasing amount of both empirical and theoretical evidence (see especially the review by Scheffé, 1959, Chapter 10, and the Norton study (1952) cited by Lindquist, 1953, Chapter 3) that the distributions of the test statistics ($t$ and $F$ ratios) and the probabilities deriving from them are remarkably insensitive to violations of these assumptions. What this means, in effect, is that these procedures yield accurate results even when some of the formal assumptions cannot strictly be met. This "robustness"

44

of the $t$ and $F$ tests is reassuring, since often either the criterion scores fail to meet these two assumptions or the data are insufficient for determining whether they do or not. In such cases it is possible to proceed in the knowledge that the test results are not markedly affected even when these formal assumptions cannot be met.

The second problem arises when for some reason the data are incomplete. We have advocated the use of complex designs as a means of exerting control and providing a basis for examining the interactions among relevant causal factors. In such designs suitable analysis procedures are available only when certain proportionalities are maintained among the cell frequencies. Sampling and random assignment procedures can be carried out so as to ensure that these requirements are met as the study begins. What can be done when subjects are lost during the course of the investigation, before the criterion measurements are obtained? If this happens early, the lost case can often be replaced with an appropriate (randomly chosen) substitute. When it occurs late in the process, however, this solution may not be feasible and other steps must be taken. Three choices are possible — undertaking a more complicated analysis, discarding additional cases at random to balance the design again, or estimating values for the missing observations. None of these decisions is very satisfying, but depending on the extent of the losses and their locations in the design one of these procedures usually can be chosen as better than the others. Discussions of these matters too can be found in several texts on experimental design (e.g., Cochran and Cox, 1957; Winer, 1962).

One should, of course, do everything possible to obtain complete data. The difficulties that arise when cases are lost, especially from complex experimental designs, are sufficiently great to warrant the use of every possible precaution to ensure that the original samples of both experimental and control subjects are carried through to the end of the study. We will describe some techniques that we have found useful in this regard when we discuss procedural aspects of outcome research in Chapter 5.

A final point we should discuss in this section concerns the use of *post factum* analyses. To some extent we dealt with this topic earlier, when we emphasized the need for explicitly formulating hypotheses to be tested *before* collecting data. As we stressed then, this step often is sufficient to indicate the specific test procedures to employ and the interpretations to make on the basis of the results. However, there may be situations in which neither the theory nor extratheoretical information is sufficient to lead one to make a specific, directional prediction about what outcome to expect among several classifications being compared.

For instance, suppose that the experimenter wants to determine which of five different interview techniques produces the greatest decrease in the number of defensive self-reports by clients. Let us assume in addition that there is no theoretical reason or evidential basis to support the belief that one of these techniques is better than any of the others. Under these conditions (and assuming a suitable criterion measure exists) an analysis of variance would be used to test the general hypothesis that no differences exist among the treatments against the alternative hypothesis that some differences do exist. Now let us suppose the study is completed and the null hypothesis of no differences is rejected. We now have evidence that the techniques differ in their effectiveness, but we still don't know which one or ones are best, *nor between which ones of the five reliable differences exist.* In short we are now interested in a more specific set of multiple comparison questions which would not have been of concern had the general test led to acceptance of the null hypothesis.

In this situation one can and should proceed to further studies comparing at least some individual pairs of treatments, but it is reasonable to expect that some information of the kind required ought to be available from the original study. In fact this is a problem that has received a lot of attention in recent years. What is usually done is to compute all the *t*-tests possible among the treatments and to interpret them in the usual manner. The trouble with this approach is that not all such comparisons are independent and the probabilities associated with these multiple *t*-tests are *not* the same as if any one of them alone were under consideration. The probability of "Type I" error — rejecting the null hypothesis when it ought to be accepted — increases very rapidly when more than a few treatments are compared in this fashion.

Alternative methods exist for carrying out multiple comparison tests of the kind described but under more appropriate sampling frameworks than the one underlying the ordinary *t*-test. We will not attempt a detailed discussion of these methods here, but the reader is referred to two excellent reviews of this problem and the alternative methods that have been proposed for conducting such analyses in the texts by Scheffé (1959, Chapter 3) and Winer (1962, Chapter 3). Since these problems arise so frequently in comparing several classifications in a single experiment, the techniques referred to deserve, and will very probably get, widespread attention in the future. For problems of comparing the effects of different counseling and psychotherapeutic treatments, these *post factum* analysis methods may prove to be some of the most useful ones we possess.

It should be clear that what we refer to as *post factum* analyses are a far cry from the kind of data-manipulating that is sometimes done in desperation upon finding that the original null hypotheses cannot be rejected. When this last occurs (and assuming the study was well designed and carried out) one has all the information that the data can provide. It is only when the general null hypothesis is rejected that these multiple comparison methods can add anything to our knowledge or provide any fruitful leads for further experimentation.

# 5

## *Technical Considerations in the Collection of Data*

---

T ECHNICAL problems arise in the attempt to implement the logic of some experimental design *in a particular situation.* The peculiar, specific characteristics of the setting in which the research is done often impose restraints and difficulties on the execution of otherwise well-designed studies. This situational specificity makes a general discussion of procedural problems and suggestions for their resolution difficult — what may be a major and perhaps irresolvable impediment to a certain study in one clinic may constitute no obstacle at all in another setting.

To provide a framework for discussion, let us consider a hypothetical setting in which a study of counseling outcomes might be done, and take up in approximately chronological order some of the problems that could arise.

Our discussion will be limited to installations of appreciable size, that is, to those with client or patient populations large enough to permit studies of some complexity. Such settings as a counseling center at a large university, a counseling or psychotherapeutic outpatient clinic in a typical veterans' hospital, or a consulting service of the kind found in many metropolitan areas, would be examples.

Discussion will be further confined to settings in which the clients or patients are not under continuous institutional care but reside outside the agency. This latter stipulation will require consideration of certain problems which one might justifiably bypass in dealing only with more easily controlled institutional environments. This is not to say that the problems discussed do not arise in residential institutions, but rather that they are simpler to deal with and more easily resolved when a high degree of institutional control is possible.

## Staff Attitudes

Agencies of the sort we have in mind are usually organized as service units and only secondarily as training or research installations. Consequently, the administrative and professional staff will be justifiably concerned that the proposed research does not unduly interfere with their service responsibilities. Research that requires major modification of the standard operating procedures of the agency is likely to be received coolly, if not completely rejected at the outset. Unless an experimenter is assured of substantial support and cooperation from the staff, research studies of any magnitude will seldom be feasible. Hence, eliciting the needed support and time commitment from those responsible for the agency's program, as well as from those who will be involved in the research program, will be an important part of the preparations for any study.

In most cases, securing cooperation will be facilitated if a procedural plan is presented which specifies in detail the manner in which existing facilities, personnel, and procedures are to be used or affected in the study. If the research is well planned and if the researcher takes the trouble to become thoroughly familiar with the agency's organization and operation, he will often be able to adapt the study to the setting in a manner that requires only minor changes in either. A certain amount of flexibility on the part of the experimenter at this stage can pay large dividends in cooperation by agency personnel.

In some cases, of course, the restrictions imposed by the setting will be such that some crucial aspect of the design cannot be implemented. If the objectionable feature of the setting cannot be changed, then the feasibility of doing the proposed study may have to be reconsidered. Seldom can one achieve, in an experimental situation, the ideal conditions as formulated in a theory, but one should not be too quick to concede defeat. Sometimes the problems are such that, while not easily overcome, they may be circumvented by a little cleverness or additional effort. The best one can ever hope to do is to approximate ideal conditions within the limits imposed by one's resources.

What then are some of the organizational features of a typical agency that warrant special attention? At what points in the planning and conduct of the study should one anticipate difficulties and how can they be resolved effectively? These are the questions which we now wish to discuss.

## Selecting Subjects

As clients first come to the agency, they are usually met by a reception-ist, who is responsible for their preliminary screening and for scheduling initial interviews. From the experimenter's point of view, this is an important step in the process. The population of subjects which he will have available will be determined by the selections made by the receptionist or intake interviewer at this juncture. In addition, the assignment of a subject to a counselor or to a control group in the study ordinarily will have to be made at this point or shortly thereafter. Special attention must be given to the individuals serving ancillary roles in the research. Adequate definition and training in their tasks as well as adequate feedback and reward for their efforts is an essential part of any continuing research program. Care taken to obtain full cooperation from such personnel will facilitate progress and eliminate many small but important difficulties.

In the preceding chapter we stated that the definition of the population of subjects and the method for choosing a sample and assigning the subjects sampled to various parts of the study are important aspects of the experimental design. More specifically we stressed that only by the use of an appropriate randomization scheme can valid results be obtained. However, ordinary random sampling of subjects from the general population is not usually possible in the applied setting, and even when it is possible the procedure is seldom appropriate. Most theories of counseling or psychotherapy pertain to more circumscribed subpopulations. These are sometimes defined in terms of personality characteristics such as neuroses or anxiety, or demographic groupings such as college class, marital status, or age.

Usually only a certain subgroup within one of the subpopulations is considered relevant, i.e., persons who voluntarily apply for help or in some cases are referred for treatment. In any case the relevant population cannot be enumerated ahead of time to permit the use of a conventional random sampling scheme. Members of the population present themselves (or are presented) serially but not in a random fashion. The persons seen at a typical college counseling center during the week before midterm examinations may be quite different from those who present themselves after they receive their grades. In other installations it is not uncommon to observe seasonal fluctuations in the kinds of complaints presented and subsequent diagnoses.

In view of these considerations one might ask how the notion of randomization can be applied. When and how can such procedures be introduced? What is their function? Although in settings such as we are discussing random sampling procedures usually cannot be used in *selecting* persons from any completely enumerable, real population, they can and must be used in *assigning* subjects to treatment and control groups. The sequential manner in which subjects become available in most counseling centers, coupled with the tendency for such groups to differ in characteristics over time, makes it imperative that experimentals and controls be designated at random from among a common series of applicants or referrals. If, for example, experimentals are chosen first in order to get them started with their interviews, and controls are picked later, there can be no assurance that the two groups are comparable or that they will be similarly affected by extraneous events occurring during the course of the study.

A convenient way to achieve a random assignment of subjects and to keep selective factors from operating is to construct a serial random assignment schedule for use by the receptionist or intake interviewer. For example, if the study is to be a simple treatment vs. control groups study in which each of three counselors treats ten subjects and fifteen subjects are held as time-lapse controls, one could construct a list of ten A's, ten B's, ten C's (representing the clients to be seen by the three counselors), and fifteen D's (representing the control subjects). These forty-five letters should then be thoroughly randomized to eliminate any serial order effects and listed for the use of the receptionist. As clients present themselves, the receptionist can assign each one to one of the three counselors or to the control group according to the next symbol on this schedule.

The introduction of relevant controlled variables or multiple classification categories into the design somewhat complicates the procedure described above. If clients from the population under investigation can be grouped or stratified into more homogeneous subpopulations and if the researcher wishes to employ a multiple classification design based on this stratification, as is often desirable, additional data must be obtained prior to random assignment.

Suppose one wishes to incorporate sex and age differences into the design as controlled variables. In addition to the two sex categories let us suppose that three age categories are chosen — 16 to 25, 26 to 35, and 36 years and older. All persons of either sex and 16 years of age or older who also meet whatever other routine screening criteria are used would constitute the relevant population. A randomization schedule consisting of six columns could then be constructed — one for each of the sex-age combinations — containing in each column a random ordering of symbols indicating experimental or control status in proportion to the numbers of each to be included in the study. When, after initial screening, a given client is judged appropriate for the study, his sex and age are determined, the appropriate column is found, and he is assigned to the treatment or control classification indicated by the next symbol in that column.

A point stressed earlier bears repeating. Once the design is chosen and a proper randomization method employed to assign subjects to treatment and control groups, any shifting or reassignment of cases can serve only to invalidate the results.

As was mentioned above, certain criteria may exist for the screening of subjects prior to their random assignment to a classification of the study. Typically many persons who make initial inquiries at counseling centers or psychological clinics never see a counselor or therapist. Some are just misdirected and simply need information on how to find the library, an academic adviser, or the men's room. These cases are easily identified and usually introduce no serious screening problem. In some experiments, however, not everyone who might be given an initial appointment by the receptionist will be considered an appropriate subject. Often the hypotheses under test dictate special features of the subpopulation from which subjects are to be drawn. When the criteria for screening are not simple and easily ascertained characteristics like age or sex, it is usually necessary to schedule a preliminary interview with the prospective subject to determine whether or not he meets the criteria for inclusion in the study.

This screening can be facilitated by using an interview schedule that incorporates all limitations on the population of subjects to be used. If a given applicant meets all specified criteria, then and only then is he assigned to the study by means of the randomized list.

The use of a screening interview, though it may be necessary to identify appropriate subjects for many studies, introduces some new difficulties. Merely seeing *someone* in an interview setting and having talked, however briefly, about what brought him to the agency may have some effect on the prospective client-subject. Such considerations are especially signifi-

52

cant when the typical treatment is of short duration. In many college counseling centers, for example, the average number of interviews per client is small and many students are seen only once or twice. The situation is probably not much different in many private or community agencies. In such brief-treatment contexts, whatever effects do result from treatment may well occur almost at once (perhaps simply as a function of some prestigeful person's indicating an interest in the client or his problem). Because of the screening interview, all subjects, both experimentals and controls, will have had an "interview" prior to the initial assessment stage of the study. Whatever effects grow out of this procedure will not be separable from any possible comparisons between these two groups of subjects.

No simple plan completely avoids these undesirable effects of the necessary screening interview. One suggestion can be made: When a prospective client is scheduled for a screening interview, it should be emphasized that it is not with a counselor or for purposes of counseling, but that the interview has some other function, such as routine personal data collection or a study of the demographic characteristics of the agency's clientele. The interviewer also should do whatever he can to dissociate himself and the screening interview from the regular treatment the client will receive, in order to minimize the spurious effects of this procedure on the experimental variables.

Another problem can arise when the same person who conducts the screening interview also makes initial assignments of subjects to the study. Knowing that the next subject to be admitted to the study will be an experimental (or a control), the interviewer may not be able to be completely objective or impartial in his application of the screening criteria. For instance, should a particular interviewee appear unusually motivated, distressed, or anxious, there is a natural tendency to admit him to treatment quickly, and it would probably be good therapeutic practice to do so. If the screening interviewer is aware that the next subject is to be assigned to control status, there might be a temptation to "overrule" the assignment schedule or to impose more stringent screening criteria, thereby excluding this subject from the study and permitting him to get immediate attention outside the study. This would, of course, constitute a breach of the randomization principle and to some (usually unknown) extent introduce an invalidating selective factor into the results. If such a client normally would be accepted as an experimental, then the only ap-

53

propriate action is to admit him to the study by strict adherence to the assignment schedule. To guarantee that unconscious selective factors do not enter into the conduct of the screening interview, the assigning of subjects should be done by someone other than the screening interviewer.

In addition to these problems that occur in the screening and assignment of subjects to the various categories of the experimental design, a related set of problems sometimes proves troublesome. Most agencies like those described above have established policies providing for the referral of certain types of clients that the agency is not equipped to treat. Some persons who are given initial appointments by the receptionist and who may see a counselor one or more times are eventually sent elsewhere to obtain the help they need, e.g., to a remedial reading service, a medical center, or a psychiatric clinic. Such decisions to refer are made in the best interests of the client and undoubtedly are justified in most instances, but the practice creates some difficulties for the experimenter. This problem again concerns the definition or specification of the population of subjects and the selective factors that can operate in the choice of the experimental sample. If explicit procedures exist in the agency for the referral of clients, the experimenter's problem can be resolved easily. He simply needs to define the population of clients as those who meet the initial screening criteria and who are not judged as appropriate for immediate referral by the agency. Any client who then is assigned an initial interview but is deemed appropriate for referral shortly thereafter may be dropped from the study and replaced by another chosen again by reference to the random assignment schedule.

In some cases, however, referral may come only after the client has had several interviews. If such a client happens to be an experimental one, a decision has to be made about his status in the study. In most instances of this kind, the client was originally accepted as appropriate for treatment of the kind available from the agency. When referral occurs only after the client has been seeing the counselor for some time, he should usually be retained in the sample and post-tested like any other terminating client. That is, terminal referral would constitute completed treatment as given in the particular setting. The question to be answered in this kind of research ordinarily is not whether the client could be made better by other kinds of treatment, but whether the treatment he received made any discernible changes in him on relevant outcome variables.

All screening and referring of potential subjects should, of course, be done on the basis of previously specified explicit criteria. If it is left to the therapists or counselors individually to decide what the criteria for screening and referral will be, or to decide whether individual clients who are referred after a number of sessions are to be included as subjects in an outcome study, idiosyncratic differences will be introduced into the selection of subjects which will quickly destroy the validity of the study.

Since the counselors or therapists ideally should not know whether they are seeing an experimental or a regular agency client, provision should be made for reporting *all* referrals to the experimenter together with the reasons for each. He may then decide on the basis of the established rules whether those who were experimentals should be replaced in the experimental design or should be followed up for final assessment.

## Procedural Problems

We have advocated experimental designs which require that each subject be assessed initially as well as terminally on the dependent variables. In addition, for designs which employ one or more classification dimensions for purposes of "controlling in" certain important sources of variation, it is necessary to obtain data on which subjects may be grouped prior to their designation as experimentals or controls in the study. The grouping of subjects cannot always be done on the basis of inspection or the intake interview. When less easily ascertained attributes than age or sex are used to classify subjects, then methods and procedures for assessing such attributes become extremely important.

Because much of what we wish to say in this regard will pertain also to the devices and methods used to obtain terminal data on the dependent variables, let us return to these matters a little later. In the meantime, there are a number of miscellaneous procedural problems that deserve at least brief mention. These include methods for scheduling appointments both for treatment and for experimental purposes, procedures for handling missed appointments, and suggestions for following up experimental and control subjects for evaluation and for equating time-lapse for the two groups.

In agencies of the sort we are considering, a central calendar is usually maintained for scheduling appointments. Each counselor or therapist has designated blocks of time in which he or the receptionist schedules appointments for his clients. A carefully kept calendar can be of considerable use to the experimenter, since it provides information on the time that

55

each counselor has available to see experimental subjects and records missed appointments and client terminations.

One of the major obstacles to employing an adequate time-lapse control group in outcome evaluation studies is the necessity of withholding treatment from the individuals in the control group for a period of time after they request it. The longer the period of treatment for the experimentals, the greater is this difficulty. It is therefore extremely important to get the experimentals into treatment quickly and to arrange for them to have interviews as regularly as possible until they terminate. A carefully kept calendar is indispensable in this regard. If the experimenter can arrange to have some control over the scheduling of appointments on the calendar, much can be done to expedite the study.

For example, in many counseling centers and psychological clinics, there is a waiting list of persons who cannot be interviewed immediately because the calendar is full for several days to several weeks (or even months) in advance. When this situation exists, the controls must wait not only for the period of time during which the experimentals are having their interviews but also for an additional prior interval while the experimentals are waiting for their initial appointments. If, in addition, the experimentals are seen only once a week or perhaps even less often after they begin treatment, the problem of maintaining an intact group of controls becomes very difficult.

But suppose that several months before the start of the study the experimenter can reserve blocks of counselor time on the calendar for the period during which the study will be in progress. Then as the study begins and subjects are selected, the experimentals may be assigned immediately to initial and subsequent appointments within the blocks of research time. There is no net loss of client-hours to the clinic entailed by this procedure. It means only that some nonexperimental clients who applied before the start of the study will have a somewhat longer waiting period. Where the number of experimental subjects is small relative to the total caseload of the agency, this increment in the waiting period for such clients may not be noticeable.

Where the usual period of treatment is brief, say fewer than ten or twenty interviews, and the typical waiting period is several weeks to a month or more, it may be possible to schedule daily appointments for the experimental subjects, get them to the point of termination, and pick up the controls for their first (post-study) interview only slightly after the time when they would have been scheduled for their first interview under the regular calendar. Where the typical treatment is not brief, the controls may have to be delayed for longer than would be customary for regular client applicants. The point is that by reserving at least part of the calendar and by making effective use of it, many of the practical objections to using a control-group design can be overcome.

Some may object that to place the experimental subjects on such an accelerated schedule as we have just described means that they will not be treated in a manner typical for the agency. We must, of course, agree. But the reason that clients are not seen more regularly in most clinics and counseling centers is a matter of practical limitations rather than preference, that is, the press for service rather than any intrinsic feature of the treatment dictates a schedule of widely separated interviews. Indeed many counselors and therapists would probably contend that the effects of treatment would be enhanced if the client could be seen on a more intensive, regular schedule than is possible in most service agencies. In any event, what we have suggested should make it possible to schedule treatment sessions as closely together as is considered optimal and simultaneously shorten the period during which the controls will have to be kept from treatment. Attempts to generalize the findings of the study would, however, have to take into account the accelerated schedule of the interviews.

We mentioned above that a carefully kept calendar can also be useful in other ways. In some cases a client will terminate by simply failing to appear for any further appointments. A regular check of the calendar will reveal which clients have failed to keep appointments. All such cases should be followed up to determine whether they have terminated without notice or whether they missed the appointment for some other reason. In the former case, the terminal assessment on the experimental variables must be scheduled; in the latter, a new appointment must be arranged. Whether a client terminates with notice or without, the experimenter must know of the termination as soon as possible after it occurs, for not only must he schedule a terminal evaluation of any such experimental subjects but he must call in the controls for their "post-testing" in the experiment and for their initial treatment sessions.

Some flexibility in these matters is provided, however, by certain features of the usual experimental designs. It is ordinarily advisable to wait for a period of time following the last appointment with a subject before

57

post-testing him on the experimental measures. The objectives of most counseling or therapeutic treatments will probably be couched in terms of at least moderately lasting changes in the client. Thus it is reasonable to permit an interval of time to elapse following treatment before a terminal evaluation is made. This temporal lag required by the logic of treatment evaluation provides the experimenter with the time needed to arrange for the terminal evaluation of the experimental subjects and matched controls.

Some designs do not require *equal* numbers of control and experimental subjects, but only numbers in each group that are proportional within each classification of the design and subjects that in some sense have comparable time intervals between the initial and final evaluations within each classification. It is not always necessary to call in a member of the control group for a final assessment every time an experimental subject terminates. One does have to be careful, however, to keep the time intervals for matched *groups* of experimentals and controls comparable. It is usually easier to do this when matching is on the basis of group parameters rather than on a subject-to-subject basis. If the means and variances of the times between assessments for matched groups are kept equivalent, this usually is sufficient.

## Assessment Devices

Now let us turn our attention to the final and perhaps the most important topic of this section — the development and use of devices to assess the effects of treatment.

Adequate assessments of changes on the dependent variable (as well as assessments of status used for classification purposes) are crucial to evaluation of the treatments. The measurements made on the experimental subjects before and after treatment provide the data on which the analyses are based. If the devices and techniques used for data collection are insensitive, unreliable, or subject to distortions or contaminating influences, interpretations of even the most carefully designed and executed studies become difficult, if not impossible.

The measurement of human attitudes — especially personality characteristics — is a large, complicated, and burgeoning field of research in its own right. We realize we cannot hope to do justice to the scope and intricacies of this area within the limits of the present discussion. However, so many past attempts to assess the effects of counseling or psychotherapy have employed evaluation methods and techniques that were, and still are, unsuitable for the task that we want to emphasize the essential place of such measurement among the *technical* problems of outcome research. In the logic of our research design the assessment of dependent variables is but one aspect of the total program; but that doesn't mean we are unaware of its own claims to intrinsic importance. Any assessment device or technique must possess certain properties in order to yield scientifically useful data. For instruments and techniques of the sort most likely to be employed in outcome research studies, *Technical Recommendations for Psychological Tests and Diagnostic Techniques* (A.P.A., 1954) provides a basic statement of such minimal requisites. One could hardly wish for a more clearly stated presentation of the need for (and means of) establishing such information about assessment devices prior to their use as routine tools for research or diagnosis. We will not attempt to repeat the criticisms and recommendations made in this document but rather will highlight some of the arguments that have special relevance to the assessment of treatment outcomes.

Experiments of the sort we are discussing are done to test hypotheses and to estimate the magnitudes of the effects identified. Such hypotheses derive from theoretical formulations of the supposed effects of therapeutic practices on certain attributes of clients. To test such hypotheses, means for assessing appropriate client attributes are required. The first and most important question to be raised about a given assessment device is the degree to which the scores it yields reflect differences on the client attribute named by the term or concept in the theory. This is the question of *construct validity*.

As Cronbach and Meehl (1955) pointed out, establishing the construct validity of a measure for a theoretical concept is no simple matter. Ordinarily no single numerical index is calculable and probably no one psychometric study is sufficient; what is required is an entire program of test development, closely tied to the theoretical system. Such a program entails the determination of various empirical coefficients and their integration into a tightly reasoned argument relating the observable test scores to components of the theoretical structure. Information about reliability (including homogeneity, stability, and equivalence), concurrent and predictive validities against various criteria, content validity, and population and situational differences in performance, all bear on the question of the

59

degree of construct validity possessed by an assessment device *relative to a stated theory.*

Certain data usually will be more important than others in evaluating the construct validity of a measure to be used in a treatment evaluation study. Of the varieties of reliability, two are of major importance.

First, in order for a device to be useful for assessing changes that take place over time, it must reflect a high degree of stability between two administrations in the absence of intervening treatment. We are assuming that the attribute being measured is a fairly stable characteristic of a person drawn from the population we are studying and not subject to marked variations in the course of normal experiences unless special influences (like therapy) are present. This will be the case for most or all personality characteristics that will be considered as dependent variables in outcome studies since treatment objectives usually are couched in terms of changes in more or less permanent attributes. If a certain level of anxiety or defensiveness is viewed as typical for a client, the device or technique used to assess the effect of treatment in modifying one of these characteristics must yield stable estimates of the status of that person at two separated points in time.

Second, an estimate of the internal consistency or homogeneity of the test may be important. If the attribute is theoretically conceptualized as factorially pure, the test should possess a high coefficient of internal consistency. If the test is factorially complex, tapping several attributes rather than only one, then interpretations based on scores from the test will be equivocal. As Cronbach (1951) has demonstrated, however, a high coefficient of internal consistency (such as *alpha* or Kuder-Richardson #20) is no guarantee of complete factorial purity. Such a coefficient reveals only that the major portion of the test variance is attributable to one factor although any item within the test (or all items) may tap it only minutely. Thus a high coefficient of internal consistency may or may not reflect homogeneity of the item content, whereas a low coefficient does indicate factorial complexity of the scores. This will be true for tests of at least moderate length which also have high reliabilities of other kinds such as those estimated by immediate retest or equivalence coefficients.

Let us turn now from questions of reliability of the assessment device to consider what sorts of validity data are relevant. When external criteria are available, correlations of test scores with such criteria are of the essence. For instance, scores on a diagnostic inventory which do not relate

60

highly to acceptable diagnostic judgments about clients can hardly be considered valuable for their stated purpose. Similarly, when test scores on a personality measure fail to agree with carefully collected judgments of this characteristic made by trained raters who have observed the subject in relevant situations, the test must be viewed with skepticism. From our point of view, empirical validations of the assessment devices to be used in treatment evaluation studies are the most important data that can be presented to justify their use.

In one sense empirical validity data can be *sufficient* for deciding the adequacy of an assessment procedure. If an acceptable criterion exists against which a test can be validated and if the test is highly related to such a criterion, then little else is important. The key to this assertion is the existence of an *acceptable* criterion — acceptable in the sense of being free from bias and other contaminants, having indisputable relevance to the theoretical concept to be assessed, and possessing at least some degree of reliability.

It should be recognized that few situations exist in which such completely acceptable criteria are available. When external criteria can be used in the process of test development, they usually possess some undesirable features or shortcomings that make their simple correlations with test scores less than fully convincing.

Ratings or judgments, especially in the area of personality assessment, have often been used as criteria for validating other assessment techniques. The accumulated experience with rating procedures not only has served to identify the difficulties to which the method is subject, but also has indicated the means by which many of these problems can be overcome or at least minimized. Guilford (1954b), in discussing rating scales, has summarized much of this information, and anyone considering the use of such data collection techniques should read this account carefully before proceeding. Other reviews, not limited entirely to rating methods of assessment, but relevant and informative nonetheless, have been published by Cronbach (1946, 1950) and by Campbell and Fiske (1959). Rating methods — self-ratings or those made by others — are particularly subject to a variety of contaminating factors because of differences in rater frames of reference and response sets of various kinds including acquiescence, position bias, and several varieties of "halo" effects. However, a number of these sources of bias and error can be eliminated or their effects minimized. Recommendations have been made to improve meth-

61

ods for training raters, techniques for designing rating schedule formats, and definitions and descriptions of the attributes to be rated.

Of course, ratings are not the only data that can be employed as criteria for the empirical validation of test devices, nor are they necessarily the most desirable. To the contrary, as pointed out above, they are often influenced by factors unrelated to the attribute to be measured, and thus often provide a rather risky basis against which to validate other techniques. Because of the ease with which ratings can usually be obtained, however, this method is the most frequently used source of criterion data. Other sources, such as behavior records based on time-sampling procedures or critical incident records, often can be employed to obtain objective performance data for validation purposes. Such techniques, when appropriately used, are free from many of the subjective aspects of ratings and for that reason may be preferable to them.

Regardless of the method used to collect criterion data, the questions of their relevance to the concepts being assessed and their freedom from bias and error are central to the interpretation of tests validated against them. Obviously, if the criterion data are open to dispute, then assessment devices based upon them must be also.

Despite these limitations, validity against such external criteria can still be the most useful kind of information for judging the construct validity of a test. The experimenter should do everything possible to obtain the best criterion data he can, but much can be learned when even the best obtainable are less than perfect. For instance, ratings by peers are always influenced by the rater's own personality and ability and by the relationships between rater and rated. Despite this subjectivity, it is difficult to imagine a more relevant kind of data to use in the validation of other techniques for assessing personality attributes. If care is taken to avoid bias and other contaminants (e.g., by using multiple raters, forced choice formats, and clearly stated instructions and scale descriptions), useful criterion data can often be obtained.

What has been said about the effects of contaminating influences on criteria pertains also to the experimental assessment devices and techniques themselves. Self-ratings by clients or judgments by therapists or counselors are sometimes employed directly as a means of evaluating treatment effects. The items or statements are taken at face value by the experimenter, and responses to them frequently are offered as evidence of treatment effectiveness. This is a hazardous practice in any psychological assessment study and especially so in the present context. Quite aside from the problem of the subjectivity of the counselors' or clients' judgments and that of getting multiple judgments, another serious difficulty exists. Clients usually apply for treatment because they perceive a problem that concerns them. Thus, when pretested on a self-report device, they are likely to indicate such feelings. However, after they have been in treatment and have terminated they may be less prone to be as frank as before, even though they feel essentially the same as they did at the beginning.

Many of the more casual approaches to the evaluation of treatment outcomes have made use of assessment techniques which were open to criticism on just this basis. The so-called "hello-goodbye" pattern (Hathaway, 1948) which plays so pervasive a part in social interchanges in our society undoubtedly exerts its influence in attempts at assessment. When someone requests help of another he is likely to give a justification for his request, and when a person or an agency has attempted to be of assistance, whether effectively or not, the client is not likely to be critical or negative in his appraisal of those efforts. There are exceptions to this principle, of course, but when evaluations of treatment are based exclusively on such "face valid" methods, there is good reason to be suspicious of the results. The researcher ought to require corroborative data from methods not subject to this kind of contamination before taking such results very seriously.

The "hello-goodbye" phenomenon is just one among many factors that serve to confound attempts at psychological measurement. However, it is probably one of the most serious for research on treatment evaluation. Perhaps because those concerned with treatment evaluation tend not to be measurement specialists, much of the research on counseling or therapy outcomes has employed methods for data collection which suffer from this defect. Certainly psychologists should be sensitive to the problems of interpreting verbal reports by either the client or the therapist at their face value. Unless additional data are presented to support their validity, interpretations of self-report questionnaires, Q-sorts, or rating scales should be viewed with caution.

Let us turn now to one final topic or class of data relevant to the establishment of the construct validity of an assessment instrument. Often the theory which contains the concept or variable to be assessed specifies the relationship of that variable to other measurable characteristics of the

63

person. Thus, if the theory implies that two personality traits are related to each other in some particular manner and if methods are proposed to assess both of the traits, then it is expected that the measures relate in the way and to the degree postulated for the attributes. If they do not, then something is at fault with one or both of the measures, with the theory, or possibly with all three. Hence, data from intercorrelational studies, factor analyses, and the like are pertinent to the development of assessment methods to be used in outcome studies, provided the outcomes are to be related to some particular theoretical framework.

As with the questions of reliability and validity raised above, information about the relationship of a measure to other measurable features of the subjects should be obtained before it is employed for evaluation purposes. Unless there is evidence that an assessment device does what it is supposed to do, i.e., provides reliable and valid assessment of the outcome variable *as defined in the theory,* there is little point in going to the effort and expense of conducting an evaluation study. As we mentioned earlier, when novel methods are proposed to assess outcomes of treatment, there is no alternative but to spend the time, effort, and resources necessary to assure oneself (and one's audience) that the assessments mean what they are supposed to mean. In many research programs, developing measuring devices and providing the data required to establish their scientific credentials may well demand as much ingenuity, time, and effort as designing and carrying out the evaluation study itself.

Finally, we wish to make a few comments on procedures for the collection and handling of assessment data in outcome studies. We have discussed the use of a screening interview to select subjects for the study. In some investigations, the selection and grouping of subjects will depend not only on interview data but also on the results of psychometric assessments of the prospective clients. When subjects are to be assigned to classifications of the design on the basis of measured characteristics, provision must be made for getting and using such data in scheduling initial appointments.

It will often prove effective to arrange a pretesting session for all prospective subjects who can pass the preliminary screening. During this session all classification measures as well as pretreatment assessments on the dependent variables can be obtained. Once the classification measures are available, the subject may be assigned to a treatment or control category of the study (or excluded from it) as his scores indicate. If the classification measures are obtained first, it will be possible in many cases to determine client status relative to the experimental design before he has finished being assessed on the dependent variable measures. This will make it possible to arrange initial appointments at once for those classed as experimentals. Since in all time-lapse control studies it is important to get the experimental subjects into treatment quickly, everything possible should be done to expedite their assignment to an initial interview. We offer the above as an example of one way to help accomplish this.

We come now to the final stage of the study. After the experimentals have terminated and a suitable period of time has elapsed, they, as well as the controls, must be assessed for the second time on the outcome variables. Scheduling such testing sessions can be troublesome if certain steps have not been taken in advance. If current addresses and phone numbers for all subjects have not been recorded or if the subjects have not been told that they will be contacted again, the experimenter may find he has lost some of his cases. Without terminal data on each subject, of course, the effort taken to balance the assignment of subjects to the design is lost. In many cases the guarantee of valid, interpretable tests based on the random assignment of cases is destroyed or markedly weakened if data are incomplete, and even if it should be possible to analyze the remaining data, the analysis may be greatly complicated when some observations are missing.

# 6

## *A Conceptual Framework*

THE complex of sequential interactions between the counselor or therapist and his client represents a demanding and challenging subject for theory, practice, and research—demanding in the sense that as a source of behavioral modification the process is highly valued in our culture. A great deal of time, money, and training is involved in becoming proficient in its practice. Nevertheless, the many current psychological theories of learning and personality have not crystallized into a useful conceptual framework for guiding counseling practice or research on the outcomes of that practice (Pepinsky, 1953; Shoben, 1953b).

As we pointed out in Chapter 2, many theories have no utility for the researcher because they deal with constructs that at least at present are untestable, or because their complex and nebulous premises prevent us from deriving testable hypotheses. Still other theories are so loosely formulated that they can account for all experimental findings. Such theories may explain (usually in hindsight) some bits of past or present client behavior, but they have not led to any systematic or ordered way of understanding the functional role of the counselor in the therapeutic process.

The lack of a framework for interpreting client-counselor interaction has several serious consequences. It impairs the value of services to clients and seriously limits the consistency and scope of programs to train and supervise counselors. Furthermore, this lack is reflected in counseling and psychotherapy research, for without an adequate framework for understanding the counseling process and its outcomes, research time, money, and energy cannot be used to best advantage. Too often the variables used in experimental investigations seem quite concrete yet are superficial, unordered, or only tenuously related to the process itself. Dressel (1953) and Wrenn and Parker (1960) have observed an inverse relationship between the significance of the variables used in counseling research and their accessibility to measurement.

Conceptual schemes must (1) broaden and deepen our understanding of the counseling process, (2) encourage critical research, and (3) permit the useful application of such research findings to subsequent counseling practice. We contend that the most productive conceptual framework will incorporate variables that are directly relevant to the *goals* of counseling or psychotherapy.

There are two general approaches to counseling research; one focuses upon the process itself and one upon the outcomes or effects of the process. The studies reported by Raskin (1949), Sheerer (1949), Stock (1949), Haigh (1949), Seeman (1949), Raimy (1948), Snyder (1945), and Carnes and Robinson (1948) are representative of the former approach. The conference on research in psychotherapy held under the auspices of the Division of Clinical Psychology of the American Psychological Association (Rubinstein and Parloff, 1959) revealed that the participants were concerned almost entirely with characteristics of the therapeutic process itself as distinct from the investigation of outcomes. Conversely, Whitehorn's introduction to the conference report stressed as the purpose of the conference and its most crucial topic the goals of psychotherapy, which he identified as the issue from which all other issues derive their significance (Whitehorn, 1959).

Dressel (1953) has observed that the counseling or therapeutic process itself is significant only in terms of the outcomes or effects in the post-counseling status of the client. From his survey of psychotherapeutic outcomes, Eysenck (1952) drew negative and controversial conclusions. Notwithstanding the critiques and comments of Rosenzweig (1954) and others, following Eysenck's article, the basic question of effects attributable to the process itself remains. Meehl (1955) has expressed the view, in which we concur, that the question of effect is a basic and troublesome one, which demands an answer quite apart from the validity of the Eysenck report. This demand is not met by labeling the problem of effectiveness as a pseudoproblem (Sanford, 1953) and restating the issue by seeking to specify what kinds of treatments with what kinds of clients and what kinds of therapists have what kinds of effects. The specification is meaningful but it implies an avoidance of the consideration of goals, in terms of which such differential conditions may be examined.

Investigations concerned with outcome variables are reported with regularity in the literature. Many of these have identified a group of variables and empirically determined the degree to which they show significant differences between treated and nontreated subjects. The limitations of such research are twofold: on the one hand many scales, signs, and indices are ambiguous and of questionable validity in themselves (Worchel, 1955); on the other hand, there is little indication that the criterion variables are clearly linked to therapeutic objectives which presumably guide the treatment experiences of the clients.

Worchel (1955) has indicated that empirical approaches have serious limitations because they do not shed light on how or why certain variables predict, correlate with, or reflect outcomes. We contend that outcome variables developing from commonly accepted therapeutic objectives will clarify in part the "how" and "why" questions, if only by first identifying the subgroup of individuals for whom the therapeutic objectives were achieved. The identification of such subgroups would seem to be a basic step toward clarifying how and why such results were obtained. Some other variable or variables, of course, may have contributed a great deal to such change. Zubin and Windle (1954) in their discussion of criteria for sound prognostic studies illustrate the potential significance of an unconsidered variable (chronicity in this instance) in accounting for contradictory findings in past studies.

Using therapeutic goals as a base for assessing outcomes presents many difficulties. Goals of socialization or social adjustment, when compared with those of self-adjustment, happiness, or lack of tension, reflect our incompatible cultural values of competition and individual achievement on the one hand and conformity on the other. The goal of social adjustment raises the additional problem of what standard counseling should present for the individual to adopt: the value standards of the counselor, the counselor's ideal standards, or standards appropriate to the client's background and socioeconomic status? Goals of self-adjustment or contentment present other problems. They may be achieved by extremely idiosyncratic or antisocial individuals (Walker and Peiffer, 1957). Some psychopaths and schizophrenics meet such therapeutic objectives. It can be answered that such a goal must not reduce the client to an unmotivated vegetative state. Clearly, the counselor must seek to reduce certain tensions without eliminating those that are useful for ongoing action. The distinction between debilitative anxiety and facilitative motivation is relevant here.

Another approach to therapeutic goals noted by Walker and Peiffer is the adoption of generalized rather than specific objectives, and multiple rather than singular objectives. The more generalized the objectives are, the more likely they are to apply to all clients and the more likely it becomes that their generalized nature will defy any operational definition.

Recognition of these limitations could lead us to abandon any specification of therapeutic objectives at this time and focus upon characteristics and correlates of the counseling process. Recognition of these limitations could also lead us to continual pursuit, identification, and assessment of objectives, elusive though they may be. The latter alternative is consistent with the prime hypothesis investigated and reported later in this book, particularly in the context of multiple goals with hypothesized interrelationships between them. The complexity of adequate analytical techniques for investigating such relationships among a number of outcome variables will be obvious. It should be noted that critiques such as that by Walker and Peiffer usually deal with one goal variable at a time. Many of these criticisms of objectives valid in the one-goal-variable-at-a-time analysis could be met by viewing therapeutic objectives along several interrelated dimensions in such a way that change on one variable would be interpreted only in relation to change on one or more related variables. Thus, change on variable $A$ might be viewed as appropriate for some clients and not for others, depending on the change in variables $B, C,$ etc. As an example, the client who becomes less anxious following counseling may do so in several ways, each of which would have different implications for his post-counseling status. If he is reducing his anxiety by developing defensive behaviors, he presents a quite different picture from the client, also less anxious, who now manifests realistic problem-solving behaviors which reduce anxiety or serve to prevent future anxiety.

Only by considering therapeutic objectives in terms of multiple facets of client behavior can we realistically conceptualize change brought about by the counseling experience.

The present conceptual framework evolved from the investigation of quite common yet critical objectives of the counseling or therapeutic processes — objectives to which the counselor subscribes as legitimate, desirable, and expected outcomes of his work with clients. Five dimensions of client behavior — anxiety, defensiveness, personal-problem-solving ability, motivation to change, and perception of counseling — form the elements of this framework. Our definitions of these dimensions and our hypotheses about their relationships to the outcomes of the counseling process will be discussed in the remainder of this chapter.

## Anxiety

May (1950) and a host of other psychologists, psychiatrists, and analysts have concerned themselves with anxiety as a prominent and significant characteristic in individual behavior having important implications for the mental health of the individual. Definitions of anxiety vary widely, for it has biological and cultural as well as psychological components. Sometimes it is treated as a stimulus or drive state (Taylor, 1951, 1953, 1956; Pepinsky and Pepinsky, 1954), sometimes as a response, and sometimes as including both. It has been treated as observable or manifest behavior and as an inferred state not overtly manifest.

Writers such as May (1950), Fenichel (1945), and Mowrer (1951, 1953) have distinguished neurotic and normal forms of anxiety. May considers normal anxiety as a reaction proportional to objective threat which does not include repression or other defensive mechanisms, and which can be coped with constructively on the level of conscious awareness.

Fenichel formulates a triple stratification of anxiety in terms of *trauma* (anxiety automatic and unspecified), *danger* (anxiety in the service of the ego, affect created by anticipation, controlled and utilized as a warning signal), and *panic* (failure of ego controls, affect becoming overwhelming, regression to the first stratum). His second level, danger, encompasses positive components through its anticipatory nature, which enables the individual to take some form of protective or defensive action.

Mowrer, in making a distinction similar to May's, views both normal and neurotic anxiety as associated with the experience of conflict in contrast to fear, which does not necessarily rest in conflict at all. Normal anxiety, he says, is a form of unconditioned response to stress, pain, or danger. Normal anxiety is also considered situational and the individual is aware of the causes of his anxiety. The individual experiencing such a reaction may deal with it constructively and rationally, or, on the other hand, dissociatively — disruptively from the point of view of the individual's problem-solving capacities. This view leads to the consideration of the goal of psychotherapy as the reversal of dissociative trends, e.g., the replacement of neurotic anxiety and its unconscious conflict with normal anxiety where components of conflict are consciously available to the individual. Similarly, counseling goals are focused on relief of conscious conflicts and of the consequent normal anxiety. While both therapeutic processes may be (and he believes they are) involved in psychotherapy, he chooses to regard them as different for these reasons. In a later paper, Mowrer (1958) questions his distinction between the two forms of helping functions. The problems are important and the attempt to sharpen definitions is commendable. However, thinking of the distinction as one of degree rather than kind has suggested to us the importance of dealing with the anxiety concept in general, while recognizing both intra- and inter-individual differences in its manifestation and components.

Relevant to this point are Shoben's (1953b) observations regarding the all-or-none concept of unconscious processes as unverbalized processes. Unconscious processes, in his view, are relative and involve variations in lack of symbolization — a broader base than lack of verbalization alone. Again, the varying extent of such symbolization and the closeness of its content to unconscious content among and within individuals have led us to avoid a conscious-unconscious dichotomy as well.

Shoben (1953a, 1953c) and Mowrer (1953) conceptualize the therapeutic process in terms of two-factor learning theory. Rogers and his colleagues (1951, 1954) have proceeded in a similar vein but use a self-concept phenomenological framework.

Mowrer (1953) has defined anxiety as a conditioned form of the pain reaction. As such it is a response which, like other responses, can itself produce additional stimuli having motivating qualities. Shoben (1953c) has sketched the development of such anxiety. While he focuses primarily upon neurotic behavior, his rationale seems equally appropriate for our purpose. Basic to anxiety is fear, a drive state of the organism derived from pain. Stimuli paired with the experience of pain may take on the capacity to elicit the affective components of the pain reaction. The affective component is labeled fear and it serves as a drive to further behavior aimed at modifying, eliminating, or escaping from the stimuli that evoked it. Repression, which can also vary in degree and pervasiveness, has immediate anxiety-reducing properties. Since repression is rarely complete in nature, the consequences of anxiety are manifested in such forms as social uneasiness and behaviors inappropriate to the situations, including the overt anxiety responses themselves.

71

In summary, anxiety, like fear, may be characterized as a response acquired through punishment, anticipatory in character, and having definite drive state properties. It develops like fear, but differs from fear in that it is more often a response to internal than to external stimuli (the principal cues eliciting it may be impulses to act in ways that have previously met with punishment); it does not involve an objective or identifiable danger; and the punishing experiences mediating its acquisition are often socially administered.

Many authors have incorporated the concept of anxiety into theories of the counseling or therapeutic process. Authors best described as neobehaviorists have dealt with the concept in the most definitive manner. Shoben (1953a) views the therapeutic process as a learning experience which has as its goal the elimination or modification of anxiety. This comes about through a counter-conditioning process in which the nonpunitive social situation experienced by the individual in the interview relationship enables him to learn new nonanxious or less anxious responses to replace his anxiety reactions.

Dollard and Miller (1950) likewise have identified fear or anxiety as one of the most important drives, pointing out that its potential strength is so great that it can easily be attached to new cues through learning, and that it motivates the inhibiting responses in most conflicts. They regard anxiety as a response to unlabeled internal cues originating in any of the common conflict-producing experiences of life and demonstrate how stimulus generalization takes place when the anxiety drive is sufficiently intense. They view psychotherapy as a process for the creation of normality; anxiety is a critical concept in their consideration of this process and its normality-inducing objectives. A drive-reduction reinforcement theory in the strict sense is not necessary to account for their conceptualizations. Indeed, they indicate that for purposes of their analysis only a reinforcement theory in the broadest sense is needed. Dollard and Miller hypothesize that a sudden reduction in the strength of a strong drive will have the effect of making acts contiguous to this drive reduction prepotent. At this time, our concern is not so much with the "how" of anxiety development and modification as with the fact that there are many concepts and procedures that stress the importance of anxiety and the therapeutic objective of modifying its impact on the individual.

Pepinsky and Pepinsky (1954) use the concept of irrelevant drive as synonymous with anxiety and describe how this helps to explain the behavior of those who seek counseling and of those who provide the counseling services requested. They define anxiety as "a state of tension produced in an organism by its inability to respond to drive-evoking events in such a way as to achieve drive reduction." (Pepinsky and Pepinsky, 1954, p. 95.) They go on to observe that this anxiety drive state and other internal and external stimuli can generalize to produce the same responses in different situations, where they are irrelevant. These responses become anticipatory in nature and, as such, operate to enable the individual to avoid manifest anxiety. The Pepinskys also discuss the question of what constitutes optimal amounts of such anxiety, citing Davis' (1947) contention that some anxiety is necessary for motivating the individual to learn a social role acceptable to the members of his reference groups.

Bordin (1955a, 1955b) similarly has noted that, in general, most schools of psychotherapy believe that some degree of anxiety over problems is essential to a client's therapeutic progress. His illustrations of insufficient, optimal, and excessive anxiety show a somewhat different typing from the normal-neurotic distinctions of May, Mowrer, and others. Bordin stresses the role commonly played by normal anxiety: experiences, conflicts, and inadequacies take their toll in anxiety, but the individual is able to endure this and adjust to environmental demands. Bordin further indicates that counseling service typically is sought by the "normal" personality only when he encounters situations that create an awareness of conflicts or inadequacies; here anxiety takes on protective, positive, equilibrium-seeking properties. Furthermore, Bordin describes how the ambiguity of the therapeutic relationship may influence the degree of anxiety experienced by the client during the therapeutic process.

Views such as these share the inevitable arbitrariness or artificiality of any distinction concerning a phenomenon which manifests intricate variations within and between client problems. Therefore, while recognizing these distinctions as having much illustrative value, we have chosen to treat anxiety as a continuously distributed variable, including among its variations its intensity, motivational qualities, and effects.

Up to this point we have focused attention primarily on anxiety as a drive state, or as a drive state giving the cue to certain internal response events. (In many instances the anxiety referred to is latent in nature.) What can be said of the manifestation of anxiety? Grayson and Tolman, in their semantic analysis of the clinical concept of anxiety, indicate the variety of definitions employed by psychologists and psychiatrists. Many of the definitions encompass both the drive state and manifest responses. They say that "all authoritative references, and practically all of the respondents in this study, view anxiety as a fear or tension state, but some emphasize the etiological factor (unconscious), some emphasize the physiological correlates, some see it as a clinical symptom and some apparently emphasize its free-floating nature (unrelated to object)." (Grayson and Tolman, 1950, p. 221.) The authors were impressed with the looseness of many of the definitions.

With the view that anxiety takes varied forms, which may range from motivating to debilitating in effect, we readily agree. We propose that overt manifestations of anxiety indicate the presence of anxiety of a type or magnitude that must be considered debilitating. It is with these overt manifestations of anxiety that we are particularly concerned. Anxiety reactions which are of a defensive nature will be discussed in the next section. However, there is a class of such responses which we see as manifestly anxious in nature themselves. Symonds (1946), reviewing expressions of anxiety, includes physical symptoms (cardiac, respiratory, alimentary, motor, and glandular disturbances), confusion and doubt in thought and speech, and variations of feeling states, including a sense of isolation, inadequacy, strain, and the like.

We view the concept of anxiety as involving both a drive state and a response class, one part of the class of responses being labeled "manifest anxiety." This view closely parallels that of Bergman (1959), who utilizes the concepts of exteroceptive and interoceptive stimuli, anxiety responses, and defensive responses in his adaptation of learning theory concepts to organize the phenomena of psychopathology and psychotherapy. Like Shoben, he sees the counter-conditioning process in the therapeutic relationship as the production and strengthening of responses which must arise in the presence of anxiety stimuli but which compete with anxiety responses, e.g., so-called "comfort responses." Bergman implies some similarity between anxiety and defensive responses. We regard the similarity between anxiety and defensiveness in this way: both function as responses to anxiety drive states, but manifestly anxious responses appear distinct because they commonly occur when defensive responses fail, or are inadequately developed to reduce sufficiently the anxiety drive state that has stimulated them. Illustrations of such manifest anxiety responses include verbal statements of discomfort and self-doubt, and such nonverbal responses as accelerated heartbeat, perspiration, and trembling.

Parloff, Kelman, and Frank (1954) and Kelman and Parloff (1957) have included a measure of client "comfort" as one of their criterion variables. This measure involves assessment of the latent or interoceptive components of the anxiety drive state, as well as its response aspect. On the other hand, the authors emphasize the overt manifestations of anxiety in assessing client status on this variable.

Manifest anxiety is a part of the client's feeling state that must be dealt with in the counseling or psychotherapeutic process. Reduction in manifest anxiety thus becomes the first variable in our conceptual framework. Our rationale in defining this variable has been to delimit the concept to those manifestations observable to people in close and continuing contact with the anxious individual. As a result, our defining properties, while stated with reasonable clarity in behavioral terms, provide a limited "map" of the anxiety concept.

## Defensiveness

Another mode of responding to anxiety stimuli is the second variable in our framework, *defensiveness*. As we have said, conceptions of anxiety have embodied notions of a drive state and of internal and external response classes. As a drive state, anxiety is a powerful motivator to action. In any situation, the response which most effectively reduces the felt need tends to be learned. Clinical observation has borne this out. Defensive behavior appears to reduce felt anxiety, although in the process it can distort the individual's relationship to reality. To the extent that such defensive behaviors reduce the strength of the anxiety drive stimulus, they are reinforced and more likely to occur again under similar stimulus conditions.

Bergman (1959) has viewed this partial or total escape from anxiety stimuli (whether labeled as avoidance or inhibition) as part of the individual's defense pattern. He believes the undoing of defensiveness should be a therapeutic objective since the protection against anxiety provided by such defensive behavior is a major obstacle to any counter-conditioning of anxiety in the therapeutic process. Although defensive responses are incompatible with anxiety responses, their reality-distorting nature keeps them from being optimal responses for providing continuing (as opposed to immediate) anxiety reduction.

Dittman and Raush (1954), in their delineation of the structure and methodology of the psychoanalytic theory of conflict, identify the derivative responses to anxiety stimuli as compromise behavior. As treatment progresses, the individual does not need to manifest such derivative behavior and can cope with his conflicts in realistic ways. These derivatives embody impulses whose direct expression would create anxiety. The use of defensive behaviors allows the individual to respond to these stimuli with minimal anxiety. The derivative behavior appears to involve more then than the defensive behavior itself. Furthermore, in analytic theory its origins lie in unconscious conflicts.

This conception of the role of defensive behavior resembles others discussed in this section. Its reference to unconscious conflicts is a restricting one which we have not imposed upon our conceptualization, believing that the awareness of conflict embodied in defensive responses will vary greatly among and within individuals. Furthermore, for those conflicts seemingly conscious in nature it does not follow that "were the associations (or sometimes the lack of them) not representative of conflict, and were they not *disguised* representatives of *unconscious* conflict (that is, derivatives), the patient would have little need or motivation for treatment — he could deal with reality as adequately as the situation allowed, and with a minimal degree of discomfort." (Dittman and Raush, 1954, p. 387.)

Difficulties in distinguishing between manifestations of anxiety and of defensiveness are quite common in the literature and in practice. The Grayson and Tolman (1950) study of the concept of defensiveness is a case in point. The textbook references they used as guiding criteria for expert judges included: (1) mechanism or symptom for tension, anxiety, or discomfort reduction, (2) means of adjustment and protection, and (3) means of restraining or counteracting painful or unacceptable impulses. The psychologists and psychiatrists queried gave widely varied definitions of defensiveness, although the psychologists predominantly preferred the first definition cited above. The definitions seem to emphasize the effect rather than the nature of the phenomenon itself, i.e., defensiveness as an inferred or manifest response or sequence of responses.

Pepinsky and Pepinsky (1954), as we have previously mentioned, discuss anxiety as an irrelevant drive, indicating that the internal anticipatory response to anxiety drive may operate as a signal enabling the person to avoid manifest anxiety; this response may, in turn, generalize. The resulting observable behaviors, which would not be described as anxious in themselves, include inflexibility of behavior, avoidance of manifest anxiety, and escape from a generalized irrelevant drive state. These behaviors fit our conception of how defensiveness manifests itself.

Cowen, Heilizer, Axelrod, and Alexander (1957) have studied the correlates of manifest anxiety in terms of several variables similar to our conception of defensiveness. They compared high ( $\geqq$ 90th percentile), middle (43rd–56th percentile), and low ( $\leqq$ 20th percentile) Taylor Manifest Anxiety Test scores with performance on the Bills Index of Adjustment and Values and with Minnesota Multiphasic Personality Inventory (MMPI) L scale scores. They found significant differences in Bills Index performance between the anxiety groups — the higher the anxiety score, the poorer the self-concept of the subject. When the subjects were categorized in terms of high and low L scores, the reverse was found — the high L scorers had more adequate self-concepts. This finding supports our conceptualization of the relationship between anxiety and defensiveness. Even when these investigators divided low Manifest Anxiety Test scores into "high" and "low" L score groups, they found that those with high L scores consistently scored in the direction of more adequate self-concepts on the Bills Index.

In a similar vein, Cartwright (1956) found that self-consistent information was better recalled than inconsistent information and that the difference in recall was related to an index of maladjustment.

Sarason (1956) has reported on the relationship of Manifest Anxiety Test score to lack of defensiveness. He found that persons with low scores on the MMPI K scale, supposedly indicating a lack of defensiveness, manifest feelings of inadequacy. Responses of a self-deprecating nature are seen as interfering responses detrimental to optimal performance. In our view of the anxiety-defensiveness relationship, we would expect such individuals, lacking defensive responses, to manifest high anxiety, which is also incompatible with optimal performance levels.

Miller (1955), in his description of the development of a general behavior system, cites a proposition which is relevant here: ". . . systems which survive employ the least expensive defenses against stress first and increasingly more expensive ones later." (Miller, 1955, p. 528.) Excessive psychogenic drives (which would include drive state anxiety) constitute stress and the system must respond readily to defend itself against such stress if it is to maintain equilibrium. Miller's proposition, which specifies the order in which defenses occur — more expensive defenses coming into play as less expensive ones prove unable to reduce the stress — is more

satisfactory than Hogan's (1952b) system of additional defensive increments, mentioned below.

One of the prominent contributions of psychoanalytic writers has been
the conceptualization of the various defense mechanisms. Such formulations have given therapeutic workers a common basis for both understanding and dealing with such self-protecting behaviors as they are ex-
hibited by clients. Our use of manifest response variables, we believe, both
exemplifies and clarifies such terms as "mechanism," "means of," and
"techniques made use of." (Freud, 1946.)

Within the theoretical framework of concept of self, Hogan (1952a,
1952b) has spelled out the meaning of defensiveness and the modification of such behaviors by counseling. He defines defensiveness as "a sequence of behavior in response to threat, the goal of which is the main-
tenance of the structure of the self against the threat." (Hogan, 1952b, p.
419.) He believes there are essentially two responses to such a threat:
". . . the individual may revise his concepts or values, and perhaps the
attendant tensions, to include the new and different experience; in this
way he would change his structure of self so that it was more consistent
with his continuing experience. Also, the individual may deny or in some
way distort the inconsistent experience in such a way so that he may see
himself in the accustomed way." (*Ibid.*) The latter kinds of responses
are termed defensive since they maintain and enhance the self-concept by
clinging to familiar values in the face of experiences that challenge them.
Other prominent characteristics of defensive behaviors are these: (1)
they reduce the awareness of threat rather than the threat itself, and (2)
they breed further defenses when resulting discrepancies with reality constitute further threats, necessitating additional defenses. Hogan concluded
that the concepts of threat and defense might well be utilized as criteria
for adjustment and maladjustment.

Haigh (1949) made use of the same framework in the University of
Chicago's coordinated psychotherapy research project. His analysis of
interview protocols revealed a decrease in defensiveness of client's interview behavior during the course of the counseling interview.

In her study using the same interview protocols, Sheerer (1949) devised elaborate definitions of the variables "acceptance of self" and "acceptance of others." These definitions are so all-encompassing that they
seem to provide a picture of general psychological adjustment. Perhaps
for this reason, some of her operational definitions bear a close resem-

blance to Hogan's definition of defensiveness, particularly the following, which we might rephrase as selected characteristics of the nondefensive person:

He does not condemn others or feel defensive when they react unfavorably toward him or other persons.

He resists domination.

He does not deny the facts of his experience nor try to overlook them.

When others criticize his behavior he evaluates the criticism objectively and does not become upset by it.

Sheerer found a marked and fairly regular increase in the measured acceptance of, and respect for, self in the client's statements during the course of the counseling interviews.

Similarly, Robinson (1950) indirectly referred to defensiveness in speaking of behavior that decreases a client's psychological readiness to deal with his problems. Discrepancies between the way a person sees himself and his environment and the way things actually are, he observed, prevent the working out of adequate responses.

In an experimental investigation of the effects of two types of therapy on clients, Ashby, Ford, Guerney, and Guerney (1957) revealed their concern with the defensiveness concept, measured in several ways. For categorizing client interview behavior, defensiveness was defined as the sum of ratings made on three other variables: guardedness, covert resistance, and overt resistance. The authors also developed a Client Personal Reaction Questionnaire, in which one 40-item scale was intended to measure defensive-subjective reactions to therapy and the therapist. Although the scale was not validated by external criteria and change after therapy was not investigated (pre-treatment measures being compared only with in-treatment measures), the identification of defensiveness as a variable in therapeutic change was noteworthy.

Murray (1954) divided the defensive interview behavior of a single client into intellectual defensive statements and complaints about a wide range of physical symptoms and discomforts, plotted according to number of interview hours. Both forms, representing alternative defenses against anxiety, tended to decrease over time. Both, however, helped the client avoid talking about areas of conflict.

As is true of anxiety, certain defensive behaviors — sublimation is one — are viewed as positive and adjustive in nature (see Fenichel, 1945, and Ellis, 1955). Rosen (1956) has reported that college students tend to re-

79

gard defensiveness (MMPI K scale) as desirable. On the other hand, in addition to earlier studies by Hogan (1952b) and Haigh (1949), Hillson and Worchel (1957), Cartwright (1956), and Chodorkoff (1954) report studies which can be interpreted to indicate that incongruity between self-perception and experience is associated with manifestations of defensiveness. Hillson and Worchel, in comparing groups of normals, neurotics anxious group), and schizophrenics (defensive group), found that the anxious group revealed significantly more self-ideal discrepancies than either normal or defensive group. Also, as hypothesized, the defensive group was not significantly different in self-ideal discrepancies from the normal subjects.

It is apparent that the concept of defensiveness, although it stems from different theoretical frames of reference and is stated in different ways, is an important variable of the counseling process in most current theories. It is one that we may expect the counseling experience to effect a change in, decreasing the manifestation of such self-protecting, reality-distorting behaviors.

As used in the present study, defensiveness is defined as response to stimuli perceived as threatening to the self, a special condition of the defensive response being that aspects of reality are denied or distorted. This distortion reduces or reconciles the perceived incongruity between reality and self-concept. Defensiveness is manifested in such response patterns as aggression, withdrawal, and the various defense mechanisms. It brings about immediate anxiety reduction with its attendant reinforcing qualities. The degree to which the individual manifests responses of anxiety, which is the affective component of internal response to threat, is one indication of the efficacy of such protective distortions.

Our brief review illustrates that some measures and some speculations suggest that defensiveness has "good" and "bad" facets. Typing of defenses has artificial, arbitrary features which we find less acceptable than viewing defensive behavior as a continuously distributed phenomenon, varying in intensity, purpose, and effect. While enhancement of certain defensive behaviors may be a justified therapeutic objective, propounding such a goal is severely limited, first, by the ambiguity and variability of definitions of types and degrees of defensiveness and, second, by the implication that this is as much as the individual can tolerate or accomplish. The reduction of defensiveness is a common therapeutic objective, though it cannot be recommended in all cases. Such reduction should result in heightened anxiety drive, internal and overt responses of anxiety, other defensive behaviors, or effective problem-solving responses. Appropriate problem-solving responses differ from anxiety or defensive responses in that their net effect is to reduce anxiety without distorting reality, leaving the individual less open to challenge in the future.

Defensiveness may be shown in both the content and the form of behavior. Thus, in an interview, we would consider defensive any behavior which indicates that problems are not to be discussed, statements are final, client interpretations are not to be altered, while we would consider non-defensive, or less defensive, any response suggesting that problems may be explored, issues are open, decisions are not final, and evaluations are subject to modification. On the other hand, defensiveness may be classified according to its form, for instance, the way in which reality is distorted for protection against anxiety. One classification of such forms includes denial, distortion, withdrawal, justification, hostility, and projection. Anna Freud has presented the classic categorization of defensiveness in *The Ego and the Mechanisms of Defence* (1946).

In essence, defensive responses achieve self-protection by so distorting some aspect of the individual's relationship with his environment that his anxiety is reduced. Thus the second variable of our framework is identified.

## Problem-Solving

The therapeutic objectives which have been reviewed thus far have been stated in negative terms, that is, the reduction of anxiety and defensiveness. Surely the process should involve a positive, developmental component, and indeed such an objective has been frequently endorsed as an outcome goal.

The term "problem-solving" as commonly used in discussing therapeutic outcomes refers to an intricate complex of human behavior. Despite its popularity, the term has no fixed or generally accepted meaning (Guilford, 1954a) either in definition or in modes of solution.

Williamson (1950b) has interpreted the counseling process as one of developmental phases that include analysis, synthesis, diagnosis, prognosis, counseling, and follow-up. He has also stated that one objective of the process is enabling individuals to make optimal use of their potentialities. He has placed much emphasis on this variable as a means of conceptualizing both the counseling process and its outcome. He views the counseling experience as "a generalized method of learning to deal with all kinds of situations." (P. 213.) The counseling experience enables the client to find a method of discovering and weighing the relevant facts about himself. The client's understanding of this method is also applied to identifying alternative courses of action and to selecting the one with the greatest probability of leading to the desired life adjustments. This approach hypothesizes the learning of a generalized method of solving problems as an outcome of counseling. Williamson implied much the same thing in writing about the social purposes of counseling which he felt were to enable the client to learn and relearn methods of realistic appraisal of self.

In the related field of general semantics, Johnson (1946) has inferred that personal adjustment is basically a matter of problem-solving. He goes on to speak of the scientific method as the one clearly effective problem-solving method yet devised.

Problem-solving is a primary objective of the counseling process to Dressel (1951). Problem-solving can refer to the particular concern, conflict, or complaint of the client, or it can have a more generalized referent, improved capacity to solve problems beyond the particular one. This counseling objective could be stated as the learning of a broadly applicable method by which the client is able to recognize, define, and resolve problems which continually confront him in his daily life. Dressel hypothesized that individuals seeking counseling are less capable problem-solvers than those who do not seek counseling. One of Bordin's (1955b) views is quite relevant here. He feels a primary question the counselor should ask himself is this: Why is this individual blocked to the point that he seeks counseling assistance, while others do not? That is, aside from the client's presented complaints, why is he unable to resolve problems for himself?

Dollard and Miller (1950), in a framework of reinforcement theory, have examined the way therapy brings about client changes, some of which appear as changes in problem-solving behavior. The therapist helps the client identify and discriminate relevant problems. As fears are extinguished, there occurs a reduction of repressions, which "restores the higher mental processes," which in turn enables the individual to engage in reasoning, foresight, and adaptive planning.

Shoben (1953a) has also referred to therapeutic changes that imply changes in problem-solving ability. The client who is relieved of anxiety can develop different instrumental social behaviors appropriate to

82

the situations he encounters. "Appropriate" acts are defined as socially reinforced responses. The individual learns under what conditions what behaviors will be followed by such reinforcement.

Perry and Estes (1953) have viewed the counseling process as "sentient problem solving," in which solutions to problems with affective components bear a striking resemblance to problem solutions of an abstract or intellectual sort. They, too, view the "problem" to be solved as more than the particular difficulty the individual experiences. Two aspects of problem-solving which these authors note are the learning of a new cognitive organization with the associated changes in affect, and a learning set (Harlow, 1949), or more generalized conception of how related problems may best be resolved. This conception involves definition, redefinition, asking productive questions, evaluating evidence, and judging alternatives for their relevance and their consistency with definition and available evidence.

Problem-solving behavior takes on another meaning when its drive or motivational origin is considered. Mowrer (1953b) has spoken of defensive problem-solving. And May (1950) is impressed by Mowrer's earlier discussions of the distinction between integrative and adjustive learning (Mowrer and Ullman, 1945). We have chosen not to treat problem-solving in this way. Anxiety and defensiveness, as well as effective problem-solving, may all be considered integrative, and the crucial distinctions among them are then lost to sight. Our approach to problem-solving makes its orientation to reality a critical property, distinguishing it from the reality-distorting technique of defensiveness. We also expect that, as anxiety is lessened in therapy and anxiety drives become less powerful motivators, newly learned problem-solving behaviors will concomitantly replace them. Though both may be called integrative, we find it more useful to emphasize the differences in adjustive effectiveness between them.

Weitz (1954, 1957) has defined the goal of counseling as problem-solving. In the earlier article, dealing with the semantics of diagnosis, he stated that the only purpose of the diagnostic process is solving the client's problems. In the later paper he discussed how during counseling anxiety is reduced by symbolic means and how new responses are symbolically reinforced and therefore learned. The experience of this process carries into the extra-counseling life of the client. According to this view, problem-solving comes about through objectification, i.e., the client's learned sym-

83

bolic behavior is objectified in actions, objects, and events. When this objectification is anxiety-reducing, the objectified behavior will also be learned. The objectification process is the reverse of the symbolic process occurring in the counseling interaction, where both counselor and client employ symbols abstracted from the objects and events of the client's past, and the counseling process.

Thorne (1953) has discussed problem-solving as a therapeutic goal. The problem-solving process, he says, provides the setting in which re-training can occur and be translated into action. This view emphasized rational problem-solving behavior and the therapist's role in counseling as a "master educator." This is similar to one of the counseling objectives of Williamson mentioned earlier in this chapter.

To Berdie (1949) counseling has a broader purpose than simply problem-oriented rehabilitation. He views it as having an educational function in meeting clients' needs — needs that do not necessarily involve deficiencies, inadequacies, or other negative connotations of "problem." Wrenn (1951), noting these maladaptive connotations, suggests that problems are manifestations of unmet needs. The person is aware of his problems; if he is not aware of his needs he has no problem. Our orientation focuses on problem-solving without taking into account degree of awareness or inferred states of need underlying the problem-solving behavior.

Investigators of problem-solving have defined and measured this variable and its correlates in a number of ways. Measures of problem-solving typically have been abstract intellectual tasks, which are related only indirectly to our concern with efficiency in solving *personal* problems. Some experimenters, however, have shed light on this latter process. Cowen (1952), for example, has investigated the relationship of psychological stress to problem-solving rigidity, hypothesizing that increased stress will elicit increased rigidity of problem-solving behavior. He employed the Luchins water jar procedure as the problem-solving task, defining problem-solving rigidity as the tendency to adhere to an induced method of solution when it ceases to be the most direct one. Comparison of groups subjected to varying degrees of stress revealed significant differences in the degree of problem-solving rigidity manifested.

We would infer that stress-induced anxiety leads to relatively inefficient problem-solving responses: the individual clings to behavior which has succeeded in the past and does not explore alternative responses to the tasks confronting him.

Presumably some degree of anxiety drive is optimal in the sense that it facilitates problem-solving. Undoubtedly, there are individual differences in the amount of anxiety that individuals can tolerate and use without resorting to maladaptive (manifestly anxious and defensive) behaviors. In our framework it is far from clear how optimal levels can be identified. A multi-variable framework does allow this descriptive proposition: "optimal" can be defined in terms of the point at which increasing levels of anxiety (present or induced) will produce a shift from effective problem-solving behavior to manifestly anxious or defensive behavior.

Gaier (1952) found a relationship among problem-solving, anxiety, and rigidity. Rigid, inadequate behavior resulting in habitual or perseverative responses inappropriate to the situation was characteristic of the individual who could not improvise new solutions to problems. Gaier found support for the hypothesis that great anxiety leads the individual to preoccupation with self and questions about personal adequacy.

Robinson (1950) differentiates the learning of skills from the learning of better adjustment to one's environment, which he considers one of the goals of counseling. He goes on to note that while this goal is achieved more readily by the happy person it may be achieved in counseling whether the client comes to feel happy or not.

The independence of the client's feeling state and his problem-solving effectiveness seems questionable. We would hypothesize that the relationship between a client's status on these outcome variables is an inverse one, even if only moderately so. Evidence in support of this interpretation of the relationship between anxiety and problem-solving is found in the monograph by Fattu, Kapos, and Mech (1954). A significant inverse relationship ($-.365$) was shown between problem-solving performance (locating defects in operation of a gear box and performance on an electromaze) and Taylor anxiety scores. The index of problem-solving performance was the number of problems solved correctly. However, other indices of problem-solving performance did not reveal significant relationships, particularly for male subjects. Thus, there is at least some evidence to suggest that individuals who manifest the fewest anxiety responses will manifest the most successful problem-solving behavior. However, the relationship appears to be quite dependent upon both the task and the problem-solving response measures employed. These researchers did not find any relationship between manifest anxiety and rigidity, as Gaier (1952) did.

85

While an increasing number of investigations of problem-solving, its measurement, and its correlates have been appearing in the literature, they present a confusing array of incompatible findings. Furthermore, their concern with abstract and depersonalized problem-solving, while appropriate for the purposes of the various investigators, makes their relevance rather remote for the individual beset with personal difficulties who wants to solve problems in his daily life. Moreover, on such depersonalized, cognitive material, the defensively responding individual for whom the content encourages a compartmentalized, intellectualized approach might show himself quite capable, despite his ineffectiveness in solving personal problems.

Problem-solving in the abstract or experimental sense occurs when an individual is presumably motivated to achieve a goal, cannot achieve it through simple actions, and must employ a mediating process, involving words, to reach a solution. In clinical situations the "problem" is more complicated because of the absence or inadequacy of problem definition and means of solution. The data to be considered and evaluated in order to understand the problem and its alternative solutions are not readily available, vary among individuals, and frequently are obscured by anxiety or defensive responses. Even the solution itself in such situations is highly complex, although when stated very generally in terms of "effective functioning," "constructive use of potentials," "understanding of self and others," and the like, it superficially appears to have an attraction.

Despite the vast amount written on problem-solving, we did not find it easy to work out operational definition and measurement of this variable. In order to use such a concept in our study of outcomes, we recognized that "problem" is itself a nebulous term, implying any kind of situation in which the individual's ongoing behavior is obstructed. However, as applied to counseling outcomes, "problem" refers more to personalized, ego-involving situations than to the practical or mathematical forms of problem which occupied Duncker's attention (1945).

There is some evidence relating reasoning to emotional attitudes. For example, Thistlethwaite (1950) gave northern and southern college students logical reasoning problems, some of which were "neutral" and some "emotive" in content, the latter dealing with Negro-white attitudes and behaviors. He found that the distortion in reasoning (the difference between the number of correct solutions to the "neutral" and to the "emotive" problems) was significantly greater for the southern students than for the northern students. However, in problem situations with only slight similarity to those which the client has faced and attempted to resolve, we may be expecting far too much of the power of generalization. This might well be the case with the mathematical equation problems, learning of artificial languages, puzzles, mazes, or, for that matter, the problems of neutral content used by Thistlethwaite.

Similarly, Marks (1951) has proposed a positive relationship between an individual's awareness of the elements of a problem and his ability to reach a solution to the problem. He views awareness as a function of analysis of the situation and the solution as a function of awareness. But in the complex personalized forms of problems with which we are concerned, loosely defined problems are common. His investigation showed that subjects were better at solving impersonal problems than personal ones. Thus, the degree of personal involvement of the subject is a critical variable in any assessment of solving personal problems.

This relationship between anxiety and problem-solving performance may be partly a function of the complexity of the learning task involved. In terms of conditioned discrimination, Hilgard, Jones, and Kaplan (1951) have found that more anxious subjects do not discriminate as well as less anxious ones. They obtained a correlation of .37 between anxiety and the ratio of negative to positive conditioned responses. No significant relationship was found between anxiety and simple conditioning. They recognize that their results reflect a complex situation involving apprehensiveness, set, and accuracy of perceptual discrimination, all of which enter into the determination of the individual's efficiency in producing correct responses to the problem situation.

Now, could all clients be provided with a common problem situation sufficiently "personal" so that the client's problem-solving efforts would be indicative of the effectiveness with which he could handle his own day-to-day problems?

To reconcile these requirements, we defined personal-problem-solving as a series of phases. While presented in some logical order here, these phases would, in reality, be manifested cyclically and concurrently during the counseling process:

*Becoming aware of a problem.* This phase refers to responses by the individual indicating that his ongoing need-reducing behaviors have been blocked in some manner. He cannot perform behaviors that have in the past been need-reducing, or he is at a loss to determine what behaviors

87

will be need-reducing in his present situation. Indications of this in the counseling process are found in the following kinds of client reactions: "I always felt that I was as good as the next student in high school, but here in college I can't seem to begin to measure up." "I don't know what to do."

*Clarifying the problem.* This phase involves determining (1) the objective to be achieved, that is, what is specifically required in a solution; (2) the facts and conditions relevant to the problem faced; and (3) the nature and location of the gap to be bridged between present status and status upon resolution of the problem. This phase also involves the identification of restrictive assumptions narrowing the individual's awareness of the problem. Besides identifying the facts and conditions, and the requirements of a solution, giving these factors a differential weighting, this phase involves putting together these data in an organized way. In vocational counseling, we could illustrate this phase by an assessment of the individual's abilities, interests, personal characteristics, aspirations, and needs, and the importance of weighting such factors in reaching a solution.

*Proposing hypotheses for solution of the problem.* This third phase of problem-solving refers to specific proposals for dealing with the situation. Proposals by the client will depend on the adequacy with which the previous phases have been developed, and particularly on the clarity with which the problem has been defined (the gap identified). Such hypotheses, which may arise at any stage in the problem-solving process, may be the joint work of client and counselor. In the case of less motivated or articulate clients, some counselors would assume more responsibility for proposing a range of possible hypotheses for evaluation by the client.

*Evaluating and selecting among hypotheses.* This phase refers to bringing together hypotheses and relevant facts to determine, first, how consistent such hypotheses are with the data at hand, and, second, what the differing consequences of pursuing such hypotheses would be. These two points overlap considerably and usually are considered simultaneously by an individual, but assessment of hypotheses on the basis of current data logically precedes determination of whether a hypothesis should be translated into a plan of action.

This evaluation process involves three aspects: bringing to bear all relevant information to provide correct premises for reasoning (this reemphasizes the importance of the early phases of the problem-solving process); rigorous "if-then" thinking to indicate the conclusions that follow logically from these premises; and testing each hypothesis to see if the plan of action would be followed by reinforcement.

Such a synthesis of hypotheses with the "givens" of current facts and conditions and requirements of solution provides the test of validity of such hypotheses for bridging the previously identified gap.

Problem-solving of the kind we have described reduces anxiety associated with the problem, with resultant differential reinforcement of the anxiety-reducing responses. In self-concept terms, effective problem-solving responses are nondefensive in nature, distinguished by their realism from the reality-distorting nature of defensive behavior.

## Interrelationships among the Variables

Together, these interrelated variables, anxiety, defensiveness, and effective problem-solving are the framework of our classification system for interpreting the counseling process in terms of its outcomes. Many relationships among these variables suggest themselves. One might hypothesize that during counseling any of these variables might vary in any direction. For instance, the breakdown of a moderately effective defense for the individual might result in an increase in manifestations of anxiety or the appearance of a new set of defenses even more marked than the initial set. Needless to say, this set of circumstances would have a potentially negative effect on effective problem-solving. However, we would hypothesize that the ultimate goal of any counseling process is to (1) decrease sustained manifest anxiety, (2) decrease defensiveness, and (3) increase the effectiveness of problem-solving behavior.

Most writers agree that the processes involved in solving "personal" and "intellectual" problems are essentially the same. Still there is a growing body of experimental literature, particularly Marks (1951) and Thistlethwaite (1950), pointing to the conclusion that personal or emotionally toned problems are less often solved successfully. The framework we have developed is helpful in understanding this.

Through all stages of the problem-solving process, there is ample opportunity for defensive behavior. "Becoming aware of a problem" is a process that defensive withdrawal frequently seems to inhibit. The recognition of unconscious hostility may produce so much anxiety that the individual denies these feelings altogether in a defensive effort to avoid the anticipated punishment. But, as we have earlier indicated, such a "solution" is often more problem-making than problem-solving. Effective counseling often depends upon the solution of a problem of which the client, because of his defensiveness, has not "become aware."

College counselors more frequently see defensiveness and anxiety interfering with the second or clarifying stage. Particularly during the phase of discovering facts and conditions relevant to the problem, the client frequently denies reality or distorts it by projection, rationalization, etc. The fact that students have frequently "overlooked" relevant information (affective and cognitive) suggests that they do not understand the nature of the problem. Thus, the individual may originally see as "feeling ill at ease with peer groups" a problem that might better be described as learning how to deal with anticipations of rejection.

The third or "hypothesis formulation" stage is likewise subject to defensiveness in the sense that certain possibilities are so anxiety-producing that they cannot be brought to consciousness. If the counseling has been thoroughly effective in the first two stages, the "touchy" defensive anxiety-reducing behaviors will have been dealt with already, and hypothesis proposal may proceed much less encumbered. As noted above, the counselor need not restrict his activities to freeing the individual so that his defenses no longer inhibit his perceptual range. The counselor's experience, training, and maturity qualify him as an expert in hypothesis proposal, and this is a valid role; but we must recognize that counselors' hypotheses are no more acceptable to the client than those he makes himself unless he is able to overcome the defensive blocks he has erected.

Because verbalization of a hypothesis may represent only the client's defensive way of dealing with the counselor, counseling must not proceed hastily through the fourth, or evaluative, phase. To guard against this tendency, the counselor must ensure that the client subjects alternative hypotheses to thorough examination and evaluation. It is never safe to assume that defensive behavior has been extinguished or weakened. Misinterpretations of probable consequences, or hasty acceptance or rejection of given hypotheses, are clear signs of defensiveness and indicate the counseling process is incomplete. The client's subsequent actions, of course, should provide the evidence that his behavior is less defensive and that effective problem-solving responses have indeed become more prepotent in his hierarchy of available responses.

Individuals may manifest varying degrees of anxiety and defensiveness. Our first inclination was to assume that the relationship between the two variables would be an inverse one, that is, continuing defensive behavior must have anxiety-reducing properties. From this line of reasoning it would follow that manifestations of anxiety indicated a lack of defensive behaviors (and effective problem-solving behaviors) to cope with the anxiety state and, conversely, that defensive behaviors were anxiety-reducing and hence lessened any indications of manifest anxiety. Subsequent investigations of the relationship between these variables did not bear out our initial assumption. Further consideration suggests that individuals may present both manifestly anxious and defensive behaviors at once. An example would be the nonverbal anxiety responses of perspiring and trembling coupled with verbal responses that all is well and nothing is wrong. Such occurrences would suggest that conceptually the relationship between these two variables is exceedingly complex, and its complexity suggests that any specification at present of the nature of this relationship may be premature.

There is some evidence that may be of help in teasing out the nature of the relationship. Many studies employing the Taylor Manifest Anxiety Scale reveal a marked bunching of college students at the low end. It is quite possible that college students, and student clients at university counseling centers in particular, are relatively homogeneous populations with regard to such variables as manifest anxiety, defensiveness, and effective problem-solving. Would neuropsychiatric outpatient clinic patients and hospitalized patients manifest the same status and variability? It would seem unlikely.

A further complication arises from the fact that the anxiety-defensiveness relationship may differ for different places on these scales. Individuals revealing relatively little manifest anxiety may exhibit any degree of defensiveness. We would expect such individuals to be more effective at problem-solving the less defensive their behavior was. Conversely, such individuals should be less effective at problem-solving behavior if they are highly defensive.

Viewing the three variables together may shed further light on the anxiety-defensiveness relationship and particularly on the question of the positive components of some defenses referred to earlier. Our conceptual framework would predict that those individuals who might be judged as manifesting "constructive" defensive behaviors would also be judged effective problem-solvers. In this sense, their defensive behavior has taken on effective problem-solving properties with a minimum distortion of reality.

91

In discussing manifest anxiety and defensiveness, we have spoken of their characteristics, antecedents, and effects. In looking at effective problem-solving, we have so far concentrated on its characteristics. Is all effective problem-solving rooted in the drive components of anxiety? Among clients seeking counseling or psychotherapeutic assistance this may be a significant source of the motivation to which reinforcing rather than punishing consequences are linked. A case might be made for the view that the drive components of anxiety are the common base from which many different responses manifest themselves — responses of a varied nature reflecting the client's prior learning. On the other hand, this would seem to overlook the role of such drive conditions as curiosity, interests, and exploration, all of which can serve as powerful motivators to effective problem-solving actions. Pepinsky and Pepinsky might refer to these as relevant drive states. "An individual becomes a client because he must deal with a situation or situations, for which there is some doubt as to the appropriateness of his responses." (Pepinsky and Pepinsky, 1954, p. 69.)

Client populations by definition reflect loss, deficit, or dissatisfaction with regard to the adequacy of their problem-solving. Effective problem-solving in this context does rise from anxiety drive, although the drive is socially acquired by learning many cultural values where subsequent failure to behave congruently with these values is anxiety-producing. Many of these cultural values (curiosity, achievement, making sense, etc.) are of a positive nature, but the client's inability to behave congruently with such acquired values evokes anxiety and anxiety-reducing behaviors. These behaviors may or may not be of an effective problem-solving nature depending upon whether more than the reduction of anxiety results.

For our purposes, it does not seem necessary at this time to decide whether anxiety is the source of all effective problem-solving, nor are there sufficient data available to do so. In any case, what happens in counseling is the same. Heretofore responses most readily available to the individual were adequate to reduce his drive tensions. For whatever reason, this is no longer true and the individual seeks help. Through the counseling relationship, the individual acquires new responses, ones that have been weak or nonexistent in his hierarchy of responses.

The stronger the habit patterns of defensiveness or anxiety responses the oftener the original responses must be made in the presence of given cues and drive states with no reduction in drive strength before the old response will be extinguished and shifts in the hierarchy of responses to such cues will occur. The length of time required for these response changes will be a function of the strength of the habitual response patterns and of the strength of the drive component of anxiety during this process. In this shift, it is to be expected that as in most new learning there will be manifestations of much vacillation and variation in responses before effective problem-solving responses become linked with initial cues and drive states.

It will be noted that we are not labeling post-treatment status in terms of any particular level of performance evaluated as "success," "good adjustment," or the like. Rather, the therapeutic objectives are cast in the form of expected *change* in client status, change in one variable not being independent of client status on the other variables. Our initial conceptions here presume linear relationships among the three variables involved. They may not prove to be so. Furthermore, these therapeutic objectives may not be relevant for every client-counselor relationship. However, given practitioners who will accept such outcomes as the ones expected from their work with clients, the framework provides a basis for assessing client change. Subsequent investigations can determine whether there are variations in the degree and direction of change which must be posited as a function of client differences.

## Related Variables

In developing the conceptual framework described in this chapter, we became aware that while these variables are goals toward which counselors and therapists work with clients, there may be other factors which could distort the degree of client change occurring as a result of the process. This led to a search of the literature and discussions among ourselves and with consultants and practitioners. We found two variables that are regarded as potentially influential in determining therapeutic movement and outcomes.

*Motivation to change self through counseling.* Bordin (1955a) has suggested that there are multiple factors which, depending on their particular character, can influence the therapeutic relationship and hence its outcome. Motivation is a popular concept that serves as an example of this kind of variable. Counselors have been prone to assume that the client must manifest motivation in order for the counseling process to be effective. At one extreme is the argument that counseling cannot take place without client motivation; at the other extreme is the belief that one of

93

the counselor's responsibilities is motivating the client for counseling. No one, to our knowledge, has stated or implied that motivation is *not* a critical variable in the counseling process.

Robinson (1950), in his painstaking analyses of characteristics of the counseling process and of immediate criteria of counseling, noted that when differences in counselor techniques and topic were held constant, there were positive correlations between clients' "responsibility-taking" and other immediate criteria of counseling. Thorne (1946) discusses how clients' low motivation influences the counselor's behavior. He emphasizes that the psychologist must vary his mode of imparting information to a client as a function of whether the client's attitude is receptive or only superficially cooperative.

Barron (1953) has developed an MMPI scale measuring various facets of personal efficiency assumed to be associated with ego strength — a concept invested with various meanings, one of which is the individual's strength to strive, at least, in the face of frustration and uncertainty. Grant and Grant (1950) have reported an initial attempt to develop a "therapy readiness" rating scale. While the ratings made of protocols on this basis were correlated only with a second judge's rating of readiness, the client behaviors identified with readiness deserve note. They include ease of verbalization, the extent to which the client expresses feelings as opposed to making unemotional statements, and the amount of work the client assumes he will contribute to the process relative to the contribution of the therapist. These characteristics seem implicit in the literature on the nature of the client's participation in the counseling process.

These types of investigations, statements, and hypotheses led us to identify motivation as one variable we felt should be related to predictions of counseling outcomes. Our definition restricts the term to motivation involving change in the client (as opposed to change in others) and change in the client through counseling (as opposed to change through extra-counseling behaviors).

We would anticipate wide individual differences in client status on this variable and would hypothesize that before the therapist can achieve the therapeutic objectives detailed earlier, the client must perceive and accept the need for change and view the counseling process as the vehicle for accomplishing change.

*Perception of counseling.* The accumulated learnings of an individual are brought to bear upon each new experience he encounters. The counseling relationship is obviously no exception. In a discussion of the critical importance of understanding client expectancies, Sarason states: "If for any kind of interaction we could determine the conditions which gave rise to the initial attitudes, if we could determine the nature of these attitudes and the behavioral changes to which they give rise both before and during the interaction — if we could make these determinations, we would then be in a position not only to say to what other kinds of interactions we can make predictions but also to state the kinds of learning conditions which might have given rise to these kinds of attitudes to this kind of interaction." (Sarason, 1954, p. 74.) Thus, a grasp of the nature of such expectancies is an integral part of understanding the client and his behavior in the interview relationship.

Bordin (1955b) notes the paucity of information available about the anticipations of a client approaching counseling. Subjective impressions from clinical experience lead him to speculate that these anticipations include expression of need for help, signs of affirmation that he has acted appropriately in seeking help, and a commitment on the part of the counselor to provide this help. These expectations are but a few of those which the new client may feel, whether overtly expressed or not. In an unpublished study, Bordin reported that clients tended to anticipate either a personal relationship with the counselor or an impersonal relationship in which their role would be one of receiving advice and information. Among the former group, clients appeared concerned about the counselor's characteristics. In the latter group, the clients seemed to regard counselor characteristics as irrelevant. Bordin's findings were that less than 50 per cent of the client group actually responded in either of these ways, which further illustrates the idiosyncrasies of such expectations — reflecting the client's personal problems, complaints, wishes, fears, and prior experiences.

In a preliminary investigation conducted through semi-structured interviews with clients before their first counseling interview, we also were impressed by the variability in content expressed and in the intensity or strength of response manifested.

Differences in expectations as a function of client problem have been observed by Robinson (1950). He found that clients with problems concerning skills anticipated a more active role for the counselor than did clients with personal adjustment problems. The latter group expected the counselor to assume more of a listening role.

95

Coleman (1948), in a paper on the psychotherapeutic relationship, stated that in the initial period of treatment few clients have any conception of the course which treatment will take, but they expect they will be met with reassurances, advice, explanations, and the like. The client perceives his role in the therapeutic relationship only when he experiences acceptance and understanding, at which time the author believes the therapeutic relationship has been established. This shift is also reflected in a change in the client's perception of the relationship from one of fearing rejection to one of trusting the therapist and utilizing this trust to motivate increasing exposure of his anxieties.

Client expectations and perceptions are further clarified by Shaw (1955) in his concept of mutuality and the upending of client expectancies. He sees the client as orienting himself to his environment (in this context, the counseling relationship) in terms of his expectations. While Shaw does not deal with expectations of the process directly, there are clear parallels. The counselor may be viewed as a strategist attempting to reorient the client's perceptions through upsetting his expectancies of himself, his potentials, his ability to cope with problems, and the like. The upending can be accomplished in various ways, each having in common behaviors which are unexpected by the client and designed to reorient the client to "try on" ways of feeling about himself and his problems which he previously had not considered.

Libo (1957) developed a projective technique to predict return or termination of clients following their first interview. From client responses to four pictures like those in the Thematic Apperception Test, he devised an attraction score to ascertain the cohesiveness of the relationship as experienced by the clients. Predictions of which clients would return were better than chance.

From these diverse attempts at description, inference, and measurement, the role of client expectation or perception of counseling as a potential contributor to client changes appears well worth assessment. Three general referent areas seem to encompass most of the characteristics mentioned: the client's perception of his own role in the process, of the counselor's role, and of the characteristics of the process itself. We have defined perceptions in evaluative terms, seeking assessment of the degree to which a client's perceptions appear appropriate for profiting from the counseling relationship. The next chapter describes the development of a measure of perception of counseling involving the use of counselor judgments as to appropriate or desirable client perceptions.

In summary, these two variables, motivation to change self through counseling and perception of counseling, emerged as potential influences on the movement of clients toward therapeutic objectives. As such, these variables were not utilized as outcome variables but served as classification measures.

The client's motivation to change may have several facets, and we would hypothesize that those clients motivated to change — but to change others rather than themselves — would reflect the least movement in counseling. Similarly, they are less likely to seek a counseling relationship unless it is forced upon them. On the other hand, these initial perceptions or anticipations may be modified as a function of experiences early in a counseling relationship. McGowan (1956), for example, compared clients' attitudes and expectations before and after the first counseling interview. He concluded that the reported changes indicated that the clients found it easier to talk, talked more, and assumed more responsibility in their interviews than they had anticipated they would. This suggests that certain perceptions are modifiable. Those perceptions which are relatively easy to alter may be less a reflection of the client's particular problems than of lack of experience or information; expectations stemming from the latter base should be most amenable to change as a result of direct counseling experience. This is not to say that such perceptions are any the less critical, since the individual holding such views would continue to do so, lacking the direct experience of initial interview contacts.

97

# 7

## The Evaluation Instruments

THE theory developed in Chapter 6 is, in part, an integration of the thinking of many outstanding teachers, the research of many behavioral scientists, and the ideas of many excellent writers and helpful colleagues. Most immediately, it is the product of a coordinated program of research which preceded it (Hoyt, 1954; Magoon, 1954; Jesness, 1955), which in turn developed from a similar ancestry of ideas.

Notwithstanding its impressive background, the theory must be subjected to evaluation before it can leave the realm of pontifical pronouncement, that is, before it can make any claim to scientific contribution. We stress this because it is so common to hear such statements as "the biggest factor in successful counseling is the counselor's personality," or "it's the relationship that counts," or "progress is dependent upon the client's motivation for change." Such statements can be verified only when reliable and valid means of evaluation are available. Only then can counselor personality, the relationship, or client motivation be related to outcomes so that we can test their importance.

Effective evaluation of the outcomes of a counseling experience requires a statement of the objectives of the treatment and methods of measuring these objectives. In Chapter 6 we outlined three variables representing outcome objectives of a counseling program as well as the dynamic aspects of the counseling process as we view it. In addition, two further considerations were specified which we felt were important *pre*-conditions of the counseling process. The second step in evaluating the effectiveness of a program based on these objectives was to develop valid and reliable measures of them.

98

We have previously pointed to some of the known methodological, design, and statistical inadequacies of research in the field of counseling. Shortcomings in the development of indicator measures from which one generalizes to important criterion behavior are even more obvious.

## Indicator Measures

The populations utilized here in developing measuring instruments were, in the main, extreme groups identified in terms of defined behavioral characteristics which, on the basis of previous work, were assumed to be related to the variable under consideration. We broke down the variables in which we were interested into unitary behavioral characteristics, so that nominations of individuals to the validity-criterion groups could be based on *manifest behavior* that was *observable in their day-to-day functioning*. We made the first of these two stipulations to reduce the vagueness and ambiguity that result when judges must choose their own criteria and levels of interpretations for such constructs as anxiety and defensiveness. The second stipulation follows from our interest in outcomes of treatment: after counseling, the client must present behaviors that are discernibly different from his previous ones in his real-life interactions. An example of our procedure may be found by comparing the definitions that follow with the actual rating form we used, which is reproduced in Schedule E.*

Rooting these measures in observable, operationally defined behaviors does not imply that the constructs we have picked as criterion variables (anxiety, defensiveness, and the ability to solve personal problems) are synonymous with the measures developed. Our measures are indicators; what they indicate, if they have been properly worked out, is some of the behaviors that we consider partial definitions of the constructs.

A major problem in developing such indicator measures is obtaining reliable judgments of the behavior of the people who make up our criterion groups. What we preferred was many independent judgments based on extended intimate observations of the nominees. Sophisticated judgments of personality traits are hard to come by, when available at all, and vary in the degree of confidence that can be placed in them.

Most past research in this area has made use of statements of clients to

---

* This schedule and the others referred to subsequently have been multilithed, and copies are available to the interested reader from the Student Counseling Bureau, University of Minnesota. Five of the most basic and frequently referred-to schedules, including Schedule E, are included as an Appendix to the present volume.

counselors about change, or of judgments about client movement made by counselors and therapists. We wanted measures other than those based wholly on the closed therapeutic situation. Whenever we used expert judgments in the development of a scale, we also tried to validate the scale by the judgments of peer groups. Our reasons for this preference were two-fold: we suspected that therapists' judgments would give undue weight to the rapport developed between counselor and client, and the ability of the client to learn the accepting, non-judgmental vocabulary of the therapist, rather than measuring actual psychological movement; and we had the initial postulate that the criteria of adjustment were to be found in the social and cultural milieu of the client, i.e., in the responses of his peers.

*Sensitivity.* Since continuous measurable criteria were not available, and since we placed greater confidence in judgmental specifications of extreme cases than in more minute classifications across the entire range, we chose Fisher's two-sample *t*-test of the mean differences between the two (*high* and *low*) criterion groups (Johnson, 1949).

The populations with which we planned to deal would not span the entire possible range on any of the major variables. Persons seen in a typical counseling bureau were not likely to be grossly pathological or, for that matter, devoid of behavior considered to be at the undesirable end of the continuum in which we were interested. Since the eventual use of our instruments was to be with the average, near-normal clients, the desirability of establishing validity for the tests within a similar range was apparent.

While the validity studies contrasted extreme groups within the near-normal range, we hoped in determining effects of counseling with our measures, to be able to detect changes of a lesser degree than those observed between criterion samples without having to use very large groups of experimental subjects. That is, since the *t*-test of significance is a function of sample size, relatively small (but real) mean differences might be demonstrated for the rather extreme validity group differences by using sufficiently large samples. However, this would mean that, in experimental clients, in order to detect smaller changes than those between criterion highs and lows, we would have to use more subjects, perhaps a great many more.

*Standard of scale acceptance.* To make possible the detection of relatively small real differences or changes in status without the need for extensive replication in future experimental designs, we attempted to construct tests which would separate validity samples by a fixed amount. The distance arbitrarily chosen was one standard deviation between the means of the criterion groups. Thus, if a test adequately represented the same behaviors the criterion judges utilized in nominating validity samples, then, assuming the variables were normally distributed, the extreme 25 to 30 per cent groups from the population of possible nominees would have test score means more than one standard deviation apart. If a test was not sensitive enough to the behavior comprising the operational definition of the variable (as interpreted by the judges) to enable us to separate by this amount the extremes of the criterion samples, then it seemed doubtful the test would prove useful for detecting the presumably more subtle, average changes brought about through counseling, given evaluation experiments of manageable size.

The following sections of this chapter will describe the development of indicator measures for the three basic criterion variables to be used in the study — manifest anxiety, defensiveness, and ability to solve personal problems. Also we will briefly discuss the two classification variables, motivation to change self through counseling and perception of the counseling process. The final part of this chapter will describe the interrelationships among these measures.

## Development of the Minnesota Manifest Anxiety Scale

In the context of the discussion in the previous chapter, we perceive anxiety as (1) a stimulus and a response, as discussed by Mowrer (1953) and Shoben (1953c), and (2) manifest behavior assumed to be indicative of "pure" or residual anxiety not masked by defensive responses. The latter point presupposes the distinctions we have made between manifest anxiety and manifest defensive responses.

*Anxiety defined.* The person with manifest anxiety is (1) *nervous*: having such mannerisms as nail-biting, knuckle-cracking, chain-smoking; (2) *tense*: restless, unable to relax, unable to concentrate, appearing to be under continual pressure; (3) *easily embarrassed*: shy, stammering, blushing readily; (4) *worried*: lacking assurance, fearful of what the next day will bring, overly concerned about the impression he makes on others. Some persons may show just one of these characteristics to a dramatic or extreme degree; others may show several of them to a lesser degree.

*Initial selection of items.* Starting from this definition, we selected an initial group of items to be used in the validity studies on anxiety.

Because anxiety is generally accepted as a core concept in personality theory, many researchers have dealt with this variable before us. Taylor (1953), Sarason and Gordon (1953), and Freeman (1953) all had developed paper and pencil tests designed to tap this variable.

Sarason and Gordon tentatively answered the important questions of generalized anxiety as opposed to specific anxieties by showing consistently positive and relatively high correlations between tendencies to report anxiety in a number of specific situations. However, their scale was devoid of subtlety, and could not be generalized to other than college populations; therefore, the scale was not considered for use in this study.

Taylor reported a scale composed of fifty items from the MMPI chosen according to a criterion of clinical judgment. Only if four of five psychiatrists agreed that a given item should measure anxiety was that item included. She showed a high test-retest reliability (.89) for this scale, and reported some indirect validity data. She included additional buffer items when administering the scale. Bendig (1953) has shown, however, that these items add little to the reliability of the scale and do not change the form of the distribution or significantly alter population means. On the basis of data available, this scale was included in our initial battery.

The Freeman Scale of Manifest Anxiety (1953) uses a somewhat different rationale than does Taylor's scale. Freeman obtained a criterion group of hospitalized psychiatric patients who clearly demonstrated behavioral signs of anxiety. A heterogeneous group of "normals" formed a comparison group. Both groups responded to a 141-item questionnaire disguised as a test of ability to judge other persons. A cross-validation study on new cases showed some promise for the validity of this test. On the basis of this evidence the Freeman Anxiety Scale was included in the initial test battery.

Mowrer, Light, Luria, and Zeleny (1953) made a plea for the use of a simple physiological measure of anxiety. Applying a chemical solution to the subject's fingers and pressing them on specially treated paper provided a measure of the amount of perspiration on the fingertips. Mowrer presented strong arguments for the use of this Palmer Perspiration Index as a meaningful measure of anxiety. An index such as this seemed to fit our conceptual framework, so it was included in the initial battery for the validation studies.

In addition, a fourth index was developed, which we called the Minnesota Manifest Anxiety Scale (MMAS). This scale was developed by providing each experienced counselor at the University of Minnesota Student

Counseling Bureau with a roster of clients he had seen at least twice during the preceding six months. Working with the definition of manifest anxiety developed for this study, the counselors were asked to choose from the list those individuals they felt they knew well enough to rate on degree of manifest anxiety present. The ratings were simply "high," "average," or "low."

Each of the three groups thus obtained was randomly divided into two sections for cross-validation. Responses to the MMPI for the two sets of three groups were simultaneously item-analyzed and items were found which significantly differentiated the highs from the lows for both sets of groups.

This random split of the nomination pool yielded three sets of clients: two high groups of 43 each, two average groups of 58 each, and two low groups of 44 each.

Item analysis using a .05 significance criterion yielded a set of 45 items significant on both sets and transitive across the average groups. An additional set of 13 items which were not transitive across one of the average samples was included in the inventory. These items were employed in the experimental study of counseling outcomes and are listed in Schedule A.*

These four tests constituted the initial anxiety battery.

*Validity.* The question of validity of the anxiety instruments was the next problem. The development of the MMAS made possible a validity study of the Taylor Anxiety Scale. Since the Taylor instrument was based on the MMPI, it was a simple matter to score our nominated individuals on the MMPI items of that scale. Significant differences were found between students judged high and low by our counselors. However, the mean differences between the high- and low-anxiety populations fell short of our desired separation of one standard deviation. This work with the Taylor scale also led us to believe that the scale confounded anxiety and defensiveness as we defined them. Therefore, further use of the Taylor scale was seriously questioned. (Hoyt and Magoon, 1954.)

Twenty-two academic fraternities on the University of Minnesota campus cooperated in a second validity study. Fraternity presidents and counselors (graduate students serving quasi-university staff roles in each house) were given our definition of anxiety and a complete roster of men in their fraternity, and asked to nominate from three to seven who best fit the two extremes of the anxiety variable. Only men independently nom-

* See note on p. 99.

103

inated to the same group by both house counselor and president were included in the criterion samples. Of the group thus obtained we got in touch with 30 highs and 27 lows.

These students, when reached by phone, were told they had been suggested by their house counselors as the type of students we needed for our study and asked to cooperate in the standardization of some tests being developed at the university. (House counselors were given standard responses of neutral content to use when asked about nominations.) Repeated phone calls were made to obtain the sample. The Freeman Anxiety Test, the MMAS, and the Palmer Perspiration Index were administered at the Student Counseling Bureau by examiners who did not know to which category the students had been nominated.

The Freeman Anxiety Test showed no promise of being a valid instrument for separating these populations and was dropped from the battery. The first form of the MMAS and the Palmer Perspiration Index both differentiated our high and low criterion populations. In neither case, however, were these instruments sensitive enough to meet our pre-set standard for acceptance. Computation of a linear discriminant function (Rao, 1952) also failed to yield a satisfactory index.

The criterion populations obtained for this study were used as a basis for further analysis of items from MMAS-1. (The results of this analysis are reported in Schedule A under the heading MMAS-2 Frat. Items with no corresponding MMPI number were developed for the defensiveness scale, to be described later in this section. These items also differentiated these "anxiety" samples.) The resulting scale was keyed and designated as form 2 of the MMAS.

The pool of subjects from the fraternity study enabled us to develop a third item pool. At this time the MMPI was administered routinely as a part of the freshman orientation battery given to each student after his admission to the University of Minnesota, so it was possible to obtain a personality inventory for each member of the subject pool. This set of data was then item-analyzed to yield a third set of analytical results designated MMAS-3 in Schedule A. The items thus obtained were held as a separate scale because of suspected instability of individual responses to these items over prolonged periods of time.

To increase item and scale sensitivity, we reanalyzed the data obtained from the initial (counselor) study. The pool of subjects submitted to counselors in the first study consisted of both men and women. The second (fraternity) study obviously included only men. We knew that the next validation study and the counseling outcome study to follow would use a male sample. Therefore, men from the subsamples of the counselor judgment study were combined into a single group and the item data were reanalyzed to yield a refined set of items. This item set is labeled MMAS-4 in Schedule A. The next step was an expansion of the item pool. After analyzing the items and examining their content, we constructed more items. These were intended to map more broadly the content areas which seemed to differentiate our populations. The items retained from this fifth set may be identified as the items in the final column of the table in Schedule A which have no previous analytical history.

A third validity study was undertaken with the cooperation of the Navy Reserve Training Unit at Wold-Chamberlain Naval Base. No member of the administrative staff felt he knew the men well enough to make comparative ratings, but since the men worked in small groups, it was assumed that there would be a ready source of informal judgments. The definition of anxiety was broken down into behavioral elements so that each man could make sociometric judgments of others in his group on each of these elements. From the nominations thus obtained, combined ratings could be made. In addition to the paper and pencil indices, the Palmer Perspiration Index was administered twice, at the beginning of the testing session and again at the end. The first time, the test was administered under standard conditions, with instructions to relieve excessive situational anxiety; the second time, the instructions were designed to induce stress or anxiety feelings.

During this study, it became apparent that many of the men had been reassigned recently and were not familiar enough with their co-workers to make usable ratings. For this reason, analyses based on these ratings were not carried out.

The Palmer Perspiration Index was, however, subjected to two analyses on the basis of this study: (1) a comparison of the fingerprints obtained with the stress and the nonstress instructions, and (2) a general comparison of these sets of fingerprints with those obtained in previous studies. Although the evidence was still supportive of the general sensitivity of this index to anxiety, the variation of fingerprints administered at different times indicated that the need for further refinement and control of this method exceeded the time and other practical limits of the present project. For this reason it was necessary to drop this index from the battery.

The final validity study on this variable preceding the counseling experiment was carried out with the enlisted men in the Naval Air Reserve Training Unit at Wold-Chamberlain Field under an arrangement like the last. The 110 men in this training unit had been living and working together for the previous 90 days as part of their summer training program. Five men from each of the eight sections, consisting of the section leader and four others randomly selected, were appointed to complete a sociometric form designed for the previously described study. These teams of judges acting independently were asked to make "high" and "low" nominations for each characteristic. From these ratings a weighted index, adjusted for the size of each section, was obtained and cutting scores were set. This procedure yielded a sample of 22 highs and 21 lows.

Analysis of various scales of the MMAS revealed that although we were able to separate the criterion groups, only the new set of items, which had been constructed in order to map more adequately the factors seeming to differentiate criterion populations, reached the goal (one standard deviation) set for acceptance of a measuring instrument.

*Final anxiety scale.* Because of the demands of the overall research schedule, no opportunity presented itself to cross-validate the above-mentioned scale. Therefore, we decided to use item rather than scale validity as a basis for inclusion in the final anxiety scale. Referring to empirical studies by Clark and Gee (1954), we planned to obtain scales of maximized sensitivity by including only items from our previous studies that differentiated criterion groups by at least 20 per cent.

In this way we selected 39 items which were both valid and sensitive for our purpose. The final Naval Air criterion samples were used for an analysis of the new "logical" items we had added, and those which exceeded a 20 per cent standard of discrimination were included in the scale. This procedure added 13 items and completed the final version of the scale, which, from the number of items in it, we call the MMAS (52) Scale.

As an additional check, we computed the correlation between the "empirical" and "logical" item sets. The result, a correlation of .60 uncorrected for attenuation, added some confidence to our use of this procedure of combining scales.

It is evident that additional validation of this scale is needed. While it compares well with scales being used in present-day psychological research, it cannot be said with any degree of assurance that it meets the standards set by the research team for inclusion in the evaluation study to be reported.

Schedule A contains a summary table of the items included in the final version of the MMAS (52). The source of each set of data has already been described. Column one presents the item number from the research inventory; column two, the MMPI item number for those items obtained from that inventory. Columns three through eight present the percentage response for each criterion group described in this section, with the percentage for the high-anxiety group appearing first in each column. The scoring key is also presented under each set of figures. The asterisk allows easy identification of studies in which the item met the "20 per cent or more" criterion for inclusion in the final scale.

Schedule B (included in the Appendix) presents the list of items which made up the final anxiety scale. Items derived from the MMPI are identified by their respective numbers in that scale. Items without MMPI numbers were developed by us as previously described.

Two further studies provide additional validity data on the MMAS (52). Both were made by colleagues who were at the University of Minnesota while this research was being done, but who were not directly connected with the project. Both investigators have graciously given permission for the inclusion of their data.

Nakamura (1959) was particularly interested in the interrelationship among scales purporting to measure anxiety. He obtained a sample of 88 men enrolled in the introductory psychology course at the University of Minnesota and administered an inventory including items from the MMAS (52) as well as items from the Taylor Manifest Anxiety Scale, and the K and F scales from the MMPI. This inventory was readministered after a period of three weeks. The product-moment correlations obtained between scales are shown below.

| MMAS (52) | TAS | MMPI K | MMPI F |
|---|---|---|---|
| First administration .......... | .81 | −.71 | .58 |
| Second administration ......... | .81 | −.72 | .50 |

The data for congruent validity obtained by Nakamura suggest a high degree of interrelationship with the Taylor scale but add no information as to whether or not we were able to increase the sensitivity of a scale of manifest anxiety in a manner designed to suit our needs. The relationships with the K and F scales of the MMPI added to our knowledge of the

MMAS (52) but because these scales were, for the most part, empirically derived, they added little to our knowledge of the anxiety construct as defined in this study. The relationships were, however, in the predicted direction in all instances.

The second study was carried out by Jewell (1958). Of importance here is the part of the study which adds descriptive knowledge regarding the construct validity of the MMAS (52).

Working with the clients used by the research team in the evaluation of counseling effectiveness described in the next chapter, Jewell selected a random sample of twenty individuals stratified to proportionally represent the case load of each counselor involved in the study. He then obtained two teams of three counseling psychologists each from the Vocational Counseling Service at Fort Snelling Veterans Administration Hospital. These counselors were not familiar with the study presented in this book. Each of these counselors was given the definition of anxiety used in the development of the MMAS and case data available to the experimental counselor at the time of the first interview (made up of test scores from the University of Minnesota freshman orientation program). He then listened to a recording of the client's first interview. On the basis of this information each of the counselors independently rated the client for presence or absence of anxiety as defined. Each team of three counselors was then asked to meet and, where differences existed, force a common team judgment as to presence or absence of anxiety. In this manner, two independent judgments were obtained for each client (one from each of the two teams). Reliability of team judgments obtained by analysis of inter-team judgment was .81.

Ordering the twenty clients by the magnitude of their scores on the MMAS (52), Jewell selected the upper five cases and, because of a three-way tie in the final position, the seven cases with lowest scores. Against a criterion of team judgments (two for each case), he concluded that use of the MMAS (52) would have led to eight instances of proper classification and two instances of misclassification; there were among the twelve two cases of inter-team disagreement. Results for the total distribution of cases were comparable and suggested that an empirical cutting score of 19 raw score points on the MMAS (52) was maximally efficient.

*Reliability.* Estimates of the reliability of the various instruments used in the validity studies were made on three occasions by drawing samples from a research pool of students available from the undergraduate psychology courses at the University of Minnesota. At each step in the test development, reliability coefficients were determined by Hoyt's (1941) analysis of variance method on the instruments under consideration at that time. The following coefficients were obtained on the scales in the initial anxiety battery: Taylor Anxiety Scale .88, Freeman Scale .66 and .63, Minnesota Manifest Anxiety Scale .91. The Palmer Perspiration Index was dropped because sets of fingerprints proved to vary in darkness over time.

The Hoyt reliability coefficient obtained on the final MMAS (52) was .74 for the Naval Air sample; the test-retest index obtained from the third psychology pool sample was .94. Nakamura, in his test-retest study with a three-week delay between administrations, obtained a reliability coefficient of .89.

## Development of the Minnesota Defensiveness Scale

In Chapter 6 we described defensive responses as maladaptive behaviors in which anxiety is reduced through the distortion of reality. Some of the more generalized attempts at anxiety measurement which group together both manifest anxiety and defensive behaviors would, according to our theoretical conceptualizations of the therapeutic process, miss one dynamic of behavioral change of great importance to the progress of counseling. A single scale sensitive both to pure anxiety responses and to defensive behaviors could lead to a conclusion of no behavioral change. This could be accomplished by an intra-index shift from anxious to depressive items, the latter in effect minimizing observable anxiety responses. We would argue that the failure of a counselor to recognize such shifts in affective behaviors would minimize his effectiveness. In terms of evaluation of outcomes of counseling the conclusion of "no change" resulting from the generalized measure would be as misleading.

*Defensiveness defined.* The defensive person (1) resists admitting mistakes or inadequacies, (2) rationalizes and excuses them, (3) avoids dealing with problems, for example by daydreaming, wishful thinking, "gold-bricking," withdrawing, changing the conversation, (4) blames others for his own failures, (5) evaluates his abilities unrealistically, in either direction, makes plans not likely to be carried out, tells tall tales about past accomplishments, (6) cannot express his feelings, has his guard up, is unresponsive or apathetic, (7) suspects the motives of others, aggressively doubts authority, consistently challenges the ideas of others.

109

Some persons may show just one of these characteristics to a dramatic or extreme degree; others may show several of them to a lesser degree.

*Initial selection of items.* Although defensiveness is nearly as popular as anxiety as a concept of personality theory, its measurement has been given little attention. Hogan (1948) did attempt to assess this variable through categorization of psychotherapeutic interview transcripts. While his method produced fairly reliable ratings of defensiveness, it is too cumbersome and expensive to be practical.

Because of the paucity of research on this concept, it was necessary to construct an initial testing instrument. Developing items on the basis of our definitions, we prepared a paper and pencil test of defensiveness. Items were included in the initial pool that we supposed represented reality for most individuals. The rationale was that it would then be a simple and direct index of defensiveness if an individual denied or distorted this reality.

An example of such an item would be: "I have felt very self-conscious at one or more times in the past." We assume this to be true of almost everyone, although it is not necessarily complimentary. If a person says "false," we judge this as a denial of a reality experience and score the item as defensive. In this way a set of 66 items was constructed and called the Minnesota Defensiveness Scale 1 (MDS-1). Complete item analysis data are presented in Schedule C.

*Validity.* The first validity study of this scale was carried out with fraternities at the University of Minnesota as described in the preceding section on anxiety.

A sample of 24 highs and 35 lows was obtained from the "agreement" nominations of fraternity counselors and presidents. Our defensiveness test differentiated the high from the low criterion populations, but not sufficiently to meet our goal of a separation of one standard deviation between means. As a result, we used the fraternity answers to analyze the item pool. This procedure yielded a set of 20 defensiveness items which met a .05 statistical significance criterion and were carried over to the second validity study. Items from this source which were used in the final defensiveness scale can be found in Schedule C in the column headed MDS-1.

Using these criterion populations we were also able to obtain MMPI answer sheets from the test battery taken by each of these students upon admission to the University of Minnesota. Item analysis of these data, again using the .05 level of significance for selection, yielded a second set of items referred to as the Minnesota Defensiveness Scale 2 (MDS-2).

In order to increase the defensiveness battery, we took three additional steps. First, we included the Subtle-Obvious items identified by Wiener (1948a, b) from the MMPI, assuming that a valid index of defensiveness could be derived by subtracting the total number of Obvious items answered in the scored direction from the total number of Subtle items answered in the scored direction. We also conducted another Counseling Bureau study like the one conducted for the initial development of the MMAS.

All counselors were given case folders of clients they had seen at least twice during the previous four months. (Clients who had not taken the MMPI as part of their counseling were excluded.) Because this study was begun more than a year after the parallel study in the development of the MMAS-1, there was no overlap in populations used. Each of the eight counselors was given definitions of the defensiveness variable and asked to rate all clients that he felt he knew well enough on the high to low continuum. This procedure resulted in a criterion population of 33 highs and 31 lows.

Item analysis of the MMPI's of these groups yielded 47 defensiveness items meeting a 20 per cent discrimination criterion. These were added to the item pool. Those remaining in the final scale are labeled MDS-3 in Schedule C.

The change to the use of a simple 20 per cent *discrimination index* between samples rather than a .05 or .01 level of statistical significance criterion has been described in the previous section. Comparatively, the discrimination index tends to load a scale with a few more items in the range of middle difficulty (or endorsement rate) and eliminate some of the items at the extreme ends of the difficulty range.

Finally, as with the anxiety scale, additional items were composed to map more broadly behaviors listed in our definition of defensiveness. Items from this source are identifiable in the table of analytical results presented in Schedule C since they appear in the final defensiveness scale MDS (63) but not in any of the other studies.

In previous studies where professional people in counseling or clinical psychology made ratings for use as external criteria, we felt confidence in our use of global judgments. In asking for peer judgments, however, we felt it necessary to modify procedures in order to lessen the burden on

111

those making judgments and insofar as possible to minimize halo effects. Detailed instructions were worked out for raters. Definitions were broken down into unit characteristics and ordered ratings were requested (e.g., who best fits this characteristic, who is the second best fit, etc.). This rating scale is reproduced in Schedule E (see Appendix). A weighting system for order of position was developed as well as a method for equating differences in group size.

By the use of this weighted sociometric method as an external criterion, 23 highs and 24 lows were selected from the Naval Air Unit described in the previous section.

Three analyses were carried out, the first using the Subtle-Obvious (S-O) scoring key for the MMPI. The items obtained from item analysis of the fraternity sample, plus the set of items obtained from the Student Counseling Bureau defensiveness study, were used to develop a second scoring key. The logically derived items developed after the fraternity study were keyed to obtain a third index of defensiveness. The S-O items differentiated the population but did not achieve the desired level of discrimination. Scores obtained for the other two sets of items proved sensitive enough to discriminate our populations at the desired level.

*Final defensiveness scale.* As described in the discussion of anxiety, it was decided to do a further item analysis using the last criterion set obtained from the Naval Air Unit. Items from both discriminating scales were subjected to analysis. Using the 20 per cent discrimination standard, we selected all items contributing to the differentiation and combined them into the final Minnesota Defensiveness Scale (63). The completed scale is reproduced in Schedule D (see Appendix).

The studies by Nakamura and Jewell described in the previous section on the development of the anxiety scale provided similar information on the final Minnesota Defensiveness Scale. The MDS (63) was included in Nakamura's battery of anxiety indices. The tabulation below presents the intercorrelations he obtained in administering this battery twice to a sample of 88 male introductory psychology students.

| MDS (63) | TAS | MMPI K | MMPI F |
|---|---|---|---|
| First administration .......... | .82 | −.68 | .64 |
| Second administration ........ | .81 | −.67 | .54 |

Nakamura's data indicate that the two scales, MMAS (52) and MDS (63), map essentially the same areas. Theoretical consideration of the constructs underlying the measures would lead one to expect different results. The interrelationships with the MMPI K and F scales are too similar to support the hypothesis that the MMAS (52) and the MDS (63) are in fact measuring two relatively independent psychological attributes. Unfortunately, use of reverse armchair analysis, that is, interpretation of the K and F scales to understand the anxiety and defensiveness scales, leaves one dealing with constructs so psychologically complex as to be of relatively little value. Interpretation of the K scale as a type of "ego strength index" as opposed to an "index of defensiveness" so confounds the conceptualization as to be of little help in understanding the original anxiety and defensiveness variables. Interpretability of the F scale in this context is no better. (Dahlstrom and Welsh, 1960.)

Jewell, using the method described in the section on validity of the MMAS (52), selected from among his twenty cases the five persons with the highest MDS (63) scores and the five with the lowest scores. These ten cases were then analyzed to see how this method of classification compared with defensiveness ratings obtained from his two teams of professional judges. The average reliability index between judges was .79. Against the criterion of two team judgments for each case, use of the MDS (63) score would have resulted in six instances of proper classification and no cases of misclassification. There were four instances of interteam disagreement. As with the anxiety scale, the accuracy of classification among Jewell's clients was encouraging and lends some credence to the experimental use of the scale.

*Reliability.* Both test-retest and single administration indices of reliability were obtained for this instrument. Indices were obtained from the validity study samples and the psychology pool samples used specifically for reliability checks.

Reliability indices on the initial Minnesota Defensiveness Scale (66) obtained from the first psychology department (test-retest) pool study and the fraternity study (Hoyt reliability index) were .84 and .85 respectively.

The estimate of reliability for the final Minnesota Defensiveness Scale (63), obtained from the Naval Air Unit study (Hoyt's method), was .81, the test-retest index from the third psychology department pool study was .89, and the final index of reliability obtained from Nakamura's test-retest administration of this instrument with a three-week delay between administrations was .90.

Development of the Indices of Effective Personal-Problem-Solving

As we defined it, effective problem-solving was the most complex, and consequently the most difficult to measure, of the three outcome variables. The fact that psychotherapists and personality theorists alike have a strong tendency to concern themselves primarily with the pathologies of behavior rather than with the more positive and adjustive responses probably accounts in part for the paucity of research on this variable.

Attempts to measure problem-solving in a more or less impersonal situation are well known through the work of Duncker (1945), Maier (1930), Luchins (1942), and others. Attempts to measure highly personalized problem-solving ability ("my" problem as opposed to "the" problem) are practically nonexistent. Marks (1951) has shown that an individual's effectiveness in the two situations may differ considerably, and that significant group differences exist.

*Problem-solving defined.* As we said in Chapter 6, we view effective personal-problem-solving as a six-phase process. First the subject becomes aware of a problem, conflict, or dilemma in which he is involved. Next, he clarifies the problem, the goal to be achieved, the resources available, and obstacles which may be encountered. Third, a set of possible solutions or alternative courses of action is formulated. Next, these possibilities are weighed and a selection is made from among them. A psychologically safe tryout is then made and by this means new information is obtained. Finally, the new information gained from the tryout experience is fed into the information complex and the process is repeated. In this way the individual attempts to achieve a closer approximation of a satisfactory solution. He does not act on impulse, he is not restricted in his planning by "single-track" thinking, and he is able to reach decisions without being overwhelmed by his problem.

*Initial development of measuring instruments: the fact-elicitation tests.* Our task was the selection of available tests, or the construction of new instruments, to assess the subjects' proficiencies in each aspect of the process described above. Since most of the clients we saw had recognized a problem situation, and the final two stages of the problem-solving model were likely to be open to direct observation, we decided to restrict the attempts at test development to the second, third, and fourth phases of our definition.

We wished to develop an instrument which would present the subject with a "real-life" problem situation that he would be free to work out in a relatively natural and unrestricted way. At the same time it was necessary to have an objective and efficient means of observing, recording, and evaluating the subject's problem-solving behaviors.

Neither the traditional paper and pencil tests of problem-solving ability nor situation tests such as those used by the Office of Strategic Services (1948) during World War II appeared adequate. The former usually deal with puzzles, occasionally clothed in verbal symbols, which could be solved by simply arranging the stated components of the problem in a logico-mathematical form and proceeding to the conclusion according to the rules of the system. These tests usually are scored on solution only, on the assumption that the subject would not arrive at the correct solution if he erred in the process.

Such tests were inappropriate for our purposes because almost none of the problems which confront clients are purely analytic. It is inductive reasoning with propositions, the "probability" of which is not precisely known, that is most often involved in solving personal problems in the counseling process. Also, it was the process we wished to assess, not merely the outcome. Finally, we felt that standard paper and pencil tests lacked a realistic, lifelike setting. To be effective a test need not be a miniature sampling of the activities one desires to test, but when such a correspondence exists, the explanatory work is simpler.

Two undesirable properties argued against the use of situation tests. In the form in which they are ordinarily employed (e.g., by the O.S.S.) the physical apparatus is expensive and the examiner and observer time required is great. Even more crucial is the difficulty of obtaining reliable, objective records and evaluations of the performances of subjects in situations which are left as flexible as has been customary. Cronbach (1956) has presented an excellent analytical critique of attempts at global assessment together with a pessimistic appraisal of them.

Thus, while the situation tests possess the desired face validity, they are inefficient and of questionable reliability. On the other hand, the paper and pencil tests, while having satisfactory scoring and reliability features, are artificial and do not allow us to observe the process itself.

We chose instead a middle ground. Having selected four areas in which the problems of clients in our setting most frequently fall — those of interpersonal relations, family relations, vocational decision-making, and social-sexual adjustment — we formulated for each area five problem situations typical of those which clients might present in counseling.

In each problem situation the person involved had to select a course of action. The facts of the situation were selected so as to balance the positive and negative consequences of choosing either of the alternatives suggested by the problem. We tried to preclude any easy solutions which would not be contraindicated by some of the available facts. Anticipating the commonest questions that would be asked in the problem situation, we prepared lists of proposed standard answers. Additional facts (such as the person's age or the size of his home town) were also included. This was done to standardize responses and add to the "reality" of the situation.

Preliminary forms for some twenty "dilemma" situations were thus constructed. These consisted of an introductory statement of the problem, a set of relevant facts, and a means for tallying the subject's questions and the examiner's responses.

In the administration of the tests, the examiner, after attempting to establish rapport, explained to the subject that this was a new type of test in which the two of them were assumed to be good friends and he, the examiner, had come to the examinee for advice on a problem that was troubling him. After the examiner had given a short, standard, and rather nebulous statement of the problem, the examinee's task was to ask questions of the examiner until he felt he had enough information to advise a course of action. To each question asked, the examiner responded with an appropriate item from the set of facts prepared for the particular situation, checking both question and response on a prepared form. To maximize the naturalness of the situation, the examiners were trained to respond as nearly as possible in a conversational manner, and to keep the test forms inconspicuous. In Schedule F the interested reader will find two complete sets of fact-elicitation problem statements and a copy of standardized procedures used by the trained test administrators.

The problem of scoring the protocol of such an interchange still remained. As an initial attempt, the members of our group independently assigned to each item of each situation a value of zero, one, two, or three according to its judged importance to a clearly formulated solution to the problem. An item which indicated a crucial aspect of one horn of the dilemma was given a weight of three points and one with no relevance to framing or solving the problem was weighted zero. These judgments were pooled and differences resolved in joint session. The rationale behind this procedure lay in the expectation that the good problem-solver would get many of the important facts about a situation and should be credited for this. By contrast, the poor problem-solver would either gather too little information or get off on a tangential or irrelevant aspect of the problem and should be penalized. Thus one index considered was total points (TP) for the information elicited. Weights used in arriving at the TP figure are given in Schedule F.

A second scoring possibility we considered was a measure of efficiency of fact-gathering. One fault we anticipated with the TP index was that a compulsive fact-gatherer, although in possession of the facts, might fail to distinguish the relevant from the unimportant. To measure this efficiency aspect we selected the ratio of total points (TP) to the total number of questions asked (TQ). This we called total ratio (TR).

We also anticipated that many of the problems could be quite easily "solved" if the subject were to ask the examiner questions requiring *him* to predict outcomes of certain actions or others' responses to alternative solutions. Thus the examiner would be making the evaluations instead of the subject. If the subject asked a question calling for a prediction or an opinion about some hypothetical or future event for which no explicit fact was given on the fact sheet, the examiner was to indicate that he "just didn't know how that would turn out." Where this response seemed unlikely some more definite item could be added so long as it was in keeping with the rest of the data and would not lead to an easy solution. These "predictions" made by the examiner were tallied separately on his report form.

Since some questions calling for predictions might be answerable by the examiner so as to give information valuable in formulating or solving the problem, we felt the subject should not be penalized as he would on the TR index. Further, without having collected any data at this point we could not decide whether correcting for compulsive questioning might better be done by some linear correction than by the ratio we had defined. To incorporate both of these points into a scoring formula, we defined a linear combination derived from the three tabulations we had available. This derived index was $D = TP - (TQ + Pred.)$.

If a question was asked that could not be answered on the basis of the given facts and that was not a "prediction" question, the examiner was to give a response in keeping with the rest of the data and to note on the report form both the question and the response given. These new items were subsequently weighted in the same manner as before, and this pool of additional information was incorporated into the standardized response repertoire of the examiners.

A final convention employed in the test administrations concerned repeated questions. It was decided to tally the question again and to make a second tally under a heading "reit" for reiterated question. Thus, on some of the indices (e.g., TR and D) the repetition of a question for which the answer had already been given would incur a penalty.

Against the possibility that the weights we had appended to the items actually would suppress results, we also, by merely giving unit values to each item of information a subject elicited, scored each subject's performance for the total number of bits of information he obtained (Bits). Correspondingly a second derived index $D' = \text{Bits} - (TQ + \text{Pred.})$ was defined and considered.

Thus we had defined five measures of effectiveness in solving personal problems (TP, TR, Bits, D, and D'), one or more of which we hoped would give us a reliable and valid measure of the fact-eliciting phase of this construct.

Because the question of equivalency of forms preceded the validation studies on this instrument, a complex analysis was used to select equivalent forms for the experiment to follow. This was necessary because five possible scoring methods, all of unknown validity, existed. The problem was to find the two fact-elicitation test sets yielding the most similar rank ordering results. For this purpose a sample was drawn from the pool of students from introductory psychology courses who volunteered for participation in experiments, and a five by five Latin square design was completed.

When the test was first developed, a design of test, treatment, test, time lapse, and test was under consideration for the study, and therefore three test sets instead of two were selected.

As an example, we present below the intercorrelation matrix for the family relationships problem area. The cluster ABD was chosen because it displayed the highest intercorrelations.

A sixth measure of effective personal-problem-solving was developed, called the Horn Index (H). This was evolved because it was possible for a subject to get a good, or at least fair, score on one of the other indices by eliciting information pertaining to only one side or one horn of the dilemma. Presumably, the good problem-solver, having been told by the examiner that there was a problem, would probe until he had information

| Situation | A | B | C | D | E |
|---|---|---|---|---|---|
| *TP* | | | | | |
| A ....... | 1.00 | .67 | .59 | .61 | .63 |
| B ....... | | 1.00 | .60 | .65 | .71 |
| C ....... | | | 1.00 | .58 | .63 |
| D ....... | | | | 1.00 | .63 |
| E ....... | | | | | 1.00 |

| Situation | A | B | C | D | E |
|---|---|---|---|---|---|
| *D'* | | | | | |
| A ....... | 1.00 | .68 | .61 | .75 | .67 |
| B ....... | | 1.00 | .64 | .70 | .74 |
| C ....... | | | 1.00 | .62 | .64 |
| D ....... | | | | 1.00 | .65 |
| E ....... | | | | | 1.00 |

| Situation | A | B | C | D | E |
|---|---|---|---|---|---|
| *TQ* | | | | | |
| A ....... | 1.00 | .70 | .59 | .50 | .71 |
| B ....... | | 1.00 | .70 | .63 | .80 |
| C ....... | | | 1.00 | .61 | .71 |
| D ....... | | | | 1.00 | .62 |
| E ....... | | | | | 1.00 |

| Situation | A | B | C | D | E |
|---|---|---|---|---|---|
| *D* | | | | | |
| A ....... | 1.00 | .55 | .56 | .62 | .48 |
| B ....... | | 1.00 | .46 | .55 | .33 |
| C ....... | | | 1.00 | .52 | .45 |
| D ....... | | | | 1.00 | .48 |
| E ....... | | | | | 1.00 |

| Situation | A | B | C | D | E |
|---|---|---|---|---|---|
| *TR* | | | | | |
| A ....... | 1.00 | .34 | .16 | .28 | .29 |
| B ....... | | 1.00 | .40 | .19 | .55 |
| C ....... | | | 1.00 | .26 | .36 |
| D ....... | | | | 1.00 | .37 |
| E ....... | | | | | 1.00 |

identifying some sort of conflict. The person who obtained data on only one aspect of the dilemma, and was thereby able to offer a relatively easy solution, ought not to receive a high score despite the thoroughness with which he elicited information on the one horn.

To identify the two subsets of items for a situation that best pointed up each aspect (horn) of the problem and when taken in opposition to each other clearly indicated a dilemma, we formulated "elegant" or pattern problem definitions (Schedule G). Each member of the research group independently identified some eight to ten items on each side of each situation. In joint session these judgments were pooled and a set of from five to seven items were selected for each horn of the dilemma. In Schedule H are presented the situation from which the item was drawn, the Horn 1 or 2 to which the bit of information was judged relevant, the item number, the code number of the information sheet from the fact-elicitation inventory, and the bit of information.

The H score was derived by counting the number of bits of information obtained from each of two subsets of items for each situation and checking the assigned score for that combination of items elicited. These were then summed across all problem situations of the test and this sum was used as the H score for the total test.

The H scores assigned to the number of such items elicited by a subject are listed below.

| Combination of Items Elicited | Situation H Score |
|---|---|
| 0–0 | 0 |
| 0–1 | 2 |
| 0–2 to 0–7 | 3 |
| 1–1 | 10 |
| 1–2 | 12 |
| 1–3 to 1–7 | 13 |
| 2–2 | 15 |
| 2–3 to 2–7 | 16 |
| 3–3 to 3–7 | 17 |
| 4–4 to 4–7 | 18 |
| 5–5 to 5–7 | 19 |
| 6–6 and 6–7 | 20 |

As the reader can easily see, the subject gets the biggest increments for identifying the two horns of the dilemma and comparatively little credit for extended elaborations of any one aspect.

*The definition-framing and solution tests.* Just as the traditional puzzle-solving tests and the elaborate situation tests had been rejected as a means of assessing the fact-elicitation phase of problem-solving, they were also rejected as a means of measuring the definition-framing and solution stages of the process. Instead, modified situation tests, in many ways similar to the fact-elicitation tests, were devised.

We took as a starting point the same four problem areas defined for the construction of the fact-elicitation tests. Again, five problem statements were devised with content from each area and a short narrative formulated about the situation. These were constructed so that the complexity of the situation would preclude easy definition and solution of the problem by anyone who took into account all of the data given.

Administration of the tests was in two stages. First, the subject was given a rather nebulous introductory problem statement and the complete set of data. He was asked to read both, then carefully but concisely to state the "real" or "most pressing" problem faced by the person in the situation.

The second step, that of solving the problem, presented a major difficulty. If the subject were allowed to solve the problem as he had defined it, the task of evaluating all possible "solutions" would be virtually impossible. For instance, one subject, having done a good job of definition, would then have a very difficult problem to solve, while another subject, having disregarded a segment of the data, might pose a grossly inadequate definition of the problem, which would be easy to solve.

We tried to scale this device by using professional judgments of definitions and solutions. But since there were marked disagreements in rankings by judges, we did not feel warranted in pursuing this scoring method further.

Since counselors' judgments of solutions were so disparate, we suspected that some standard definition would have to be made for use in the second or solution stage. Thus on the basis of the formulations we had used to construct the situations, as well as some additional definitions offered by the counselors, we framed what seemed to be adequate yet concise problem definitions for each of the twenty situations. After the subjects had formulated their definitions of the problem these were collected and a second sheet was given to them. This second sheet gave the same introductory statement and body of data, together with the standard problem definition, and the subjects were asked to solve *this* problem rather than the problem they had previously defined. Schedule I presents a sample set of five problem situations in the vocational area and the solutions developed for each.

For each situation we constructed a rating scale by considering what kinds of modifications of this inclusive definition might be acceptable. In addition, special "ground rules" were set up for certain situations, consisting of downward corrections for such faults as neglecting stated minor facts or implying a tactless manner in dealing with persons in the situations, and upward corrections for taking cognizance of related side issues as side issues, and the like. A person's score was called his Dn score for "Definition."

Taking the standard definitions as a starting point, we then constructed a similar scale for scoring the solutions for each situation. This was called the Sn score for "Solution." With these scoring scales, Dn and Sn, for reference, three members of our group independently assigned a value to each definition or solution to be scored and any disparities were resolved in joint session.

We next selected two or three equivalent sets of definitions and solutions, drawing one from each of our four content areas. This analysis of equivalent forms was done with the same sample from the student pool of volunteer subjects maintained by the psychology department that we had used for the selection of the fact-elicitation test forms. From each of

121

the four content areas, we chose clusters of three situations and constructed test forms by drawing at random one situation from each cluster.

*The logical reasoning test.* In addition to the fact-elicitation, definition, and solution tests that were developed to assess the several aspects of problem-solving effectiveness, a fourth instrument modeled after one described by Thistlethwaite (1950) was constructed. In his original test, he selected a series of six syllogistic forms and composed items substituting verbal statements for the elements of the syllogism. Thistlethwaite selected the content of these verbal statements from two areas — "neutral" and "ethnocentrically emotive." An equal number of items from each of these two areas were constructed for each of six reasoning forms and these 72 items constituted Form I of his test. Each item from the emotive area was constructed so that the "ethnocentric" subject would tend to judge it incorrectly (i.e., invalid if it was valid and valid if it was not), if he based his judgment on the conclusion only rather than on the logic. Further, an attempt was made to match each pair of emotive and neutral items not only for syllogistic form, but also for sentence length and comprehensibility of the terms.

The rationale underlying the test was that persons with strong attitudes and beliefs with respect to minority groups would experience an interference in their reasoning processes when faced with problems couched in terms of these groups. The neutral items were included as a control on the level of reasoning ability, providing a base level, as it were, of syllogistic reasoning proficiency from which the effect of the "loaded" material could be computed for each subject. The index employed was a function of the difference between the number of errors on the emotive items and the number made on the neutral items. The test was presented to the subjects simply as a test of reasoning ability.

In view of this test's reported success in measuring group differences in ethnocentrism, we constructed a modified form of the test, on the grounds that a strong emotional attitude of clients might be reflected in impaired reasoning with content from the areas in which the attitude centers. To the four areas in which fact-elicitation, definition, and solution situations were constructed — Family Relations (FR), Interpersonal Relations (IR), Vocational Decision-Making (V), and Social-Sexual Adjustment (S), we added a fifth, Academic (A). Of the six syllogistic forms employed by Thistlethwaite, we used only four, omitting the two longest and presumably most difficult, and for each of the remaining four forms we constructed sets of neutral and emotive items. This inventory (Schedule J) is keyed for correct response and problem area.

Some of the "ethnocentrically neutral" items from the Thistlethwaite test seemed inappropriate as non-emotive items for assessing differences in our problem areas. These we culled from the original test's neutral items, substituting in their stead items of similar form but different content. This modified set of 24 neutral items was then used for computing the base level of reasoning proficiency of the subjects. A completely new set of emotive items was composed with content selected from our five areas. We felt that the one-to-one matching of neutral and emotive items had been an unnecessary refinement of the original test and that, in a preliminary experiment to determine whether the test could be used to separate good and poor problem-solvers, the essential features desired were a set of neutral items to establish a reasoning base level and a set of emotive items with a nearly proportional number of items of each syllogistic form.

As a preliminary form, a test was constructed of 24 neutral and 29 emotive items. The test was scored for the number of errors committed on the neutral content items, N; the number of errors on the emotive content, E; and a difference score, $20 - (E - N)$.

*Validity.* The procedure for establishing the validity of our measures of problem-solving effectiveness was similar to that used for the validation of our other variables. First a subpopulation was selected in which multiple judgments of the members could be obtained on our criterion rating forms. From these ratings, subgroups of highs and lows were identified and contacted to solicit their aid without divulging to them the actual nature of the study. After the testing was complete, mean differences were computed between the high and low nomination groups and tests of significance were run to ascertain whether the measure had met the validity criterion previously set.

A validity study, described earlier, was conducted on samples drawn from the 22 academic fraternities on the University of Minnesota campus. As with the other dimensions, criterion groups of effective and ineffective problem-solvers were obtained from each of the participating fraternities. This procedure yielded 31 highs and 24 lows who were eventually contacted for testing. Of these, complete data on all four tests of this variable were obtained for 28 highs and 22 lows.

Because some of the men had been nominated for the criterion groups

123

on more than one of our variables, we decided to use only one set of fact-elicitation tests and only one situation from the first set of definition and solution tests in this study.

The primary analysis of the results consisted in the computation of $t$-tests of the mean differences between the high and low criterion groups on each of the previously defined indices for the several tests. These results are summarized in Table 1.

Since the "Bits" variate reversed to a small degree it was dropped from any further consideration and the derived index, $D'$, was accordingly also eliminated. Although one of the variates, total ratio ($TR_4$), was validated at close to the criterion difference set, in general the results were not satisfying. In the first place, even though the $TR_4$ mean difference was statistically significant, the mean difference was only 0.7 sigma. Secondly, we felt that on theoretical grounds the $TR_4$ index did not encompass all we meant by effectiveness in solving personal problems and we had hoped to use it only in combination with some of the other problem-solving indices.

Because these results were disappointing, we attempted to develop other indices which might prove more sensitive than the initial ones. These included subsets of two and three fact-elicitation situations selected in an attempt to minimize error variance. Analyses of these yielded no evidence of improved sensitivity.

Table 1. Mean Differences and Tests of Significance for the Problem-Solving Variates Based on the Fraternity Validity Study Samples

| Variate | Test | Number | | Mean Difference | $t$ | Probability Level |
|---------|------|------|-----|-----------------|-----|-------------------|
| | | High | Low | | | |
| $TP_4$[a] . . . . . . . . . . . | F.E. | 31 | 24 | 3.48 | .261 | $.70 < p < .80$ |
| $Bits_4$ . . . . . . . . . . . | F.E. | 31 | 24 | $-.65$[b] | $-.089$ | $.90 < p < 1.00$ |
| $TR_4$ . . . . . . . . . | F.E. | 31 | 24 | .21 | 2.573 | $.01 < p < .05*$ |
| $D_4$ . . . . . . . . . . . . | F.E. | 31 | 24 | 3.61 | .665 | $.50 < p < .60$ |
| $H_4$ . . . . . . . . . . . | F.E. | 31 | 24 | 3.70 | .849 | $.40 < p < .50$ |
| Dn . . . . . . . . . . . . | Dn | 28 | 22 | .80 | 1.061 | $.20 < p < .30$ |
| Sn . . . . . . . . . . . | Sn | 28 | 22 | .79 | 1.067 | $.20 < p < .30$ |
| E . . . . . . . . . . . . . | L.R. | 30 | 23 | $-2.97$[c] | $-1.975$ | $.05 < p < .10$ |
| N . . . . . . . . . . . . . | L.R. | 30 | 23 | $-1.96$[c] | $-1.728$ | $.05 < p < .10$ |
| $20 - (E - N)$ . . . . | L.R. | 30 | 23 | 1.01 | 1.127 | $.20 < p < .30$ |

* Significant at the .05 level.

[a] The subscript "4" indicates that these scores are based on all four fact-elicitation tests in set I.

[b] A reversal in means but of very small magnitude relative to the standard error.

[c] An error score, hence not a reversal in means.

In planning the study we had intended to select the most promising measures derived from the tests of each aspect of the problem-solving process and to compute from these a linear combination to be used as a simple measure of effectiveness in solving personal problems. The linear discriminant function (L.D.F.) of R. A. Fisher provides an effective means for constructing such a linear combination, and when used in conjunction with a generalized distance function ($D^2$) this method provides tests of significance both for the total set of variates and for the contribution of each to the separation of the groups (Rao, 1952). Since the individual variates were not highly significant, the hope was entertained that perhaps the $D^2$-L.D.F. analysis might provide us with some linear function, the members of which, though not all separately significant, might in combination yield satisfactory criterion group differences. Ten such analyses were run on the fraternity samples, using in all cases only the 28 highs and 22 lows for whom complete data were available.

The results of the generalized distance and linear discriminant function analyses are summarized in Table 2.

Table 2. Sets of Problem-Solving Variates Combined into Linear Discriminant Functions and Tests of Significance for the L.D.F.'s on the Fraternity Samples (Highs, N = 28; Lows, N = 22)

| Variates Combined | $F$ | Probability Level |
|---|---|---|
| $TR_4, 20-(E-N)$ | 4.308 | $.01<p<.05$* |
| $TR_4, 20-(E-N), N \times E$ | 3.375 | $.01<p<.05$* |
| $TR_4, 20-(E-N), N, E$ | 2.334 | $p>.05$ |
| $TR_4, 20-(E-N), N \times E, N, E$ | 2.017 | $p>.05$ |
| $[TR_4 \times 20-(E-N)], N \times E$ | 3.787 | $.01<p<.05$* |
| $TR_4, 20-(E-N), 50-(E+N)$ | 3.183 | $.01<p<.05$* |
| $TR_4, 20-(E-N), TP_4$ | 2.848 | $.01<p<.05$* |
| $TR_4, 20-(E-N), 50-(E+N), TP_4$ | 2.371 | $p>.05$ |
| $(H \times TR)_3, 50-(E+N)$[a] | 2.031 | $p>.05$ |
| $(H \times TR)_3, 50-(E+N), H_3$[a] | 1.861 | $p>.05$ |

* Significant at the .05 level.
[a] Only the IR, FR, and S situations of the fact-elicitation test were used.

Only the most tentative and cautious interpretation can be made at this point. Of the ten originally defined measures only one showed reliable differences and that at a degree of separation below what we had set as minimal. Of a set of fourteen additional measures, at least some of which were defined after a careful inspection of the data for the most promising contrasts, only three met a significance level of .05 or less. Finally, of the

125

set of ten L.D.F.'s computed, exactly five showed separations that were statistically significant at less than the .05 level, though all were less than one L.D.F. sigma in magnitude. Since these represent optimal *sample* separations, some diminution of which is to be expected in subsequent applications, our confidence in the ability of one of these functions to stand the test of cross-validation was not great.

The second validity study was concerned only with the validation of the fact-elicitation and logical reasoning problem-solving measures and made use of criterion samples drawn from two subpopulations within the university.

From the Student Activities Bureau of the Office of the Dean of Students, a list was obtained of student leaders who had been nominated for all-university recognition. This list was circulated among the staff members of the Activities Bureau together with the definition of the effective problem-solver and a set of instructions. Each of these professional persons was to nominate any student on the list whom he felt he had come to know well and who fit the description presented. This yielded a list of 50 nominees with from one to eight nominations each. From this list were culled all graduate or adult special students and any student previously given the problem-solving tests. This left a pool of 38 of whom 19 had been nominated at least twice. From these 19, 15 were eventually tested together with ten of the single-nomination subjects for a total of 25 people in the high group. (We decided that single mention was more likely to indicate specialization and consequent lack of interaction — on the part of nominators or nominees or both — than doubtful status as a problem-solver.)

The other criterion sample was drawn from the men's dormitory groups. Here the definition of the poor or ineffective solver of personal problems was given to the dormitory director, a person with considerable psychological training and sophistication. One of the responsibilities of the director's job was to meet once a week with each dormitory group counselor to discuss each resident under the counselor's charge. A record of each student's behavior, academic progress, and personal characteristics is kept and brought up to date at these weekly sessions. Because of dormitory regulations, we were not able to get independent judgments from both the dormitory director and the group counselor. However, by working through the director in his meetings with the counselors, a list of pooled-agreement nominees was obtained. After culling this list by the same criteria used for the student leader group there remained 52 students of whom 24 were tested.

The testing of both highs and lows consisted of two sessions a week apart in which a fact-elicitation test and a logical reasoning test were given at each session. The test-retest reliability coefficient for the two forms of the fact-elicitation test was .60; for the two administrations of the logical reasoning test, it was .78. It should be noted that these coefficients were obtained from a selected rather than a random sample of the college population, and generalization of these data is therefore limited.

The results of the first testing are summarized in Table 3.

Table 3. Mean Differences and Tests of Significance for the Problem-Solving Variates Based on the First Testing of the Student Leader and Dormitory Samples (Fact-Elicitation Set I)

| Variate | Test | Number High | Number Low | Mean Difference | $t$ | Probability Level |
|---|---|---|---|---|---|---|
| $TP_4$ .............. | F.E. | 25 | 27 | 29.12 | 2.865 | $.001 < p < .01$** |
| $TR_4$ ............. | F.E. | 25 | 27 | $-.11^d$ | $-1.123$ | $.20 < p < .30$ |
| $H_4$ .............. | F.E. | 25 | 27 | 7.41 | 1.781 | $.05 < p < .10$ |
| $(H \times TR)_4$ ......... | F.E. | 25 | 27 | 9.96 | 1.256 | $.20 < p < .30$ |
| $TR_3{}^a$ ............. | F.E. | 25 | 27 | $-.15^d$ | $-1.397$ | $.10 < p < .20$ |
| $H_3{}^a$ .............. | F.E. | 25 | 27 | 6.90 | 2.169 | $.01 < p < .05$* |
| $(H \times TR)_3{}^a$ ....... | F.E. | 25 | 27 | 8.20 | 1.171 | $.20 < p < .30$ |
| $TR_3{}^b$ ............. | F.E. | 25 | 27 | $-.14^d$ | $-1.364$ | $.10 < p < .20$ |
| $H_3{}^b$ .............. | F.E. | 25 | 27 | 5.70 | 1.614 | $.10 < p < .20$ |
| $(H \times TR)_3{}^b$ ....... | F.E. | 25 | 27 | 7.04 | .985 | $.30 < p < .40$ |
| $(H \times TR)_2{}^c$ ....... | F.E. | 25 | 27 | 7.98 | 1.415 | $.10 < p < .20$ |
| $TR_4 \times [20 - (E - N)]$. | F.E. & L.R. | 25 | 24 | $-1.75^d$ | $-.599$ | $.50 < p < .60$ |
| E .............. | L.R. | 25 | 24 | $-1.60^e$ | $-.811$ | $.40 < p < .50$ |
| N .............. | L.R. | 25 | 24 | $-1.72^e$ | $-1.386$ | $.10 < p < .20$ |
| $20 - (E - N)$ ....... | L.R. | 25 | 24 | $-.12^d$ | $-.116$ | $.90 < p < 1.00$ |
| $50 - (E + N)$ ....... | L.R. | 25 | 24 | 3.31 | 1.068 | $.20 < p < .30$ |
| $N \times E$ ............ | L.R. | 25 | 24 | $-24.33^e$ | $-.912$ | $.30 < p < .40$ |

* Significant at the .05 level.
** Significant at the .01 level.
[a] Only the IR, FR, and S situations were used.
[b] Only the FR, V, and S situations were used.
[c] Only the FR and S situations were used.
[d] Reversal in means from expectation.
[e] Error scores, hence there is no reversal in means.

Comparisons of these results with those obtained in the fraternity analysis, including the ad hoc sets, indicate that none of the variates cross-validated, and only three, i.e., $TP_4$, $N \times E$, and $H_3$ for the IR, FR, and S situations, have mean differences that are consistent in sign across both studies with the .05 criterion met in at least one.

For several reasons, the indices $TP_4$ and $H_3$ were considered superior to $N \times E$. First, the error product on the logical reasoning test is extremely subject to changes with a course in formal or symbolic logic. A second reason for dissatisfaction with $N \times E$ was the difficulty of interpretation. The rationale presented by Thistlethwaite would indicate that the product of neutral and emotive errors would be a measure of some type of interaction between our constructs of personal-problem-solving ability, anxiety, and defensiveness. The nature of this interrelation could not be investigated within our time schedule.

The H and $TP_4$ indices for the fact-elicitation tests seemed to be readily interpretable and as far as we could tell did not seem to be so easily affected by formal training. These measures, to be sure, do not on any rational basis explain all problem-solving as we have conceptualized it, but in lieu of other evidence they seem to be the best indices available for whatever aspects of the global construct they tap. Further work needs to be done in the validation of the fact-elicitation test indices and on the definition and solution tests.

There yet remained a possibility that some linear function of the variates might cross-validate. However, a mere inspection of the tables of results for the two studies showed that the variates which worked best in one study were relatively weak, if not reversals, in the other.

The second set of fact-elicitation tests was also given to the student leader and dormitory groups and the logical reasoning test was administered a second time to this sample. This constituted the first validation study on the second fact-elicitation set. The results of this testing are summarized in Table 4.

From a consideration of this table, two things are clear. First, the results are generally more positive than were the findings for the first set of tests in either study, and second, there seems to be a greater correspondence between the results of the two testings on the same sample with different fact-elicitation forms than for the two studies using the same test forms. As before, the selection of which fact-elicitation situation to drop from the set of four to improve the discrimination was made after plotting some of the fact-elicitation variates by situation; hence, the separations indicated on $H_3$ and $(H \times TR)_3$ are likely to prove spuriously high.

For both fact-elicitation sets, the $TP_4$ index did exceptionally well in

128

Table 4. Mean Differences and Tests of Significance for the Problem-Solving Variates Based on the Second Testing of the Student Leader and Dormitory Samples (Fact-Elicitation Set II)

| Variate | Test | Number High | Low | Mean Difference | $t$ | Probability Level |
|---------|------|------|-----|-----------------|-----|-------------------|
| $TP_4$ ............... | F.E. | 25 | 26 | 29.23 | 2.594 | $.01<p<.05$* |
| $TR_4$ ............... | F.E. | 25 | 26 | $-.20^b$ | $-2.082$ | $.01<p<.05$* |
| $H_4$ ................ | F.E. | 25 | 26 | 9.70 | 2.481 | $.01<p<.05$* |
| $(H \times TR)_4$ ........ | F.E. | 25 | 26 | 14.17 | 1.801 | $.05<p<.10$ |
| $TR_3{}^a$ ............. | F.E. | 25 | 26 | $-.12^b$ | $-1.463$ | $.10<p<.20$ |
| $H_3{}^a$ .............. | F.E. | 25 | 26 | 8.15 | 2.784 | $.001<p<.01$** |
| $(H \times TR)_3{}^a$ ....... | F.E. | 25 | 26 | 14.08 | $2.235^d$ | $.01<p<.05$* |
| $E$ ................ | L.R. | 25 | 24 | $-3.26^c$ | $-1.584$ | $.10<p<.20$ |
| $N$ ................ | L.R. | 25 | 24 | $-1.75^c$ | $-1.179$ | $.20<p<.30$ |
| $20-(E-N)$ ....... | L.R. | 25 | 24 | 1.50 | 1.452 | $.10<p<.20$ |
| $50-(E+N)$ ....... | L.R. | 25 | 24 | 5.02 | 1.460 | $.10<p<.20$ |

* Significant at the .05 level.
** Significant at the .01 level.
[a] Only the IR, FR, and V situations were used.
[b] Reversal in means from expectation.
[c] Error score, hence no reversal in means.
[d] Assumption of homogeneity of variances could not be met. Reported $t$-value is derived from the Cochran and Cox criterion.

separating the high and low groups in this study, although essentially zero differences were observed on this same index for the fraternity samples. It is also true that the high group in the present study asked far more questions than did the lows, whereas this was not true in the former study. The two fraternity groups and the student leader high group all asked appreciably more questions than did the dormitory lows.

To compare the derived weights, we ran $D^2$-L.D.F. analyses on the second set of fact-elicitation tests, using only the IR, FR, and V situations. The sample was composed of 25 student leader highs and 24 dormitory lows. The results are shown below.

| Variates Combined | $F$ | Probability Level |
|-------------------|-----|-------------------|
| $(H \times TR)_3$, $50-(E+N)$ ........ | 2.444 | $p>.05$ |
| $(H \times TR)_3$, $50-(E+N)$, $H_3$ ..... | 2.503 | $p>.05$ |

The discriminations based on the set $(H \times TR)_3$, $50-(E+N)$, and $H_3$, even when capitalizing on random errors, are not significant at the .05 level here or in either of the two previous analyses using Fact-Elicitation Set I situations. It is instructive to compare the L.D.F. weights for these three variates when derived from each of the three analyses.

129

| Variate Tested | Fraternity (F.E. Set I)[a] | Student Leader-Dorm (F.E. Set I)[a] | Student Leader-Dorm (F.E. Set II)[b] |
|---|---|---|---|
| $(H \times TR)_3$ ......... | .0372 | −.0196 | −.0279 |
| $50 - (E + N)$ ....... | .0488 | .0067 | .0127 |
| $H_3$ ............... | −.0568 | .0955 | .1199 |

[a] Only the IR, FR, and S situations used from F.E. Set I.
[b] Only the IR, FR, and V situations used from F.E. Set II.

The L.D.F. weights for the two sets of fact-elicitation tests based on the same samples look more alike than do those for the same fact-elicitation tests based on different validity samples. This corresponds to what was observed on the unitary indices earlier and suggests rather strongly that the two sets of validity samples were actually drawn from populations which differ in ways related to our indices of problem-solving effectiveness.

Jewell (1958) provides some additional information on the validity of one of the problem-solving variables. As with the other variables, he used the $H_3$ index to select from his sample of twenty cases the five individuals with the highest $H_3$ scores and the five individuals with the lowest $H_3$ scores. From his data it is possible to see how each of these people was classified independently by each of the two teams of counseling psychologists. The highest scoring individual was classified as an effective problem-solver by both teams. Two other highs received one judgment each as effective problem-solvers. The other two were classified as ineffective problem-solvers by both teams, as were all five of the low-scoring individuals. Jewell notes that of the judgments made for all twenty cases (forty judgments in all) only five team judgments of effective problem-solving were made, four of which are accounted for above. Whether this fact is to be attributed to the low incidence of effectiveness in solving personal problems among those persons seeking counseling or to unrealistic expectations by the teams of professional judges is, of course, open to conjecture.

## The Classification Variables

The next two variables, we hypothesized, were definable conditions related to the outcomes of the counseling process, rather than outcomes themselves. Under the time pressure of our research program these variables did not receive the attention given to the measurements of outcome variables. However, because of their prominence in most discussions of counseling outcomes it was our decision to develop preliminary measures

130

of the "perception of counseling" and "motivation to change self through counseling" variables, and use them as classification instruments in the counseling experiment. We recognized that under these conditions caution would be needed in interpreting any experimental outcomes related to these categorizations.

*Perception of counseling.* As we have stated, clinical experience suggests that client expectations play a very important part in counseling. Specifically, the client's view of his own role, of the counselor's role, and of the process itself partly serves to determine his behavior. We have also hypothesized that wide discrepancies between expectations and practice will disrupt rapport and impede therapeutic progress.

As an initial step toward the examination of these hypotheses, the Perception of Counseling instrument was developed. First, a member of the research team interviewed thirty students selected at random from clients waiting in the Counseling Bureau reception room for their first counseling appointments. The interviewer established rapport in a manner designed to minimize his connection with the bureau. The interview (Schedule K) was an intensive semi-structured procedure covering a multitude of areas concerning the counseling relationship.

From these protocols all attitudes expressed toward counseling were culled and reworded in a common form. This list was then submitted to our counseling staff requesting any additional expressions of expectations not covered in the item pool.

The resulting list of 379 statements was given to forty practicing counselors to rate. We asked them to consider the items as perceptions that clients might have that would make them ready or unready to benefit from counseling, and to rate the items along a scale ranging from −5 to +5. We asked them to give the lowest rating to perceptions that a poor client would have (attitudes that would detract from his readiness to benefit from counseling) and the highest rating to perceptions that an ideal client would have (attitudes that would enable him to benefit from counseling). The judgments were to apply to any client, regardless of his specific problem.

To pick the items that would best represent each point on the eleven-point scale we computed the mean rank and the variance for each statement. This gave us 167 usable statements. We administered the scale by asking the client to read each statement and decide if he might make such a statement. In each case he could give any one of four responses, "Strong-

131

ly Agree," "Agree," "Disagree," and "Strongly Disagree," but in scoring we combined the first two and scored them alike, and followed the same course with the last two.

The client's score on the inventory was a simple summation of the weighted item scores. Instructions for administration, the item pool, the scoring key, and the item weights are reproduced in Schedule L (see Appendix).

The inventory was then administered to a large sample of students taking tests in the Student Counseling Bureau Testing Room. The mean score of this population was used for classifying subsequent clients as high or low for assignment within the various cells of the counseling experiment population.

*Motivation to change self through counseling.* To measure this second classification variable we used a procedure like the one used in developing the anxiety and defensiveness tests. We formulated a definition of "motivation to change self through counseling" (MTC) that included such points as these: Has the client thought of new information that bears on his problems? Has he reflected on his own behavior? Is he willing to take the initiative in probing into the self, considering alternative courses of action, learning to understand himself? Does he come to interviews on time and without skipping any? Is he amenable to referral? The kinds of change that the client should envision in himself after counseling included greater self-understanding, greater ability to make decisions, less dependence, reduced conflict, improved skills, and greater knowledge.

Counselor judgments of male clients whom they had seen at least three times in the previous eight weeks and whom they felt they knew well enough to judge produced 47 students rated as highly motivated to work on their problems and 45 rated as poorly motivated.

Personality tests taken during counseling were then item-analyzed. The highly motivated students were randomly divided into subgroup A and subgroup B; in like manner the poorly motivated students were divided into subgroup C and subgroup D. Analysis of items between groups A and C and between groups B and D yielded 70 items meeting the criterion of statistical significance in at least one of the subgroup comparisons and in all cases discriminating in the appropriate direction in the other subgroup comparison. (See Schedule M, reproduced in the Appendix, for a copy of this inventory and its scoring key.) This scale was then scored for a large sample of counseling clients to determine cutting scores for use in the experimental classification of subsequent clients. (Schedule N contains items, key, and MMPI item number as well as the results of the item analysis described above.)

## Interrelationships among Experimental Variables

A question of major interest was the expected theoretical relationships among the experimental variables. No single question stimulated more discussion among members of the research team. Some conjectures on the anxiety-defensiveness relationship will illustrate this.

If one considers these two variables apart from the counseling situation one could say that in the absence of anxiety stimuli there is no need for manifest anxiety or defensive behavior on the part of the individual and therefore no affective impairment of efficient problem-solving. With the introduction of the anxiety stimulus we would expect, within our framework, a rise in manifest anxiety followed by an increase in defensive behaviors. However, considering the dynamic nature of individual behavior we would expect a vacillation, within some as yet undefinable range, among the expressions of discomfort as well as among the maladaptive and partly effective modes of dealing with these feelings of discomfort. Only when manifest anxiety or defensive behavior dominates the actions of the individual might we expect a negative correlation between measures.

A second aspect of this question is statistical. Developing indicator measures in the manner previously described, we would expect a "normal" level of manifest anxiety and defensive behavior to exist. What should the relationship be in this "normal" range? What ranges or levels of these behaviors are represented in the criterion and experimental populations used in this study? It would seem reasonable to expect this range to be limited when compared with the maximum possible range.

At the present level of development of our measuring instruments, we are reluctant to draw on currently available empirical evidence for future theoretical structure, yet that is where working hypotheses must come from.

In the pretest–post-test experiment to be described, it is sufficient to state that knowing the levels of these variables on the indicator measures at the beginning of therapy, assuming on the basis of the data presented that these measures have some reasonable degree of validity, and accepting the stated goals of counseling, we know the direction those levels

133

should move in, on the average, if present therapeutic techniques are effective.

The following data are examples of relationships obtained between these variables throughout the experimental program. With the instruments used in the counseling experiment, an intercorrelation of .53 was obtained between the anxiety (52) and defensiveness (63) scales with the Naval Air Unit population. In the third psychology student pool study correlations between the same two scales were found to be .47 and .49 for the first and second administrations of the test battery. Nakamura (1959) reported a correlation of .73 in the first, and a correlation of .67 in the second administration of these two scales to his experimental pool.

The counseling experiment provided the only opportunity to obtain a complete correlation matrix for all the experimental variables; this information is shown below.

| | Perception of Counseling | Anxiety | Defensiveness | Problem-Solving |
|---|---|---|---|---|
| Motivation to change ........ | −.18 | .76 | .56 | .03 |
| Perception of counseling ...... | | −.12 | −.12 | .11 |
| Anxiety .................. | | | .65 | .00 |
| Defensiveness ............. | | | | .06 |

A second intercorrelation obtained in the experiment was that between pretest and post-test measures on each of the instruments. These were as follows: anxiety, .82; defensiveness, .77; and problem-solving, .60. The last index, that for problem-solving, compares with a correlation of .78 for the leader-dormitory administration of the two forms of the same test. Comparing this set of data with reliability estimates reported for the individual scales would not indicate that treatment effects in the experiment affected the ordering of individual scores to any marked degree beyond the expected stability of the various instruments.

The only major change noted which was an exception was that in the relationship between the initial defensiveness (MDS-1) and anxiety (MMAS-1) scales. These yielded a correlation of −.53 in the fraternity study, compared to the correlation of .65 noted above for the final defensiveness (63) and anxiety (52) scales.

This finding is of course related to the changing nature of both scales throughout the various validity studies. The defensiveness scale (66) included only the denial of reality items, whereas the later defensiveness scale (63), on the basis of empirical derivation, maps a much broader set of behaviors.

134

The question of independence of the scales drawing items from the same basic item pool (MDS, MMAS, and MTC) has not yet been dealt with. At this point all items meeting the item criteria established for the various scales remain in the scales with no concession to the fact that they may appear in more than one scale. Neither theory nor available data provided sufficient understanding on which to base a decision to drop items, let alone *which* items to drop—all common items? all common items scored in a given direction? etc. The rationale of inclusion permits subsequent alternative scoring methods where exclusion would not. In Schedule O, items which overlap two or more scales are identified and the nature of the overlap, in terms of direction of scoring, is specified.

# 8

## *The Experimental Design and Its Execution*

B EFORE proceeding with a report of the counseling experiments, we shall summarize the previous sections on theory development and measurement as they relate to the experimental programs.

The three major variables of the theoretical framework are manifest anxiety, defensiveness, and problem-solving effectiveness. We viewed counseling as a means of reducing manifest anxiety and defensive behaviors and of increasing the client's ability to solve his problems. These outcome variables were the ones identified as the most widely held general objectives of counseling in a review of the literature, a survey of practicing therapists, and discussions with counselors and consultants.

Two auxiliary concepts or variables, motivation to change oneself through counseling (MTC), and perception of counseling (POC), were seen as side conditions — placing, perhaps, a limitation on the effectiveness of *any* attempted treatment or possibly representing a prior situation that had to change before counseling could be expected to have an effect. According to this view, the more highly motivated the client is to make some change in himself by means of counseling, and the more nearly his expectations of what counseling entails correspond to a set of "ideal" perceptions, the greater or faster should be his progress on one or more of the major outcome dimensions.

Objective tests were developed for assessment of each of these five variables. Itemized tests containing biographical or self-report items were constructed from a large pool of such items for the manifest anxiety, defensiveness, and motivation to change variables. These tests were keyed empirically on the basis of proportion of response differences by criterion

136

groups of highs and lows for each dimension. The perception of counseling inventory was constructed using a modification of the Thurstone equal-appearing interval scaling method for attitude items (Edwards and Kilpatrick, 1948). Finally, the problem-solving variable was quantified by means of a semi-structured situational interview test.

Although, in our estimation, these tests represent a significant improvement over the usual means employed to evaluate the effectiveness of counseling or psychotherapy, we consider them as tentative, pending further development, cross-validation, and extension through validation and standardization for other populations.

## Experimental Design and Procedures

Much of the ambiguity of research in this and in other areas of psychology stems from a failure to design experiments in advance so that they yield the most rigorous set of answers possible. Since the decision-making devices incorporated in tests of significance and the procedures of estimation are contingent upon statements of precisely what hypotheses are to be tested, and to what population the results will apply, the first and most vital step in the design was to list, in order of their relative importance, the questions to be answered from whatever data we might be able to obtain. A lengthy list of such questions was compiled and from this list were culled: (1) those for which no means of collecting data by careful, objective methods were available; (2) those judged to be *relatively* unimportant; and (3) those which would be of interest only if the results of the present investigation, and later replications of it, indicated confirmation of the major hypotheses. The experimental questions which remained were these:

1. Does counseling produce a differential *average change in status* beyond that of mere *time lapse* on any of our three major evaluation variables? That is, do counseled clients move more, and in the predicted direction, on our variables than a *comparable* group of *similarly motivated* persons used as time-lapse control subjects? This was by far the most important of all the questions for which answers were sought in this study.

2. Do different counselors produce different average amounts of movement on the outcome variables for comparable groups of clients? This second question was not intended to determine which counselors might be most skillful at producing such changes, but rather as a preliminary test to isolate those counselor behaviors, personal characteristics, or orienta-

137

tions leading to greatest movement. Many detailed questions would arise subsequent to the identification of those counselors, if any, who produced positive results and these questions would have to await later studies for definitive answers. However, if a particular counselor was found to be outstandingly successful with a certain type of client, the case notes and tape-recorded counseling protocols for his experimental clients of this type would be a valuable source of hypotheses for subsequent experiments.

3. Do different *perceptions* or *expectations* that a client may initially have about the counseling process, his role in it, or the role of the counselor, affect his subsequent movement on the outcome variables?

4. Do clients whose *motivations* to change themselves through counseling differ initially exhibit different average amounts of movement on our variables?

5. Finally, do any of the combinations of these classifications (i.e., treatments, expectations, and motivation) *interact* to produce differential movement?

For example, it was conceivable that clients who were highly motivated to change might show positive movement in counseling whereas those not so motivated might actually react against the counseling treatment with negative results. However, if those in the control group showed no such effects or showed opposite and compensating effects due to variation in motivation, this fact would not be detectable in any of the usual "main effect" tests of treatment or motivation. The fact would become apparent, however, in a test of interaction effects.

A replicated three-factor factorial design seemed to be the most efficient frame in which to collect the needed data. Figure 1 is a geometric representation of the experimental design employed. This design had the advantage of providing rigorous tests of a large number of hypotheses for a relatively small average number of subjects. In the present study 11 hypotheses about average effects under various conditions were tested on each of 3 variables for a total of 33 tests based on data from 80 experimental and 20 control subjects.

On the other hand, the practical difficulties of assigning subjects at random to the cells of such a design become progressively greater as the design becomes more complex, especially when the subjects must be taken in sequence as they apply for counseling. The sequential placing of all individuals who met experimental conditions was, of course, important since

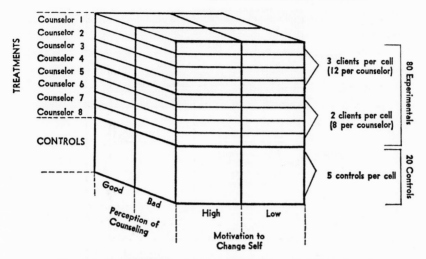

*Figure 1.* Graphic Representation of the Counseling Experiment
(a 9 x 2 x 2 replicated orthogonal factorial design)

we hoped to generalize to the effectiveness of counseling in our particular service center. Since experimental data of this sort are so expensive to obtain, and since the major issues were contingent on auxiliary variables which had to be controlled simultaneously, the additional difficulty involved in utilizing a complex experimental design was well worth the effort. Furthermore, in order to make rigorous tests of hypotheses about the interactions of effects, it was necessary to employ some form of replicated factorial design.

As can be seen from Figure 1, the "treatments" factor was divided into eight experimental subgroups (one for each of the counselors who took part in the study) and one control group. In all of the analyses involving the "treatments" factor, the orthogonal contrast between the control group and the pooled experimental group was tested separately by partitioning the degrees of freedom and sums of squares appropriate for this contrast. The residual information was then used to test for differences among counselors and for interactions of counselors with the factors of perception and motivation. This breakdown was made to obtain a set of tests involving the experimentals vs. the controls without having to resort to any of the usual secondary tests, particularly since these contrasts were seen as the most important subset of results.

Figure 2 presents a diagram of the procedural design employed in the experiment.

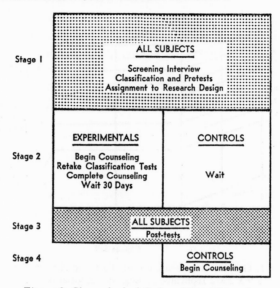

*Figure 2.* Chronological Order of Procedures for
the Counseling Experiment Subjects

The population of subjects involved in the study was limited to men who were enrolled at the University of Minnesota at the time they sought counseling and who were willing to follow through with all the experimental procedures. Those who anticipated leaving the university in less than two academic quarters were rejected, since the follow-up of such subjects is inordinately difficult. The primary reason for restricting the experimental population in this way was that instruments for evaluation had been standardized and validated for this population. A more detailed description of the screening process is given by the instructions for the screening interview in Schedule P.

The perception and motivation tests were administered after the screening interview (at the same time that the pretests for all the evaluation variables were given) and were used as independent or classification variables to place the subjects in the cells of the research design. Subjects who scored above the estimated medians on both these tests were assigned to a cell in the "high-good" column. Subjects with both scores below the established cutting points went at random into one of the "low-bad" cells. The others were assigned to the "high-bad" or "low-good" treatment cells according to the pattern of their scores. Thus, the assignment of an applicant for counseling to a certain cell of the design was a function of his

140

pattern of scores on the two classification tests and an assignment schedule developed before the experiment on the basis of a random number
table. Since all subjects were to be offered counseling eventually (after
post-testing in the case of the controls) and all were told at the initial
screening interview that there might be a delay before we could place
them on a counselor's calendar, we think it unlikely that any of the subjects were aware of their status as a control or an experimental or even
knew that this was a feature of the study. Of course, none of the test data
were available to the participating counselors or to the subjects.

The post-testing of each experimental client was done as close to thirty
days after his final counseling interview as possible. Control subjects were
contacted for post-testing in such a way as to make the total elapsed time
between pretestings and post-testings equivalent to that of their classification counterparts in the experimental group.

Before the experiment or screening procedures started, the entire experimental program was charted on paper — who would see the clients,
the nature of these contacts, the functions each staff member would have
to perform, what data would be assembled by which people, how these
data would be handled, secondary contacts the client might have which
would bear on the outcomes of the experiment, etc. This was done in an
effort to anticipate as many contingencies as possible so that standardized
methods could be developed for dealing with situations as they arose.

Written instructions were prepared for everyone involved, i.e., experimenters, counselors, receptionists, psychometrists, and administrative and
advisory staffs in the various counseling offices. The instructions dealt with
topics as basic as "who will be included in the experiment" and ranged to
"how to answer questions about why the student is requested to sign a
permit to record his interviews." All procedures were discussed with the
appropriate staff members, revised, and discussed again. This was done
not only to standardize the program but also to gain the support of all
staff and to impress upon them the importance of their part in the success
of the experiment. As the experiment progressed, all unanticipated contingencies were referred to a single authority, and his decisions became
a part of the written instructions. Examples of these procedural instructions may be found in Schedules P and Q.

We have used the term "movement" in framing the experimental questions to signify changes in the test scores between the pretesting and post-
testing sessions. The appropriate analysis of such data is provided by the

analysis of covariance on the post-test scores *adjusted for initial status* on that variable. Because one of the classification variates (motivation) is highly correlated with both anxiety and defensiveness, an ordinary analysis of variance performed on the simple difference scores between pretesting and post-test status would lead to a spuriously high probability of making a Type I error, that is, of falsely rejecting true null hypotheses (especially in the set of interaction tests of motivation with the other factors). This would happen simply because the difference scores do not take into account the differential regression of extreme pretest scores toward the mean on a second testing.

In addition to determining the occurrence and amount of *average* movement between pretestings and post-testings, a set of hypotheses about *changes in variability* during this time for subjects in various classifications was a major experimental concern. For instance, the effects of counseling with a given counselor might serve to produce a sizable positive change in one client, but, for some reason, a compensating negative change in another. Such changes would not be detected as a shift in averages but would appear in an analysis of the variability of the covariance-adjusted post-test scores. Welch's $L_1$ test, used in conjunction with Nayer's tables of critical values of $L_1$ (Johnson, 1949), provided a means of testing such hypotheses and was employed for several breakdowns of the data for each of the evaluation variables.

As a final step before the experiment, the participating counselors were asked to indicate the extent to which they accepted change in the three major variables as objectives of their counseling procedures, rated both as global evaluations and as items we regarded as components of them. (See Schedule T.) The ratings indicated a high degree of acceptance by the counselors of changes in these variables as appropriate objectives of their counseling. In other words, the counselors felt that the majority of outcomes they were trying to achieve could be accounted for within the theoretical framework of the experimental program.

In another phase of the experiment, each of the participating counselors prepared a set of rankings and a set of scale ratings of his experimental clients. These represented his judgments of their status on each of the classification and evaluation variables and of the amount of movement each client had shown during the course of his interviews. The counselor was provided with the case folders for all his clients and any of the recorded interview tapes he wished, together with the set of rating scales (a copy may be found in Schedule R), and detailed definitions of the dimensions on which he was to rate his experimental subjects. (A copy of these definitions is in Schedule S.) These judgments were collected after the counselor's final interview with his last experimental client, but before he knew any of the experimental test results for these clients. This was done in order to obtain judgmental data for comparison with assessments by previously validated psychometric instruments to determine whether the counselors could accurately estimate the effects of their own treatment.

In addition to the data collected on each of these more or less specific questions, all of the counseling interviews were tape recorded. This was done to facilitate any subsequent process analyses which might seem promising.

## Analysis

*Changes in mean status: analyses of variance and covariance.* The results of the analyses of variance and covariance for the hypotheses having to do with *average* changes on the three outcome variables are summarized in Tables 5, 6, and 7. Of the 33 null hypotheses tested by analysis of covariance, only one — that of no significant difference between experimental and control groups for the problem-solving variate — could be rejected at the .05 level. From the theoretical considerations outlined earlier we would have expected that clients who received counseling would show a greater average increase on this variate. Exactly the reverse happened! The magnitude of the mean difference between the experimentals and controls on the post-test was about 20 points, or two-thirds of a standard deviation, whereas the group means had differed by only .05 of a point on the pretest. We compared these means with others from one of the validation study samples, and found that the change was due to an actual increase in the scores of the control subjects rather than to decreases in those of the experimentals.

We are frankly at a loss to explain this finding. As far as we can determine, nothing in the selection of subjects, experimental regimen, testing, or analyses accounts for such a result. The theory which prompted the test of the hypothesis, far from explaining the outcome, predicts its opposite. One might conjecture about why this result occurred. For example, the motivated controls (who did not receive help at once) may well have been forced to solve their problems without the aid of a counselor, thereby learning the necessary skills better than would the experimentals who may

143

Table 5. Results of Analyses of Variance and Covariance for the Manifest Anxiety Outcome Variable

| Source of Variation | Original | | | | Adjusted | | | | |
|---|---|---|---|---|---|---|---|---|---|
| | df | SS(Pre) | XP(Pre-Post) | SS(Post) | df | SS | MS | $F^a$ | Concl. |
| Error .................... | 64 | 1708.9667 | 1305.3667 | 1779.9333 | 63 | 782.8500 | 12.426 | | |
| Between experimentals and controls ............. | | | | | | | | | |
| controls ............. | 1 | 63.2025 | 27.0300 | 11.5600 | 1 | 6.8874 | 6.887 | <1.0 | n.s. |
| Among counselors ....... | 7 | 426.0125* | 375.4167 | 442.1667* | 7 | 116.0367 | 16.577 | 1.334 | n.s. |
| Between POC ........... | 1 | 34.8100 | 47.2000 | 64.0000 | 1 | 11.9601 | 11.960 | <1.0 | n.s. |
| Between MTC ........... | 1 | 1656.4900** | 1505.9000 | 1369.0000** | 1 | 17.7481 | 17.748 | 1.428 | n.s. |
| (Experimentals + controls) × POC ............. | 1 | 63.2025 | 99.3750 | 156.2500* | 1 | 39.8396 | 39.840 | 3.206 | n.s. |
| Counselors × POC ....... | 7 | 156.9458 | 42.5916 | 84.7166 | 7 | 108.0181 | 15.431 | 1.242 | n.s. |
| (Experimentals + controls) × MTC ............. | 1 | 11.2225 | 5.0250 | 2.2500 | 1 | 1.1138 | 1.114 | <1.0 | n.s. |
| Counselors × MTC ...... | 7 | 347.1125 | 309.3583 | 413.1166 | 7 | 142.0888 | 20.298 | 1.634 | n.s. |
| POC × MTC ............ | 1 | 1.2100 | -.6600 | .3600 | 1 | 2.0727 | 2.073 | <1.0 | n.s. |
| (Experimentals + controls) × POC × MTC ...... | 1 | 73.1025 | 44.4600 | 27.0400 | 1 | 1.6983 | 1.698 | <1.0 | n.s. |
| Counselors × POC × MTC . | 7 | 81.5125 | -50.1833 | 60.9668 | 7 | 178.1262 | 25.447 | 2.048 | n.s. |

* Significant at the .05 level.
** Significant at the .01 level.
[a] With 1 df in the numerator of the variance ratio and 63 df in the denominator, $F_{.05} = 3.99$ and $F_{.01} = 7.06$; with 7 df in the numerator and 63 df in the denominator, $F_{.05} = 2.16$ and $F_{.01} = 2.94$.

Table 6. Results of Analyses of Variance and Covariance for the Defensiveness Outcome Variable

| Source of Variation | df | Original | | | Adjusted | | | | |
| | | SS(Pre) | XP(Pre-Post) | SS(Post) | df | SS | MS | $F^a$ | Concl. |
|---|---|---|---|---|---|---|---|---|---|
| Error | 64 | 2485.6000 | 1653.0333 | 2281.3000 | 63 | 1181.9602 | 18.761 | | |
| Between experimentals and controls | 1 | 3.8025 | 5.5575 | 8.1225 | 1 | 2.4086 | 2.409 | <1.0 | n.s. |
| Among counselors | 7 | 429.1542 | 418.1125 | 444.8625 | 7 | 72.5019 | 10.357 | <1.0 | n.s. |
| Between POC | 1 | 34.8100 | 25.9600 | 19.3600 | 1 | .2236 | .224 | <1.0 | n.s. |
| Between MTC | 1 | 1069.2900** | 928.6800** | 806.5600 | 1 | 30.9391 | 30.939 | 1.649 | n.s. |
| (Experimentals + controls) × POC | 1 | 2.1025 | 7.9025 | 29.7025 | 1 | 20.1044 | 20.104 | 1.072 | n.s. |
| Counselors × POC | 7 | 387.8875 | 314.4042 | 490.0958 | 7 | 242.3581 | 34.623 | 1.845 | n.s. |
| (Experimentals + controls) × MTC | 1 | 11.2225 | 9.8825 | 8.7025 | 1 | .5191 | .519 | <1.0 | n.s. |
| Counselors × MTC | 7 | 197.3541 | 266.2708 | 461.0292 | 7 | 187.3570 | 26.765 | 1.427 | n.s. |
| POC × MTC | 1 | .0100 | .3600 | 12.9600 | 1 | 12.4855 | 12.486 | <1.0 | n.s. |
| (Experimentals + controls) × POC × MTC | 1 | 29.7025 | 48.7775 | 80.1025 | 1 | 28.0261 | 28.026 | 1.494 | n.s. |
| Counselors × POC × MTC | 7 | 183.6542 | 3.5792 | 31.7625 | 7 | 102.9631 | 14.709 | <1.0 | n.s. |

** Significant at the .01 level.
<sup>a</sup> With 1 df in the numerator of the variance ratio and 63 df in the denominator, $F_{.05} = 3.99$ and $F_{.01} = 7.06$; with 7 df in the numerator and 63 df in the denominator, $F_{.05} = 2.16$ and $F_{.01} = 2.94$.

Table 7. Results of Analyses of Variance and Covariance for the Effective Personal-Problem-Solving Outcome Variable

| Source of Variation | df | Original | | | df | | Adjusted | | |
| --- | --- | --- | --- | --- | --- | --- | --- | --- | --- |
| | | SS(Pre) | XP(Pre-Post) | SS(Post) | | SS | MS | $F^a$ | Concl. |
| Error | 64 | 95,297.1667 | 58,272.0000 | 101,435.2000 | 63 | 65,803.2280 | 1,044.496 | | |
| Between experimentals and controls | 1 | .0400 | 16.4900 | 6,798.0025* | 1 | 6,777.8481 | 6,777.848 | 6.489 | Reject* |
| Among counselors | 7 | 16,739.2917 | 3,689.4166 | 14,002.1541 | 7 | 15,366.5565 | 2,195.222 | 2.102 | n.s. |
| Between POC | 1 | 6.7600 | 102.4400 | 1,552.3600 | 1 | 1,429.5068 | 1,429.507 | 1.369 | n.s. |
| Between MTC | 1 | 116.6400 | −172.8000 | 256.0000 | 1 | 510.3139 | 510.314 | <1.0 | n.s. |
| (Experimentals + controls) × POC | 1 | 5,595.0400 | 2,202.8600 | 867.3025 | 1 | 250.6007 | 250.601 | <1.0 | n.s. |
| Counselors × POC | 7 | 6,078.4583 | 4,299.4164 | 8,225.7209 | 7 | 5,237.1454 | 748.164 | <1.0 | n.s. |
| (Experimentals + controls) × MTC | 1 | 153.7600 | 455.7000 | 1,350.5625 | 1 | 849.3836 | 849.384 | <1.0 | n.s. |
| Counselors × MTC | 7 | 27,987.9250* | 21,893.6994 | 18,377.4875 | 7 | 1,881.9941 | 268.856 | <1.0 | n.s. |
| POC × MTC | 1 | 961.0000 | −378.2000 | 148.8400 | 1 | 960.9920 | 960.992 | <1.0 | n.s. |
| (Experimentals + controls) × POC × MTC | 1 | 25.0000 | 38.2500 | 58.5225 | 1 | 21.0866 | 21.087 | <1.0 | n.s. |
| Counselors × POC × MTC | 7 | 10,017.1583 | 9,132.3676 | 14,232.8875 | 7 | 6,724.0171 | 960.574 | <1.0 | n.s. |

* Significant at the .05 level.
a With 1 df in the numerator of the variance ratio and 63 df in the denominator, $F_{.05} = 3.99$ and $F_{.01} = 7.06$; with 7 df in the numerator and 63 df in the denominator, $F_{.05} = 2.16$ and $F_{.01} = 2.94$.

146

have had solutions handed to them. However, such an ad hoc explanation is too easy and merely serves to suggest hypotheses for future tests.

At present the best course is to suspend judgment until a replication of this test is performed and until more validation and normative data are available for our evaluation instrument on this and other populations. Another explanation, of equal value to that above, is that this result might be due to one of those unfortunate and perverse composites of random errors which, though unlikely, sometimes occur. If in a replication of the experiment the finding is confirmed, however, some other rationale will have to be found.

Leaving for the moment this one very discomforting result, we find that the rest of the hypotheses related to average or mean change fared but little better. None of the differences on any of the remaining 32 hypotheses of this set concerning average change could be considered as due to anything but random variation.

Looking over the analyses of variance for the pretests and post-tests themselves, we found largely what we had expected. Since the motivation to change test correlated highly with both the defensiveness and manifest anxiety tests, the "between MTC" hypotheses were rejected for both variates on both testings. The rejection of the "among counselors" hypothesis for both testings on the anxiety variate indicated simply that some counselors had groups of clients who were more (or possibly less) anxious than the average (i.e., they were not representative of the population sampled relative to their manifest anxiety). This is a case in point for the use of the analysis of covariance method, for without the pretest information and covariance analysis one would have concluded (erroneously) that significant mean effects had been achieved between counseled and noncounseled clients and that different counselors produce differing amounts of movement on the anxiety variate. This follows since one assumes that the randomization procedures give "representative" sets of subjects for each treatment classification in such a design.

The final asterisk in Table 5 (for the post-test analysis of the interaction of treatments by perceptions) is, on the face of it, a little hard to interpret. Apparently, since the pretest $F$ was greater than one (1.0) but not sufficiently large for us to reject the null hypothesis, and since the post-test hypothesis was rejected (though not that for the adjusted post-test scores), whatever changes occurred to yield the significant results must have supplemented the minor variation already present at the time of

147

pretesting. Hence when the analysis of covariance was employed to remove the effect of initial status, the changes which had yielded the rejection were too small to be reliable.

The rejection indicated for the "counselor by motivation" classification in Table 7 on the pretest, which does not hold up in the post-test and adjusted post-test analyses, must be interpreted in much the same way. The only difference is that the randomization procedures apparently yielded initially noncomparable groups for the "counselor by motivation" breakdown and that whatever random movements occurred between testings served to attenuate rather than supplement the original differences.

*Changes in variability ($L_1$ tests).* All of the analyses just discussed are predicated upon a set of assumptions. One of the more crucial of these is that the variabilities or scatterings of the scores within each of the classifications being contrasted are equal or homogeneous. Minor differences in variability are usually ignored, but the variances should not be significantly different in the statistical sense. Of the several procedures available, we used Welch's $L_1$ test to determine the tenability of this assumption of no significant difference for each analysis of variance and covariance.

If the analyses of average movement are to be considered exact, then it is necessary that the appropriate $L_1$ null hypotheses for the post- and adjusted post-test scores shall not have been rejected, i.e., that the assumption of equal variances for the set of contrasted groups is a tenable one. Where this assumption is not met, the usual analysis of variance and covariance test procedures cannot be derived from statistical theory.

Table 8 lists the $L_1$ values calculated for some major breakdowns of the data and the corresponding criterion values. (In contrast to the usual situation, a calculated $L_1$ value must be lower than the tabled one for the hypothesis to be rejected.) The assumption is justified for all of the problem-solving analyses. This is important since the one significant result on the previous tests of movement was with this variable and it was not invalidated by these results. However, a number of the anxiety and defensiveness breakdowns do yield significant $L_1$ values for adjusted post-test covariance analyses. In addition, one of the anxiety contrasts (MTC by POC) also shows a significant $L_1$ for the unadjusted post-test distributions. Hence, the three anxiety hypotheses and the three for defensiveness corresponding to these $L_1$ rejections are not exact tests and the results are not strictly interpretable in the same sense as the others.

These results become more important when considered as tests of hy-

Table 8. Results of Analyses of Variability on the Post- and Adjusted Post-Test Scores for Anxiety, Defensiveness, and Problem-Solving

| Breakdown | $L_1$ Rejection Points Post $L_1$ (.01) | Post $L_1$ (.05) | Adj-Post $L_1$ (.01) | Adj-Post $L_1$ (.05) | Anxiety Post $L_1$ | Anxiety Post Concl. | Anxiety Adj-Post $L_1$ | Anxiety Adj-Post Concl. | Defensiveness Post $L_1$ | Defensiveness Post Concl. | Defensiveness Adj-Post $L_1$ | Defensiveness Adj-Post Concl. | Problem-Solving Post $L_1$ | Problem-Solving Post Concl. | Problem-Solving Adj-Post $L_1$ | Problem-Solving Adj-Post Concl. |
|---|---|---|---|---|---|---|---|---|---|---|---|---|---|---|---|---|
| Treatments (T) | .773 $(9,9)^a$ | .819 | .747 $(9,8)^a$ | .798 | .8839 | n.s. | .7102 | Reject** | .8354 | n.s. | .8028 | n.s. | .9382 | n.s. | .8852 | n.s. |
| Motivation to change (MTC) | .926 $(2,49)^a$ | .957 | .924 $(2,48)^a$ | .956 | .8754 | n.s. | .9274 | Reject* | .9681 | n.s. | .8707 | Reject** | .9836 | n.s. | .9813 | n.s. |
| Perception of counseling (POC) | .926 $(2,49)^a$ | .957 | .924 $(2,48)^a$ | .956 | .9995 | n.s. | .9617 | n.s. | .9855 | n.s. | .9169 | Reject** | .9737 | n.s. | .9681 | n.s. |
| MTC × POC | .883 $(4,24)^a$ | .917 | .878 $(4,23)^a$ | .914 | .8656 | Reject* | .8762 | Reject** | .9184 | n.s. | .8025 | Reject** | .9554 | n.s. | .9518 | n.s. |
| T × MTC | .605 $(18,4)^a$ | .660 | .504 $(18,3)^a$ | .567 | .7185 | n.s. | .7413 | n.s. | .8156 | n.s. | .6070 | n.s. | .7217 | n.s. | .6424 | n.s. |
| T × POC | .605 $(18,4)^a$ | .660 | .504 $(18,3)^a$ | .567 | .7889 | n.s. | .8606 | n.s. | .8054 | n.s. | .6782 | n.s. | .7869 | n.s. | .6478 | n.s. |

\* Significant at the .05 level.
\*\* Significant at the .01 level.
[a] The numbers in parentheses show the number of degrees of freedom in the numerator of the variance ratio and in the denominator respectively.

potheses about the effects of counseling, motivation, or expectations rather than simply as tests of assumptions supplemental to those about average movement. That is, a rejected $L_1$ hypothesis for the adjusted post-test scores indicated that some differential movement took place between the two testings. If the means for the groups being contrasted were not different (as they generally were not here), then the differential variability which we observed must have been due to the fact that persons *changed in ways we would not expect on the basis of regression phenomena alone.* However, the change was not systematically up or down since this would be apparent in the tests described earlier.

We pose this interpretation tentatively. A subsequent examination of the regression coefficients for each subgroup where significant $L_1$'s were found would yield more easily interpretable results. There may be some unanticipated effect due to the high correlation between the motivation classification test and those used for each evaluation. If these further analyses sustain the conclusion of counseling effects, it will be worth going back to the protocols to see what can be teased out to account for this unpredicted differential scattering in some classifications.

*Counselor ratings vs. test scores.* The final set of outcomes of this particular analysis related counselor judgments of status and change to the psychometric assessments of these same characteristics. The ratings obtained from the counselors were correlated with (1) the post-test scores, (2) the adjusted post-test scores, and (3) the simple pretest and post-test score differences. These correlations are summarized below.

|  | Anxiety | Defensive-ness | Problem-Solving |
|---|---|---|---|
| Status: rating vs. post-test score.............. | .44 | −.04 | .27 |
| Change: | | | |
| Rating vs. adj. post-test score.............. | .00 | .13 | −.04 |
| Rating vs. pretest-post-test difference......... | .10 | .16 | .21 |

The ratings for both status and change were collected using twelve-category descriptive rating scales (see Schedule R). However, the effective range of the scales used by the counselors in making the status judgments was greater than that for the change rating on all three variables. This may, in part, account for the lower correlation for change. Corrections for restriction of the range and for unreliability of tests or judgments were not applied. It seems unlikely that such corrections would alter appreciably the conclusions to be drawn from these findings.

Combining the results of this aspect of the study with those reported in

Chapter 7 leads to several ad hoc hypotheses. The high agreement reported in Jewell's study (1958) between the judgments of initial status on the anxiety and defensiveness variables and test scores as reported in Chapter 7 lends some strength to the conclusion that the tests are to some acceptable degree valid indicators of anxiety and defensiveness as defined and interpreted by the judges used. As to assessing movement or change in status on these variables, many questions are left unanswered.

The data could be used to support two alternative and opposing hypotheses: (1) The instruments are sensitive enough to make a valid ordering of individuals according to their status on the dimensions with which the study is concerned, but they are not sensitive enough to detect the moderate degree of movement which can reasonably be expected from the treatment provided. (Because of the method used in the development of these instruments, no data were gathered which could be used to support or refute this conclusion.) (2) Lacking any absolute base from which to make the necessary judgments, the counseling psychologist can, with validity, provide only a gross ordering of individuals on the dimensions of behavior under consideration and should not be expected to provide the refined estimates of movement required by this aspect of the study. Again, we are aware of no data which would support or refute this conclusion.

The available data suggest some degree of validity in the tests used as indicators of status and movement on the variables described, and insofar as the counselors were required to make judgments which would map the same aspects of the variables as the tests, the low correlations indicate that counselors' judgments of change or improvement do not constitute a satisfactory assessment procedure. It may be that for other variables, clients, therapies, or counseling procedures, such judgments might have more validity, but there seems to be little basis for this contention in the present setting.

## Discussion

Viewing these aspects of the study from the perspective of the theoretical framework from which they evolved, we must conclude that the results are generally negative. However, considerable caution must be used in interpreting and generalizing from the data. To conclude that counseling and psychotherapy as performed in this setting produce no desirable outcomes would be wholly unwarranted, as well as a gross violation

151

of the courtesy and cooperation extended by professional service personnel to the researcher who attempts, through probing and examination, to better understand the dynamics or outcomes of a complex process. Conclusions must be limited strictly to the data at hand and the observable processes involved in the treatment methodology.

In this experiment only *three general outcome variables* were subjected to investigation. The counseling or therapy was brief: the mean number of interviews was a little over three and the range was from one to thirteen interviews. The treatment was not of any one systematic type. The researchers had established only a general acceptance by the counselors of the objectives of treatment, not the means of realizing those objectives. The psychometric instruments had only tentatively established validity as partial indicators of the general constructs by which they are named. Finally, we dealt with a population which is known to differ in many important ways from the general population both in intellectual and attitudinal variables and in its range on the personality variables under investigation. For this reason the data are interpretable and generalizable only to this group.

As these questions about the outcomes of this study are raised it must be emphasized that *they are questions, not answers*. It is too easy to assume that had there been more interviews with each client the results would have been different. To our knowledge, the only variable correlating highly with number of interviews is time expended by counselor and client.

We feel it is more reasonable to ask what it is legitimate to expect from an experiment such as the one described, and how the experiment fulfilled these expectancies. First of all, one can of course conclude that the ultimate was not achieved — we did not accurately describe, measure, and demonstrate the process and outcomes of counseling as conducted in this setting. We do feel, however, that we were able to describe and demonstrate a model for the development of a carefully controlled, complex experiment for the evaluation of counseling effectiveness. This study demonstrated that experimentation of this sort is possible, not only in principle, but in fact. A model has been provided which can be, with only minor modifications, applied to the study of similar problems of evaluation in other settings, for other types of therapies, and for other client or patient populations.

Of prime importance is the interpretation of the data of this study as they relate to the future development of this research program and the research of others who are interested in pursuing questions raised in this study. At this point, should one revise the original theory in view of the data now available? Should one conclude that revision of theory would be premature and concentrate instead on further development of the indicator measures? Or, should one conclude that current treatments are not achieving desired outcomes and concentrate on the development of counseling methods which would better accomplish these ends?

We will return to these questions and discuss them more fully in Chapter 10. However, additional data are available from related studies and from follow-ups of the present study which bear directly on any interpretation. These will be discussed in the next chapter.

# 9

## Related Studies

---

Two former graduate students working under Dr. Ralph Berdie and with the cooperation of Dr. Volsky have dealt with research questions arising out of the original study. Their work is summarized and reviewed here with their consent (Jewell, 1958; Vosbeck, 1959). In addition, a number of follow-up studies have been made on the subsequent academic histories of both the experimental and control populations used in the study reported in the preceding chapters, in an attempt to obtain data which would direct further research.*

### The Jewell Study

Early in the evolution of the theoretical framework described in Chapter 6, some colleagues took issue with the schema being formulated by the research team. While they agreed about the importance of the variables manifest anxiety, defensiveness, and solving of personal problems, they felt that the direction of desired movement could not be pre-specified, but should be uniquely specified after diagnosis of the individual case. For example, in one case anxiety should be increased, defensiveness should be reduced, and problem-solving skills should improve; while in another case anxiety should be decreased, defensiveness increased, and problem-solving skills left alone. Walter Jewell very early in the program held this alternative view.

To specify outcomes different from those hypothesized in the original study is more difficult than might appear at first. The difficulty is, of

* Appreciation and thanks are due to Miss Marian McGrail and Miss Eleanor Steele; it was mainly their efforts that made these additional data available.

154

course, related in part to how the experimenter chooses to define his variables and in part to the adequacy of measuring instruments. If anxiety and motivation were seen as two segments of a common personality variable, Jewell's conceptualization could be defended easily on a rational basis. In the original theoretical framework anxiety was defined as debilitative and defensiveness as maladaptive. However, the data as reported in Chapter 7 (not available when the theory was developed) indicate a high positive correlation between the anxiety index (debilitative) and the motivation index (facilitative), and the results of the experiment showed no significant movement of mean scores, but significant variance effects on the anxiety variable. This supports the alternative theoretical framework. However, both points of view are based on untested theories which need experimental verification.

The data gathered for the original study provided Jewell with an opportunity to test his hypothesis. For his Ph.D. dissertation, he designed an analysis which attempted to verify his point of view. Critical to this alternative framework was the need to judge, prior to treatment, which client should move in which direction.

Jewell selected twenty cases at random from the original experimental pool and gathered all case notes, test scores, and interview recordings for each of these clients. He then obtained the cooperation of two teams of judges (three counseling psychologists on each team) from a veterans' hospital counseling staff. None of these counselors were involved in the original study or familiar with its procedures or outcomes.

The tasks set for the teams were as follows: Team 1 had all data available to the original counselor at the time of the first counseling appointment, plus the counselor's notes from the first interview and the tape recording of that interview. First, they were to rate each case for the presence or absence of ability to solve personal problems, manifest anxiety, and defensiveness on a three-category scale of "present," "absent," or "cannot say." (The original definitions were used for these variables.) Second, they were to indicate their judgment of what should be the counselor's goal for each variable — "increase," "decrease," "remain the same," or "cannot say."

Team 2, working from the same set of data, replicated the first task of Team 1, as described above. Their second task was to review all case notes and all case data (excluding experimental data), listen to the first and last interview recordings and any intervening ones they wished, and

155

then judge what movement had taken place on the three variables during the course of counseling.

The intricacies of the procedures by which Jewell arrived at a single judgment are complex and not of major relevance to this presentation. They are well documented in his dissertation. General comments are, however, in order. All ratings were made independently, at a common time, with common exposure to all data and recordings. A majority rating was used to represent the team rating. Pooled reliability ratings of the individual judges ranged from a low of .69 to a high of .81. On the judgments performed in common by both teams (pre-counseling status on each variable), between-team agreement ranged from 75 to 80 per cent. Summary data derived from these ratings bear directly on evaluation of the alternative frameworks of the original study and the Jewell investigation.

In judging initial status, Team 1 and Team 2 rated 75 and 90 per cent of the individuals respectively as *not* evidencing effective problem-solving ability as originally defined. The two teams agreed on 80 per cent of the cases. However, because an exceptionally high number of judgments fall into the single category "not evidencing effective problem-solving ability," this percentage of inter-team agreement cannot be shown to be significant by the use of the *t*-test. Team 1 judged that for all cases the counselor's goal should be to improve the problem-solving skills of the individual.

For the defensiveness variable, Team 1 believed that 50 per cent and Team 2 that 75 per cent of the individuals were evidencing maladaptive defensive behaviors at the time of the first interview. The two teams agreed on their judgments in 75 per cent of the cases. This level of inter-team agreement exceeds the .05 level of significance. Team 1 judged that in 40 per cent of the cases the counselor should attempt to decrease the individual's defensiveness level, and that for the remaining 60 per cent of the cases the defensiveness level was not a matter of concern to the counselor. In no instance was a judgment made that defensiveness, as defined, should be increased.

These data suggest a number of hypotheses and tentative conclusions. Even under instructions to seek goals contrary to the basic postulates of the original study, there was no evidence in Jewell's study that the improvement of problem-solving ability, as defined, was not a generalized goal of counseling. Similarly, in the case of defensiveness, there were no data contrary to the initial formulation. The data do suggest possible modification of the framework in regard to the defensiveness variable.

One form such a modification might take involves qualification of the construct relating to defensive behaviors. For example, when at least a moderate degree of defensive behavior is present, a generalized outcome goal of counseling is to selectively reduce this behavior. Jewell's data indicate however, that there is no reason to expect maladaptive defensive behaviors to be present in even a majority of the clients involved in this study. This finding suggests that a more powerful test of the theoretical framework would be to include only those experimental subjects in whom such maladjustive defensive behaviors were observable. This course of action would naturally restrict generalizability of any obtained results.

If one is to attempt to evaluate a *representative sample* of the entire clientele of a psychological or psychiatric service, the theory, design, and all related evaluative activities would have to be expanded to include appropriate outcome variables to cover the "inappropriate cases" and also the conditions under which these alternative outcomes should be expected.

It is important to note that if the former direction is followed, the question of evaluation of counseling, psychotherapy, or casework would no longer be germane, but rather the question would become one of investigating the effectiveness of specific treatment methods on pre-specified client populations.

Only in the case of manifest anxiety do the Jewell data raise major questions about the need for restatement and clarification of the initial framework. Both teams of judges agreed that 60 per cent of the population was evidencing anxiety as defined in the original study. Inter-team judgments agreed in the classification of 80 per cent of the individuals. The first team felt that the counselor's goal should be to increase anxiety for 10 per cent of the cases, not attempt to alter the anxiety level for 53 per cent of the cases, and decrease anxiety for 37 per cent of the cases. These data support the contention that sophisticated judges looking at specific cases were not willing to accept the generalization that it should be the counselor's goal to decrease anxiety in all instances, even when it is manifestly present.

The judgments obtained do not permit one to decide between the two alternative possibilities which occur to us. Were the judges seeking some optimal level of manifest anxiety, or were they interjecting a clinical variable into the definition of anxiety presented to them and seeking the reduction of certain "types" of anxiety and the increase to optimal level of other "types"? As a result of his work, Jewell tends to the latter view in spite of the operational definition that was used to describe anxiety in both studies.

The combination of these empirical data with data from the initial study emphasizes the need for critical reappraisal of this aspect of the framework.

Two more sets of data obtained by Jewell are of major interest. First, did the judges feel that the counselors had obtained any movement on the variables under consideration, and second, what was the degree of congruence between the movement attained and the movement which the initial team of judges felt desirable?

The ratings of counselor achievement were reported to be as follows: (1) For the problem-solving variable, 25 per cent of the cases were considered improved, 65 per cent remained unchanged, and 10 per cent were judged to have become less skillful. (2) Thirty-five per cent of the clients were judged to be more defensive, 55 per cent unchanged, and 10 per cent less defensive. (3) Twenty per cent were judged to have increased anxiety levels, 65 per cent remained as they were, and 15 per cent decreased in anxiety level.

The congruence between movement and desired movement (as specified by the judges) was 25 per cent for problem-solving, 50 per cent for defensiveness, and 65 per cent for manifest anxiety. Jewell reports, however, that major congruence for the latter two variables existed in the "don't change" and "no change" categories, and he tends to question the efficacy of counselors' abilities to achieve desired movement.

As might have been hypothesized from the data previously described, intra-team agreement on the judgments of achieved movement was much lower than that obtained for the judgments of initial status on the outcome variables. Jewell's investigation also revealed no significant relationship between the judgments of movement made for his study and the estimates of change by the counselors in the initial experiment who judged accomplishment with their clients at the termination of the interview sequence. This conclusion was drawn from the data by reducing the counselors' twelve-category scales to three-category scales and making a direct comparison of congruence between the two sets of measures. Keeping in mind that one-third agreement could be expected by chance alone on any variable, Jewell reported the following results: 45 per cent agreement for ability to solve problems effectively, 55 per cent agreement for defensiveness, and 35 per cent agreement for anxiety.

At least three major points can be made about these findings. First, it is doubtful that the above data provide a fair test of the framework which Jewell set out to examine, since he was seeking effects of counselor treatments which in some cases were diametrically opposed to the stated commitments made by the participating counselors before the experimental treatments began. In these cases (e.g., seeking to attain increased anxiety level) movement could have been accomplished only in spite of the reverse commitment on the part of the counselor. Second, the data have emphasized again that the problem of assessing movement is not the same as appraising initial classification. This shows the need for more attention to the assessment of movement than is usually paid to this problem in the development of such instruments. Third, both the original data and the Jewell data direct attention to a commonly ignored problem in the assessment and evaluation of counseling, psychotherapy, and casework treatment methods. It is currently popular to assume that only two possible outcomes exist in these fields, i.e., either positive movement or no movement. If there is sufficient validity in the evaluations made by Jewell's judges, and since the original researchers were willing to commit themselves to judgments of "good" and "bad" dimensions of behavior relative to both process and outcome variables, the results obtained by Jewell and the variance effects noted in the initial study suggest the possibility of negative effects. To conclude that such is the case is not our intent. However, we must point out that this possibility cannot be ignored in further research.

## Academic Outcomes Studies

So far we have directed attention to the basic framework and to the indicator measures. A third major area for further research has only been suggested. What of the adequacy of the treatment provided?

Treatment settings and client expectancies determine to some degree what specific outcomes of the personalized helping process should be. The social setting leads clients to expect certain kinds of help from university counseling centers and certain others from vocational rehabilitation centers or mental hygiene clinics. These outcomes can be specified and indicator measures can be developed. Improved academic outcomes are certainly a part of the expectancies of both clients and others in the university and the related community. Owing to a fortuitous circumstance (from the experimental point of view) we were provided with groups of counseled and noncounseled clients for whom we could compare academic performance.

The circumstance requires explanation. As described in the introduction to Chapter 8, the research design called for holding clients in the control category only until post-testing had been completed (see the timetable in Figure 2, Chapter 8), and then giving them priority on the caseload calendar for counseling. The experiment, as is typical, lasted longer than anticipated and the research team called in the controls for post-testing and subsequent counseling late in the spring quarter, close to the summer vacation period. The combination of circumstances — the long wait, the approaching final examination period, the closeness of the vacation period, or whatever other experiences might have influenced them — led all of the controls without exception to refuse counseling when it was offered. Continuing follow-ups of these controls revealed that *none* sought formal counseling during the remainder of the time they spent at the university!

This event in and of itself must be considered significant. It raises the question: What are the effects on motivation of withholding counseling help for some time after it has been requested? It is not atypical for a person seeking help to wait as much as six weeks or more to see a professional person: there is a shortage of staff available to meet the service demands in many settings. Neither is it uncommon under these conditions for individuals to refuse appointments that far in the future, or to fail to keep their scheduled appointments. Therefore, the situation which we have described varies from the typical situation only in that the individuals who received help and those who were asked to wait were selected by a random assignment schedule rather than by the happenstance of availability of counselor time when the individuals decided to seek such help.

In the long-term follow-up data reported here, it is legitimate to ask an atypical question. The usual questions asked of research similar to this relate to the need for a motivated control group to establish a base from which to judge experimental outcomes. In this case the question to be asked but not answered is: What were the effects on relevant variables of withholding services when they were requested? One must further ask: If there are effects related to the withholding of services, what can be used as the placebo comparable in all dimensions except the relevant "treatment variable" in subsequent experimentation? It may well be that comparisons of variations in treatment methods with the random assignment of prediagnosed clientele are the legitimate limit of classical experimental methods in this area of investigation.

The unexpected event of having controls refuse counseling even under moderate pressure to accept it provided an opportunity to follow up the subsequent academic history of the experimentals and controls (counseled and noncounseled). The fact that this was not a part of the original design of the study in many ways limits what can be said about these data. However, in the sense that there are no limits to where one may seek cues on which to base theory revision or subsequent research hypotheses, the information is of value.

In the main, problems presented by clients in this setting are in the academic realm, e.g., fear of academic failure, finding a vocational interest that will provide personal satisfaction, resolution of situations that hinder academic performance. A simple count of specific presented problems as stated by both counselor and client placed more than 70 per cent of the subjects in the general category of having educational-vocational problems. The question arising from the original data relative to the significant increase in the mean score of the controls in ability to solve personal problems also provides a stimulus to pursue these data further: Is there evidence that when help is withheld an individual will seek out a way to solve problems on his own and by so doing become a better problem-solver?

Because of these stimulating questions, a number of follow-up studies were conducted on the academic histories of all the subjects involved in the original study. It was decided initially that these follow-ups would continue until each subject either had attained his bachelor's degree or had terminated his academic pursuits at the University of Minnesota. No formal estimate was made of how long this would take; however, without exception, all informal estimates were underestimates.

*The Vosbeck study.* The first formal analysis of these data was performed by Phyllis Vosbeck (1959), whose principal interest was investigating unexamined interrelationships among available sets of data which might provide direction for subsequent research. She also was interested in examining the relationship of client movement on the experimental variables to academic outcomes.

161

Rather than examining changes in mean or variance scores as was done in the original study, this researcher undertook an analysis of changes in individual scores within the various sub-populations of the study. Establishing criteria for what constituted a change in anxiety, defensiveness, problem-solving, and honor-point ratio, she analyzed the percentage and direction of individual shifts on these indices. Of twenty hypotheses tested by chi-square analysis, five significant differences were found.

Vosbeck reported that significantly more experimentals than controls changed anxiety level. On an examination of the contingency table, she concluded that "counseling is related to change . . . both increase and decrease . . . in anxiety level as measured by the Minnesota Manifest Anxiety Scale. However, the counseled students do not differ from the non-counseled students when compared on decreased anxiety. Thus, although counseling may change the level of anxiety it is not changed consistently in one direction." (Vosbeck, 1959, p. 45.)

Such a change was not found for defensiveness. She reported significant effects when she tested for change in either anxiety or defensiveness or both, and a similar result when she compared experimentals and controls for change on one or more of the three variables — anxiety, defensiveness, and problem-solving. The tests performed were not for interaction effects as the author implied, but rather were disjunctive (either-or) tests in which changes in one variable (anxiety) could account for all of the significant results reported. Analysis of the problem-solving variable indicated that fewer than the expected number of counseled students improved on this measure while more than the expected number of non-counseled students improved. This finding was statistically significant at the .05 level. These data in the Vosbeck study support the findings in the original analyses.

In addition, Vosbeck was able to examine the relationship of these three indices to academic outcomes. To carry out this latter study in the same methodological format used in the analysis reported above, she adopted certain conventions. Pre-counseling and post-counseling (excluding the academic quarters in which experimental treatment was in progress) academic honor-point ratios were computed and compared. If a student improved his honor-point ratio by one-tenth of a point and remained in school, or if he maintained a 3.00 (B) average or better he was labeled "improved." If he did not meet these conditions, he was placed in a "not improved" category. Post-counseling grades were computed, including all grades obtained in the three academic years following the conclusion of the initial study.

The data below show that the difference between counseled and non-counseled students was not great enough to be statistically significant ($\chi^2$ = 2.25 for 1 df, not significant at the .05 level, 3.84).

|  | Improved HPR | Did Not Improve HPR |
|---|---|---|
| Counseled students (N = 80) ...... | 53.75% | 46.25% |
| Noncounseled students (N = 20) ... | 35.00 | 65.00 |

The differences in honor-point ratio before and after counseling were analyzed, using algebraic summation:

|  | N | Mean Difference | Variance | t | Conclusion |
|---|---|---|---|---|---|
| Experimentals ........ | 80 | .2513 | .364 | 3.73 | p<.001 |
| Controls ............. | 20 | .0250 | .585 | .146 | n.s. |
| Between experimentals and controls ........ |  |  |  | 1.231 | n.s. |

This analysis indicates that in the experimental population a significant improvement was evidenced. No similar shift in average grades was found for the controls. However, a comparison of post-counseling differences for experimental and control groups indicated that the differences of the magnitude found were not sufficient to meet minimal criteria of statistical significance. The question of interpretation is, of course, wide open.

Is the difference attributable to chance alone, or is there evidence of a real counseling effect? A second question is also of relevance. If there is a real effect, does this effect have any practical meaning? For those who work in the academic setting, this question brings forth a qualified response. If the difference is real (not attributable to chance) and the mean achievement of the group is close to the critical pass-fail average of 2.0 (C), a shift of this much (with variances of the magnitude reported) would be of practical importance. If the mean achievement is sufficiently above or below a C average, a difference of this size would be of no consequence. It was first necessary to ascertain whether there was a significant difference in pre-counseling grades between experimentals and controls. As shown below, the difference found was not significant. The differences in post-counseling HPR, also shown, are therefore not linked to pre-counseling differences.

If the effects we have reported are attributable to counseling and tend

| | N | Mean Pre-Counseling HPR | Mean Post-Counseling HPR | Pre-Counseling Variance | t | Conclusion |
|---|---|---|---|---|---|---|
| Experimentals .... | 80 | 2.09 | 2.34 | .554 ⎫ | .045 | n.s. |
| Controls ........ | 20 | 2.07 | 2.09 | .318 ⎭ | | |

to generalize to some degree, and if grades and grade improvement are normally distributed, they would in fact be of practical importance. For some students, counseling would mean the difference between passing and failing.

In the Vosbeck study, an attempt was made to assess the effect of counseling on academic progress. Was there any evidence that counseling had an appreciable effect on attaining a college degree? At the time that Vosbeck made her study, many more of the students participating in the original study were still enrolled than she had anticipated. If those who had been graduated were compared with those who left school, a large number of students would not be placed in the matrix. For this reason, she divided the students into two categories: (1) those who had obtained a degree or were in school and in good standing; (2) those who had dropped from school or were in school but in academic difficulty.

| | Counseled | Noncounseled |
|---|---|---|
| Satisfactory progress .......... | 74% | 35% |
| Unsatisfactory progress ........ | 26 | 65 |

$\chi^2 = 10.70$ for 1 df, significant at .01 level (6.64)

These data indicate that the fact of counseling is related to successful progress in the university. Vosbeck does point out one qualification in her study, however. The question arose of what to do with students who had received the two-year associate of arts degree and sought no further schooling. There were seven such students, all in the experimental category (which must be considered a significant event in itself). These cases were included in the success category because an honor point ratio of 2.00 or better is required to obtain the degree. It remains a qualification; however, eliminating these persons or shifting them to the unsuccessful category would not alter the statistical conclusions drawn from this analysis.

A final set of relevant analyses carried out by Vosbeck was an attempt to investigate interrelationships among movement on the generalized outcome variables and improvement in the grade achievement and graduation criterion indices. Her analyses yielded no evidence of a systematic relationship between her classifications of "improved" or "unimproved" grades and the generalized outcome variables. That is, there was no evi-

164

dence that improved grades were related to any of her classifications of the variables used to assess outcomes in the original study, i.e., decreased or increased anxiety, defensiveness, or problem-solving. It is, however, doubtful that the data available to her were adequate for the task.

Before presenting the data from the succeeding follow-up studies, it is important to try to answer this question: Can the apparent differences in academic outcomes be related to preconditions not related to the experimental program? Inasmuch as the equating of such variables as academic ability was left to random assignment within cells of the design, would unexpected differences account for the suggested differential outcomes? No systematic attempt was made to gather data on this matter. However, since virtually all high school students in Minnesota take an academic aptitude test and an English achievement test as part of the cooperative program of the Minnesota Association of Colleges and the state's high schools, scores on these measures were available for most students, along with the percentile rank in the high school graduating class, which is used for admission purposes at the University of Minnesota. All students in the sample had at least one quarter in residence at the university before the experiment began and thus college achievement data were available.

In the tabulation below the compared means are presented. Most in this group had taken the 1952 form of the American Council on Education Psychological Examination (ACE) and Form Z of the Cooperative English Test; a few individuals had taken alternate forms of these tests and their raw scores were converted by means of conversion tables developed for this purpose by the Student Counseling Bureau at the University of Minnesota. The variation in numbers of students is a function of the number of out-of-state students who had not taken these tests or for whom the high school rank (HSR) was not available.

| | ACE | | Cooperative English | | HSR | | HPR | |
|---|---|---|---|---|---|---|---|---|
| | N | Mean | N | Mean | N | Mean | N | Mean |
| Experimentals ...... | 71 | 110.8 | 71 | 151.0 | 75 | 65.8 | 80 | 2.09 |
| Controls ........... | 17 | 111.8 | 17 | 151.5 | 17 | 70.6 | 20 | 2.07 |

No significant mean or variance differences were found in these comparisons. Although the data are not complete, there is no evidence that pre-counseling differences in academic potential would account for the apparent post-counseling differences in academic history.

*Later follow-ups.* Two subsequent follow-up analyses were made of the indices described above. The purpose was, first, to observe the indices as more of the students completed their academic programs, and second, to observe these commonly used criterion indices as they might vary over time. The reader is cautioned to recognize that the subsequent use of statistical tests repeated on the above data pool plus data added to that pool add no meaning to the findings already reported. Any additional tests represent examination of the significance of hypotheses arising from the data pool itself and as such would be a gross violation of assumptions underlying the statistic in use. The data are, therefore, only descriptive and suggestive of the time-related variation in the observed criterion indices.

The data given below were gathered three, five, and seven years after counseling. At the time of the final perusal of the records, only one experimental subject and one control subject remained in school, requiring only two judgments. There is, however, no guarantee that others will not return subsequently. A recent 25-year follow-up of counseling being conducted in the same setting indicates that some people actually pursue their bachelor's degree over a period of more than 25 years!

Below are presented the honor-point ratios computed for the experimental and control groups before counseling, during counseling, and for each of the time periods following counseling.

| | Pre-Counseling | During Counseling | Post-Counseling | | |
| --- | --- | --- | --- | --- | --- |
| | | | *3 yrs.* | *5 yrs.* | *7 yrs.* |
| Experimentals .......... | 2.09 | 2.01 | 2.34 | 2.46 | 2.42 |
| Controls .............. | 2.07 | 2.00 | 2.09 | 2.16 | 2.27 |

Had statistical analysis been conducted at any of the above times other than after the three-year follow-up, the conclusions mentioned on page 163 would not have varied. Inspection of the most recent set of grades, however, does suggest interesting hypotheses in that students in the experimental group who dropped from school and later returned for a second, third, or fourth try, on the whole tended to lower the overall average of their group, while those in the control group who returned were found, on the average, to raise the group mean.

The data in Table 9 about graduation are presented in slightly different form than that used by Vosbeck and one further category is added — those who dropped from school while making satisfactory progress.

Given sufficient time, a criterion index of "obtaining a degree" might fade as a significant correlate of counseling. At the same time an alterna-

Table 9. Academic Progress of Experimental and
Control Populations

| Follow-Up and Status | Experimentals | Controls |
|---|---|---|
| Three-year follow-up: | | |
| Dropped or unsatisfactory progress | 26% | 65% |
| Degree or satisfactory progress | 74[a] | 35 |
| Five-year follow-up: | | |
| Dropped | | |
| Low grades | 25 | 35 |
| Grades O.K. | 3.5 | 25 |
| A.L.A. degree | 7.5 | 0 |
| B.A., B.S. or satisfactory progress | 64 | 40 |
| Seven-year follow-up: | | |
| Dropped | | |
| Low grades | 14 | 25 |
| Grades O.K. | 14.5 | 30 |
| A.L.A. degree | 7.5 | 0 |
| B.A., B.S. or satisfactory progress | 64 | 45 |

[a] Includes holders of A.L.A. degree.

tive criterion index of "average time taken to obtain a degree" could be of practical value for this population. Because the information in Table 9 was obtained from observation of the data themselves, no statistical test was possible for this hypothesis. Also, because at the time of this experiment subjects had been in school for varying amounts of time, no simple pictorial representation of this observation seemed possible.

Finally, it must be pointed out that the adoption of universal criteria of grade-getting, obtaining a degree, or time taken to obtain a degree is no more a fair criterion index than the universal assumption of lowering anxiety might be. Problems relating even vaguely to academic performance were not present in *all* cases. Interview tapes also reveal that where "academic problems" were present, counselors often worked against themselves (if measurement of success is to be estimated by the above indices) in that they often sought to help the individual select alternative goals not requiring a college degree. In some instances counselors were at the very least not discouraging to the individual who decided to take time out from college because of problems related to maturational development or situational or environmental press.

# *10*

## *Reflections*

T HIS concluding chapter is, we believe, an unusual one. It grew
out of our discussions concerning how we might convey some general and
some quite specific impressions gained during and after the investigations
we have described. Our intent is to enable the reader to share with us
some of the frustrations and insights which close involvement with research into the methods and outcomes of counseling leaves with the investigators. Perhaps these reflections will stimulate future, more incisive
research.

While we will touch upon many topics which should be explored in discussing goals, methods, and outcomes in counseling research, our intent
is not at all to provide a comprehensive review. Rather it is to present, in
an informal fashion, selected issues which strike us as compelling in the
light of our labors of several years. There are four of these: clients and
the process, criterion problems, control methods, and future developments.

### Clients and the Process

Our investigation began as an exploration of outcome goals of the
counseling-casework-psychotherapy process. Reams of material have
been written about these processes exploring their similarities and their
relative or absolute uniqueness. Where the truth lies among such a variety
of interpretations, we don't know. We feel that in many cases the alleged
difference is a difference that doesn't make a difference. We also feel that
perhaps our proneness to lump the processes together made more sense
in the abstract than it did in the concrete operations of our investigation.

168

One of the greatest virtues of experimentation is its demand for precise definitions of generalities, whether they concern client characteristics, the treatment process, or its goals. Our concepts seemed to make a certain amount of sense for treatment processes regardless of their disciplinary labels, and they still do. Why then are there difficulties? Let us look at several possibilities.

First we may ask, is it appropriate to refer to a process as counseling or casework or psychotherapy when the clients' primary concern is indecision about their educational and vocational futures and treatment averages between four and five interviews? Little is gained by the usual pat answers with which our professional literature is replete. At our present stage of knowledge we do not have definitive, mutually exclusive concepts of these processes. A common approach to such concepts contrasts processes of education and re-education rather than examining different levels of personality organization. Yet Phillips (1956) views this approach as having little to offer, operationally, for experimentation or practice. He suggests conceptualizing the treatment process as one of purposeful interference with learned ways of behaving. Can counseling, casework, and psychotherapeutic processes be defined in mutually exclusive terms? Perhaps. Are they so described at present? No. Our belief that no such exclusive definitions are available influenced us to seek out and use as variables those which seemed to synthesize or integrate many present descriptions of process and outcomes.

How realistic is it to expect change in attributes such as those selected for this study over a span of four or five interviews? The data are inconclusive. Hindsight, of course, has a habit of reaching 20-20 acuity. One cannot usually anticipate the length of treatment which will evolve. Perhaps of more import is the empirical question of what constitutes a realistic time period in which to accomplish specified changes. Recent work on time-limited therapy raises questions about the influence of treatment length on outcomes and particularly about the effect of employing length as a manipulable variable.

Reduction in interview contacts per se does not appear to us to be the critical variable in such investigations. One cannot assume that because there is a similarity in the absolute length of time involved in counseling treatments and some types of time-limited therapeutic techniques that the nature of the relationship involved will also be similar. Perhaps the foreknowledge by client and counselor of at least a tentative limit to the number of interviews would have significant effects upon *any* type of treatment without regard to absolute number of contacts or the nature of the interview content. In other words, foreknowledge or expectation of a time limit may account for a significant proportion of the variance in degree of change. Typical counseling cases are not pointedly structured as limited (even tentatively) to three, four, or five interviews; rather, they tend to "come out" that way. Counseling might achieve the same degree of change in fewer interviews if the limit was known when the interaction began.

What about the nature of the problems that clients present? At first glance it might appear to the practicing psychotherapist that the majority of these problems are foreign to the mainstream of the psychotherapeutic process. At second glance it may still look this way — we are not sure. We are sure that client problems in the experiment were dealt with in a variety of ways, some very different from the intra-psychic techniques most familiar to some caseworkers or psychotherapists. This variation in technique might be a basis for arguing that such problems can be viewed superficially and treated in a like manner. It might also indicate that process techniques may vary widely while treatment goals show much less variability among different practitioners.

We are impressed with the fact that in the helping process many facets of the client's life are operative, relevant, and subject to joint exploration. Some of these facets will reflect pathology, some will reflect assets, and some will be difficult to classify in either category. Differences between individuals could be reflected in no other way. In the counseling setting, in their present situation, or in their life histories, clients can be sick, well, realistic, unrealistic, strong, weak, comfortable, or anxious. The detailed analyses made by White (1952) in his longitudinal studies of a number of individuals bear this out. Such intra-individual differences are a major contributor to the looseness of efforts to define the helping process.

A second question we may ask is whether it is appropriate to utilize global variables (e.g., anxiety, defensiveness, problem-solving) in assessing the outcomes of treatment. A purely empirical justification (investigate and determine what changes occur) is a valid one, but it is only partly relevant. These variables were global because of our efforts to find themes or common denominators underlying practice, theory, and research. To us these concepts fit. In retrospect we are concerned about their appropriateness for each individual case. For example, there are clients for whom more rather than less anxiety might be judged beneficial, or clients for whom increments in defensiveness might be judged as a gain, or others for whom no change would be so regarded. Also, we can imagine clients whose treatment has led them to be so open about their inadequacies that they are able to depict themselves in a light suggesting more anxiety, more defensiveness, or poorer problem-solving than they could admit before or during the early stages of treatment.

Some of these difficulties reflect problems in the conceptualization of interrelationships among the three variables. Perhaps we established a framework which was erroneous or overly ambiguous. Even granting this possibility, let us consider the variables independently of each other. We have indicated above a few instances which we see as not fitting the nature of changes which we had predicted would occur during counseling. These understandable, but unpredicted, changes seem too common to be ignored or explained away as chance errors of measurement, remote instances of individual differences, and the like. Of course, one alternative explanation of more substance lies in the nature of the criterion measures. While a great deal of work was done to maximize the reliability and validity of each of the measures, it goes without saying that each was imperfect, and the imperfections were not the same for all the measures.

An obvious difficulty with the problem-solving measures lay in the complexities involved in situation-testing procedures generally as well as in locating criterion groups which were as different as we desired. The most frustrating characteristic of the anxiety and defensiveness measures was their substantial positive intercorrelation. Individually they met one or more of the validation standards we had established, but our conceptualization predicted an inverse relationship between them. Early in our investigations we concluded that the best explanation for their positive correlation was our oversimplification of a complex relationship. We subsequently concluded that any combination of scores on these two measures was both possible and understandable *except* high scores on both measures (i.e., extremely high manifest anxiety and extremely high defensiveness). This conclusion followed from the position that manifestations of defensiveness should serve to reduce anxiety manifestations. Similarly, extreme manifest anxiety would indicate that defensive mechanisms either had not been employed or had failed as anxiety-reducing reactions.

The most likely sources of trouble with the measures would seem to be the inadequacy of the initial validation procedures and the related fact that our criterion groups for validity studies were not as different as they might have been. The latter point is treated in the next section.

A further consideration about the overall value of these variables warrants attention. We did not impose these outcome variables upon the processes in which the psychologist-counselors were engaged. These common denominator variables were presented to the counselors in the context of this question: "Do you subscribe to these goals (i.e., lessening manifest anxiety, lessening defensiveness, enhancing problem-solving) in your work with clients?" The counselors agreed that one or more of these were objectives toward which their interactions with clients were oriented.

Perhaps we were overly persuasive (albeit unintentionally), or perhaps the more global the variable, the greater will be its acceptance among practitioners — regardless of whether empirical results suggest any achievement of such objectives! It is certainly obvious that relatively little attention has been given to investigating more specific outcome variables, reflecting such client complaints as inability to sleep, lack of assurance, uncertainty of educational or vocational goals. More than twenty years ago the work of Williamson and Bordin (1940) suggested that the identification of more specific, less global attributes of change in clients might be a profitable stratagem in assessing client changes associated with counseling. Little has happened along this line since.

A likely reason for the paucity of research on specific outcomes is the current preoccupation with theory building and testing. Perhaps concern has become more centered upon assessing theories (or quasi-theories) than upon assessing clients and their changes. We do not mean to imply that these objectives are mutually exclusive. However, conceptualizations and theories reflect an integration of evidence (from experience or prior research) — an integration which leads to clearer understanding of interrelationships, and predictions of further events under various conditions. Theories should emerge when that evidence is sufficient in nature to be integrated, and not, as at present, when the status that theory building enjoys is great. Perhaps the combination of a relatively young field plus a Zeitgeist valuing theory building leads to (1) premature concern with theory building at the expense of empirical data gathering, (2) more concern with assessing theories than with assessing characteristics of clients and their changes, and as a result (3) fewer significant increments in knowledge.

172

Many investigations of counseling outcomes have borne another burden which is reflected in the investigation reported here. As the investigations are planned the question arises of the population to which the results may be generalized. Our intention was to conduct an investigation which would permit generalization of results to all clients coming to this particular counseling center. It seemed appropriate to view casework and psychotherapy as identical in terms of our conceptual framework of objectives. Where, one might ask, is the problem? In much outcome research the entire service setting has been the subject of evaluation. These investigations (including the present one) identify subjects prior to the course of counseling treatment, and once identified as subjects the individuals remain as such regardless of the nature of counseling. This procedure is essential if one is to evaluate an agency's total service program; however, it introduces complicating and self-defeating elements, because of the diversity of both problems and treatments. The great heterogeneity of client complaints, problems, expectations, and length of treatment increases the difficulty of moving to a sufficiently molar level to provide generalizations which can be applied meaningfully across this array of heterogeneity.

There is a quite different alternative, one which is more modest in scope, but perhaps more productive. This alternative involves selecting facets of the service program and subjecting them one by one to intensive study under optimal conditions. One illustration of this alternative may clarify the distinction. For purposes of this illustration let us consider definitions of clientele, treatment type, and length of treatment which will limit the heterogeneity of the experimental subject pool.

The investigator might limit himself to clients who wanted to change their vocational plans and were uncertain about the appropriateness of alternatives. Furthermore, he might choose only clients with few or no symptoms of intrapersonal emotional conflicts. With regard to treatment, the investigator could specify what elements must be present in the process for the case to be included. If certain testing or demographic data were stipulated, then clients would be included or excluded from the investigation accordingly. A similar action would be taken regarding particular counselor orientations toward work with clients. The investigator could also determine the minimum number of interviews necessary for a case to be included in the investigation. This determination would depend in large part upon the decisions reached regarding the significant elements mentioned above. Another decision might involve the manner of termination, e.g., it might be decided that only those cases terminating by mutual agreement of client and counselor would be included. Again, clients who terminated after fewer interviews or terminated in other ways would be excluded from the investigation.

The net effects of this alternative approach to outcome research would be several. First, more would be known about the characteristics of the treatment process because these characteristics had been built into the design. Second, the subjects as a group would be considerably more homogeneous for the same reason. Third, because of the first two effects, more specific criteria and their criterion measures could be applied relevantly to all of the subjects involved.

The alternative approach to the study of counseling-psychotherapy outcomes just illustrated should produce clear findings regarding this relatively pure constellation of client-treatment characteristics. The findings would be more limited, to be sure. However, successive investigations of similarly delimited facets would accumulate a body of evidence as to outcomes. These results could be far more impressive, taken together, than repeated investigations of the traditional variety which try to take giant strides and in so doing often fall short because they have attempted too much at one time.

## Criterion Problems

Having discussed some of the problems associated with the measurement of more global criteria, we shall now consider alternative criterion variables and their associated rationales and problems.

The more global the criterion variable, the more difficult are the problems of measurement. The investigation reported in the previous chapters employed rather global criterion variables. These were not easy to define, particularly the one with an asset orientation, effective problem-solving. We found it much more difficult to conceptualize and measure asset-oriented variables than those connoting disability or pathology. This difficulty is reflected in the considerable imbalance in the literature on these types of variables. Jahoda's monograph in the series of the Joint Commission on Mental Illness and Health illustrates the same problem. She undertook to identify and organize current concepts of *positive* mental health. She found that "knowledge about deviations, illness, and malfunctioning far exceeds knowledge of healthy functioning. Even apart from the issue of application, they [scientists] maintain, science requires that the previous concentration on the study of inappropriate functioning be corrected by greater emphasis on appropriate functioning, if for no other reason than to test such assumptions as that health and illness are different only in degree." (Jahoda, 1958, p. 6.)

Jahoda identifies six approaches to criteria of mental health: (1) attitudes toward self, (2) growth, development, and self-actualization, (3) integration, (4) autonomy, (5) perception of reality, and (6) environmental mastery. These concepts need operational definition and measurement attention. In some situations, one or another of these variables might be most relevant. For conceptualizing mental health generally, a multiple criterion approach seems most promising. This approach could incorporate Smith's (1950) conception of optimal mental health. The multiple criterion approach appears appropriate even within limited situational contexts, such as in counseling, because this approach can be most sensitive to individual and environmental differences. It clarifies the task of the counselor and the investigator who have to make decisions about the inclusiveness and mutual exclusiveness of criterion variables on which to assess client status.

The compass of any criterion is not determined by its conceptual definition, of course. "Environmental mastery" concepts could lead to operational definitions and criterion measures of various degrees of specificity. More will be said on this point shortly. What these concepts do stress is an orientation toward assets rather than liabilities. For our purposes they bear upon the question of whether to seek counseling changes expressed as decreased manifestations of disability or as increased manifestations of assets.

Some criterion variables can be viewed as serving both orientations — for example, the adjustment index of Dymond (1954). This index represents a pool of "adjustment related" items which Dymond had judges classify into "good adjustment" and "poor adjustment" categories. The subject is asked either to Q-sort the items or to dichotomize them in terms of being "more like me" or "less like me." The scoring of the index consists of allowing one point for each good adjustment item placed in a "more like me" category and one point for each poor adjustment item placed in a "less like me" category. This index was employed with clients in the studies reported by Rogers and Dymond (1954). The clients in these studies averaged about 30 interviews. The same index has been employed by Williams with clients in "brief educational-vocational counseling." The counselor's orientation was described as "moderately nondirective," and "in the great majority of cases, counseling was terminated after the second interview." (Williams, 1962, p. 20.) Williams reports significant post-counseling changes in the counseled group, a group (1) not significantly different in pre-counseling status from a client control group, and (2) significantly different from the pretests of a non-client control group. Post-testing of all three groups revealed the counseled group to be (1) significantly different from the client control group, and (2) not significantly different from the non-client control group. Thus, in a very abbreviated form of treatment, significant changes were manifested with this adjustment index, indicating that the instrument has quite broad applicability for assessment of change.

This type of index is relatively specific in one sense. The stimulus statements are clear and there is empirical evidence on how different subgroups of individuals are inclined to respond to them. In another sense there are troublesome problems involved with such instruments. The first is reflected in comments made by Snyder (1962) with reference to Williams' study. He raises the question of how dependent the results are upon the item content of the Q-sorts used. His comments seem to be indirect references to validity issues. One answer, of course, involves the judgmental criterion by which the items were originally classified, another involves the observation that non-client groups perform differently, and significantly so, from clients. The overlap, however, may be considerable. Snyder also raises a question about the tendency of such self-concept-based indices to encourage socially desirable responses. As he puts it, the problem is the perennial one of the potentially distorting influence of what Hathaway termed the "hello-goodbye effect." (Hathaway, 1948.) The extent of this influence in any given investigation is difficult to assess, but it is clear that such effects will be minimized to the extent that criterion measures are subtle rather than obvious in their meaning; empirical rather than a priori logic is employed in their scoring; criterion measures rely on observable behaviors rather than client self-report; and criterion measures and the assessment of client status on them appear divorced from the conditions under which the client received counseling.

A different problem with such an adjustment index rests in the ambiguity or non-specificity of "adjustment." What is *not* included in this global concept? Cannot the six concepts identified by Jahoda all be subsumed under this label? To the extent that it is all-inclusive, so also it is non-definitive.

Let us consider a specific situation, e.g., clients seeking vocational counseling. Does such an index serve as a more feasible measure of assessing change than that of assessing changes in clients' vocational plans and corresponding behavior? Or, given evidence of significant changes in "adjustment," may we assume corresponding changes in more specific client attributes? Or is the adjustment index a different approach to assessment of change, exploring a broader impact of counseling, quite apart from the particular concerns of the individual who seeks counseling assistance? In short, while X's adjustment indices may reveal significant changes after counseling, we cannot help but be intrigued by the lack of information they provide on such questions as these: Were there changes in the clarity of X's plans, or the appropriateness of his plans? Were there changes in his overt behaviors which were relevant to and consistent with such plans?

In our investigation we avoided the use of criterion variables which were specific to the problems of clients. The reasons for doing so were several. First, problems presented may differ from problems developed during counseling. Pre-counseling assessment of client status on such criterion variables would not be possible except for problems presented. Any alteration in the nature of client problems during counseling would not allow comparison of pre-counseling and post-counseling status. Similarly, any such problems evolving as a function of experience in counseling would not be comparably available from assessment of the controls, regardless of the kind employed — own controls, client controls, or non-client controls. Second, the more specifically the criterion variables were tailored to the problems of the clients, the greater would be the resulting number of criterion variables. This prospect would have seriously hindered our attempt to create a conceptual framework of criterion variables which could be applied appropriately to all clients. Third, we were puzzled as to how we could establish comparable units of different levels of status on the array of specific criterion variables that would result. Fourth, we were uncertain about how psychologically meaningful — that is, conceptually clear — such criterion variables would be.

In retrospect, our commitment to a broad conceptual framework meant that we searched no further for specific criterion variables and their measures. As a result, with the exception of the academic outcomes studies, we did not measure, before or after counseling, the concerns that led clients to seek counseling or that were considered (perhaps at length) during the course of counseling.

We came to view specific criterion variables as symptoms or constellations of symptoms. Symptoms have connotations of heterogeneity and unpredictability and do not offer a basic understanding of client status or change in status. Perhaps we overstressed the superficiality of the symptom approach and were too inclined to adopt a disability-criterion model — a model wherein lessening manifestations of anxiety or defensiveness appeared as patently acceptable outcomes of counseling. Perhaps, also, we were overly impressed with the fact that alteration in one symptom during treatment can result in the appearance of other symptoms. No research has shown that this hydraulic theory of personality is a predictable trend in counseled clients, or that symptom changes are without implications for the individual's degree of disability or productivity. Symptom differences are just as real as individual differences.

In retrospect, we might make a much greater commitment to investigation of symptom variables, on the basis that (1) symptoms are behaviors, not "something else," and (2) modification of such behaviors is a treatment goal. This issue is in no way identical with the issue of how to effect such modification. Undoubtedly, one reason for such an inclination is the paucity of conceptualization and indicator measures for variables reflecting positive mental health, the paucity noted by Jahoda.

In further retrospect, we are inclined to agree with the view that a promising approach to criterion variables for assessing counseling outcomes is found in specific variables — variables which have a certain face validity stemming from their direct reflection of client concerns in seeking and in experiencing the treatment process. This approach may also influence our criterion definitions and measures to encompass the positive portion of the disability-asset continuum.

Another advantage of this approach lies in the greater emphasis which it places upon specific, overt, observable behaviors. This emphasis appeared in the Williamson and Bordin (1940) investigation where a post-counseling follow-up study was made of the actions taken by clients and the consistency of these with counselor judgments, case data, and decisions reached during the course of counseling. Similarly, Magoon (1954) utilized counselor judgments of verbal reports of clients as to their post-counseling actions relevant to the problems manifested at the beginning of their counseling. Also, there are the numerous follow-up studies — only infrequently involving pre-counseling assessment of status — of counseled clients on such variables as employment, educational achievement, marriage, admission to hospitals, or recidivism. In a like vein is Brayfield's (1962) observation that both practice and research have given insufficient attention to individual *performance* (in contrast to inner affective states, self-conceptualizations, etc.) as the basis on which an individual is evaluated as adequate or inadequate in our society.

This distinction brings to mind a clarifying point with which Jahoda introduced her treatment of concepts of positive mental health. She said that "one has the option of defining mental health in at least one of two ways: as a *relatively constant and enduring function of personality,* leading to predictable differences in behavior and feelings depending on the stresses and strains of the situations in which a person finds himself; or as a *momentary function of personality and situation.* Looking at mental health in the first way will lead to a classification of individuals as more or less healthy; looking at it in the second way, will lead to a classification of actions as more or less healthy. The relevance of this distinction can be illustrated with an example concerning physical health. Take a strong man with a bad cold. According to the first, he is healthy; according to the second, he is sick. Both statements are justifiable and useful. But utter confusion will result if either of these correct diagnoses is made in the wrong context — that is, if he is regarded as a permanently sick person or as one who is functioning healthily. Much of the confusion in the area of mental health stems from the failure to establish whether one is talking about mental health as an enduring attribute of a person or as a momentary attribute of functioning." (Jahoda, 1958, pp. 7–8.)

This kind of distinction helps to clarify the meaning of criterion variables. It may be that outcome goals can be considered more clearly in terms of such a distinction. Variables which are act-oriented may be more relevant for brief-contact counseling or psychotherapy. Both kinds of orientations may be relevant for longer treatment processes, but they should not be confused with one another.

Stemming from quite different origins, principles of operant conditioning have been extended to counseling and psychotherapy. An inherent emphasis of this orientation falls upon observable behaviors, their identification, emission rates, and changes in emission concomitant with various schedules of reinforcement. As Lindsley (1961) has indicated, free operant conditioning and the counseling or psychotherapeutic process

have several critical features in common. These include emphasis on behavior modification and control, dealing with the single individual, dealing with observable changes in the individual over time, using response
frequency measures of status and change in status, and concern with consequences of behavior and with functional relationships between the individual and his environment. Furthermore, the verbal and nonverbal
acts of the counselor-psychotherapist in the traditional treatment process
can be interpreted as an unknowing or at least unsystematic approach to
the operant conditioning of certain responses of his clients. The applicability of verbal conditioning techniques to the wide array of therapeutic problems remains to be demonstrated. Such techniques may be used
to enable clients to control their own behavior, verbal and nonverbal,
through their own verbal stimuli. A first level of investigation here would
be to determine whether relevant client behavior can be brought under
control of the counselor-therapist; upon this issue may depend what client behaviors may be amenable subsequently to control by the client himself.

## Control Methods

The value of a control group for outcome investigations rarely has
been considered a debatable issue and needs little elaboration here; how
one goes about establishing such a control group for observational and
comparative purposes is another matter. Variations on the "own control"
and "matched group" designs have, because of their frequent use, been
subjected to more critical review than the idealized method of random assignment to experimental and control groupings from a pool of motivated
subjects. The descriptive information reported in the previous chapter
suggests some of the limitations of the latter method. Certainly at some
unknown point in time the fact of withholding treatment from a motivated
group can have an effect on readiness to seek or willingness to accept help.
Also, uncontrollable situational factors have, in this study, demonstrated
their effects.

On the other hand, the usual criticism of designs comparing motivated
experimental groups with non-motivated matched control groups cannot
be made of the descriptive information reported in Chapter 9. To assume
that academic differences found in favor of experimental subjects can be
attributed solely to their state of motivation would seem, from this information, to be untenable. It is clear that the subjects in the experiment,

both controls and experimentals, were in academic trouble, and were motivated to seek help. Experimentals who received help had a better than expected chance of resolving their difficulties, while the controls who did not receive such help fared worse than would be expected for university students in general, despite the statistical finding related to problem-solving skills.

There is, of course, no suggestion here as to the best solution to the control problem. To effect a design method psychologically parallel to the placebo technique in other fields would undoubtedly have limitations. To find "counselor-controls" equivalent in all respects to trained counselors or psychotherapists except in the "training" variable might shed some light on the significance of training itself, but would tell us little about the effects common to the two sets of practitioners. Comparison of alternative treatment methodologies, while currently the most rigorous design scheme that is available to the researcher in this field, suffers from the same limitations.

The random-assignment design method certainly has its strengths, which should be neither undersold nor overestimated. The brief time-span of some counseling and psychotherapy treatment modes is a promising feature as far as use of this scheme is concerned. The relative brevity means greater feasibility of maintaining effective control groups for the period of time needed to complete experimental treatments and post-testing programs. In other words, equality of time is maintained with minimal distortion of the relationship for either group, and without compromise of ethical considerations. Conversely, it is difficult to see how adequate controls could, by this method, be employed to cover treatment modes whose duration was one or two years, or even as short as six months.

As the students of modern philosophy of science inform us, it is highly unlikely that a single critical experiment will be the means by which scientific knowledge in the field of psychology will advance. It is also highly unlikely that a single design technique will provide the answer to all of our problems. Each method can add some information to our body of knowledge, and a multiplicity of approaches can add a variety of facets to our knowledge of a common point of concern. The potential for eliciting a closer approximation to the truth lies in a review of all these various approaches to a common problem rather than in the use of any single approach.

## Future Developments

Taking as a guide the fact that future behavior is best predicted by past behavior, we can envision some interesting future directions for outcome research. The counseling-psychotherapeutic process itself has changed and will change more over time; indeed, it is possible that dramatic changes will arise from the use of other media of communication. Film or video tape, for example, may have important consequences for the counseling process itself, quite over and beyond their uses in counselor training.

In contrast to changes in the process, goals will probably remain quite constant. Jahoda's conceptions will no doubt be subjected to operational definition which in turn will lead to the development of criterion measures. There will be increasing conceptualization and investigation of asset-oriented variables, as approaches not only to preventive intervention but also to skills and techniques oriented toward optimal development and productivity of the individual. Our evolution away from the "absence of disease" goal has been slow indeed, perhaps because our mental health activity has stemmed to a great degree from the clinical-medical-rehabilitative-curative model. Current cultural emphasis on community-wide involvement in mental health objectives, services, and facilities may accelerate this evolution. The application of operant conditioning principles and techniques to the treatment processes, to attitude change, and to information and skill acquisition will accelerate this evolution. If these applications are successful, as a small number have been to date, their importance could be considerable, since these principles and techniques bring with them no carry-over of the clinical-rehabilitative halo that has been so pervasive in the past.

What about a conceptual framework or theory regarding counseling or psychotherapeutic goals? We are inclined to believe that it is premature to expect the development of an empirically useful generalized model for these processes. Undoubtedly this belief is partly produced by the heterogeneous clientele with which we have worked. We have discussed the considerable advantages of taking a much more modest approach to the identification of goals and the assessment of outcomes specific to these more limited counseling or therapeutic objectives. With greater homogeneity of experimental subject pools, treatment methods, and treatment objectives, theorizing may be quite productive. In practice, the future will no doubt find both atheoretical, data-gathering empiricists and theory builders and testers hard at work. This is as it should be.

# APPENDIX, REFERENCES, INDEX

# *Appendix*

FIVE of the most basic and frequently referred-to schedules mentioned in this book — schedules B, D, E, L, and M — are reproduced in the pages that follow. A multilithed set of all the schedules discussed is available from the Student Counseling Bureau, University of Minnesota.

### SCHEDULE B. MINNESOTA MANIFEST ANXIETY SCALE (52)

| *Biographical Inventory Item No.* | *Scoring Key* | *Item* |
|---|---|---|
| 3 | T | I sometimes feel that I can't accomplish what I'm expected to. |
| 4 | T | In almost any group, there are some people who often irritate me. |
| 6 | T | MMPI Items 21 and 308. |
| 8 | T | Being successful in the eyes of others is important to me. |
| 9 | T | MMPI Item 26. |
| 10 | F | I never put off until tomorrow what I could do today. |
| 12 | T | MMPI Items 32 and 328. |
| 13 | F | I am not nervous when meeting a person in authority (employer, teacher, etc.) |
| 31 | F | Failure is very hard for me to take. |
| 35 | T | I wish I didn't worry so much. |
| 36 | T | MMPI Item 82. |
| 39 | T | MMPI Item 86. |
| 42 | T | MMPI Item 89. |
| 44 | T | The things I can do the best seem the most important to me. |
| 49 | F | I am not considered to be a "fussy" eater. |
| 51 | T | MMPI Item 94. |
| 55 | T | I am less popular than the average person. |
| 63 | T | MMPI Item 106. |
| 64 | T | I do my best work when the pressure is really on. |
| 66 | T | MMPI Item 124. |
| 68 | T | I don't seem to get the breaks that others do. |
| 73 | T | I am the type who makes long-range plans. |

| *Biographical Inventory Item No.* | *Scoring Key* | *Item* |
|---|---|---|
| 76 | F | I often relax just by sitting and doing nothing. |
| 77 | T | I wish that I could change parts of my personality. |
| 85 | T | I often use "white lies" to save myself from embarrassment. |
| 95 | T | In order to be successful, a person should always be worried about doing the wrong thing. |
| 98 | T | MMPI Item 171. |
| 113 | T | I try to avoid being too much like other people. |
| 114 | T | MMPI Item 217. |
| 123 | T | MMPI Item 509. |
| 128 | F | MMPI Item 242. |
| 130 | T | MMPI Item 244. |
| 146 | F | MMPI Item 287. |
| 148 | T | MMPI Item 290. |
| 151 | T | I am more careful than most people with my money. |
| 159 | T | I often act as though I were nervous. |
| 162 | T | MMPI Items 317 and 362. |
| 164 | F | MMPI Item 500. |
| 165 | T | It takes a big man to admit his mistakes. |
| 172 | T | MMPI Item 357. |
| 175 | F | I'm interested in too many things to confine my attention to any one thing for very long. |
| 177 | F | MMPI Items 20 and 310. |
| 182 | T | MMPI Item 397. |
| 183 | T | At times, having nothing to do becomes unbearable. |
| 198 | T | MMPI Item 455. |
| 200 | F | MMPI Item 463. |
| 204 | T | MMPI Item 487. |
| 223 | T | MMPI Item 206. |
| 241 | T | MMPI Item 301. |
| 247 | T | MMPI Item 382. |
| 255 | NS* | MMPI Item 488. (drop) |
| 274 | T | MMPI Item 541. |

\* NS = not scored.

## SCHEDULE D. MINNESOTA DEFENSIVENESS SCALE (63)

| *Biographical Inventory Item No.* | *Scoring Key* | *Item* |
|---|---|---|
| 2 | F | Sometimes I've felt that people don't recognize my good points. |
| 12 | F | MMPI Items 32 and 328. |
| 13 | T | I am not nervous when meeting a person in authority (employer, teacher, etc.) |
| 20 | F | I never have been stubborn enough to stick to my point even when I knew I was wrong. |
| 21 | T | MMPI Item 41. |
| 26 | T | I often feel that others have strange ideas and ways of doing things. |

186

| Biographical Inventory Item No. | Scoring Key | Item |
|---|---|---|
| 34 | T | When someone asks me to do something, it is easy for me to say "no." |
| 36 | F | MMPI Item 82. |
| 37 | T | I seldom set deadlines for myself. |
| 42 | T | MMPI Item 89. |
| 54 | F | MMPI Item 96. |
| 59 | T | I have done some things that I would not want anyone to know about. |
| 64 | F | I do my best work when the pressure is really on. |
| 74 | T | Often in the past others have tried to make me look bad. |
| 75 | T | MMPI Item 131. |
| 76 | T | I often relax just by sitting and doing nothing. |
| 81 | T | I have often felt that others look down on me without justification. |
| 86 | F | MMPI Item 152. |
| 87 | F | It is hard for me to be "natural" around people I don't know too well. |
| 92 | T | MMPI Item 167. |
| 98 | F | MMPI Item 171. |
| 103 | T | If a person is very sensitive, the reason is that he has a fine character. |
| 109 | T | You've got to have influence to get anywhere these days. |
| 112 | T | MMPI Item 216. |
| 114 | T | MMPI Item 217. |
| 116 | T | MMPI Item 222. |
| 124 | T | MMPI Item 238. |
| 125 | T | Few people see me as I see myself. |
| 130 | T | MMPI Item 244. |
| 138 | T | MMPI Item 266. |
| 142 | T | MMPI Item 277. |
| 144 | T | MMPI Item 284. |
| 146 | T | MMPI Item 287. |
| 148 | T | MMPI Item 290. |
| 150 | F | MMPI Item 295. |
| 159 | T | I often act as though I were nervous. |
| 160 | T | MMPI Item 316. |
| 163 | T | In a group, I usually get a chance to have my say. |
| 180 | T | MMPI Item 394. |
| 181 | F | I would not say that I am a nervous person. |
| 210 | F | MMPI Item 329. |
| 214 | F | MMPI Item 3. |
| 215 | T | MMPI Item 40. |
| 216 | T | MMPI Item 99. |
| 223 | F | MMPI Item 206. |
| 228 | T | MMPI Item 241. |
| 232 | T | MMPI Item 279. |
| 235 | F | MMPI Item 289. |
| 240 | T | MMPI Item 320. |
| 242 | T | MMPI Item 322. |
| 245 | T | MMPI Item 345. |
| 246 | T | MMPI Item 335. |

| Biographical Inventory Item No. | Scoring Key | Item |
|---|---|---|
| 249 | T | MMPI Item 416. |
| 252 | T | MMPI Item 439. |
| 255 | F | MMPI Item 488. |
| 257 | T | MMPI Item 505. |
| 258 | T | MMPI Item 396. |
| 259 | T | MMPI Item 506. |
| 263 | T | MMPI Item 518. |
| 265 | T | MMPI Item 544. |
| 267 | F | MMPI Item 137. |
| 268 | T | MMPI Item 161. |
| 269 | T | MMPI Item 334. |

## SCHEDULE E. SOCIOMETRIC FORM DEVELOPED FOR ANXIETY AND DEFENSIVENESS VALIDITY STUDIES

We are about to give you some illustrations of different ways people commonly act. *Everyone* acts like this to some degree. On the basis of your experience with the men in your section, we are asking you to indicate those men whose behavior is *most similar* and those whose behavior is *least similar* to the following descriptions.

By "most similar" we mean what men in your section show the most and the least of these behaviors. We are not interested in who is a "good guy" or a "jerk." Instead, we will describe some of the ways everyone acts at one time or another, and it is your job to decide which men in your group *act like this, the most and the least.*

You are to judge only the men in your section who are taking the test, and forget about those like yourself who are making these ratings. Do not list yourself or the other 4 men making the ratings.

### What to Do

1. Read over the first characteristic on the next page, two or three times.
2. Look over the men in your section who are taking the test and decide *which 3 men in your group act the* MOST *like this.*
3. Print their names in the space marked "Behave MOST like this," putting the man who best illustrates this as 1st, then the 2nd, and then the 3rd in that order.
4. Now look over the men in your section who are taking the test, and decide *which 3 men in your group act the* LEAST *like this.*
5. Print their names in the space marked "Behave LEAST like this," putting the man who acts the least like this as 1st, then the 2nd, and then the 3rd, in that order.
6. Now go through the same steps (Nos. 1–5) for the other ten characteristics. The same person may be listed under more than one characteristic if this seems appropriate to you. Of course no man can be listed under 'Most' and 'Least' for the *same* characteristic.
7. After finishing, check to make sure that you have *3* men listed in each space.

NOTE: After you have started to make your ratings, if you have any questions, the test examiner in the room with your section will be glad to answer them.

When you have finished and checked over your ratings, give them to the examiner in the room.

Characteristic 1:
*Unwillingness to admit mistakes or inadequacies.*

(For example, denies he had been given responsibility for a job that was not done.

188

Explains failure to meet a deadline on basis of not knowing there was one. Unwilling to admit he doesn't know the score or that he has failings common to almost everyone, etc.)

*Behave most like this*          *Behave least like this*

_____          _____
_____          _____
_____          _____

Characteristic 2:
*Acts suspicious or aggressive.*

(For example, suspicious of the reasons behind others' efforts to help him. Doubts authority. Consistently challenges others' ideas, etc.)

*Behave most like this*          *Behave least like this*

_____          _____
_____          _____
_____          _____

Characteristic 3:
*Nervous.*

(For example, mannerisms such as nailbiting, knuckle-cracking, chain-smoking, etc.)

*Behave most like this*          *Behave least like this*

_____          _____
_____          _____
_____          _____

Characteristic 4:
*Explains away his own mistakes or inadequacies.*

(For example, always has an excuse for not doing a better job in class, on the job, with girls, makes excuses for his lack of dates, not having a better job, etc.)

*Behave most like this*          *Behave least like this*

_____          _____
_____          _____
_____          _____

Characteristic 5:
*Unresponsive or apathetic.*

(For example, unable to express how he feels. Doesn't act the way he seems to feel. Has his "guard up" much of the time, etc.)

*Behave most like this*          *Behave least like this*

_____          _____
_____          _____
_____          _____

Characteristic 6:
*Tense.*

(For example, unable to relax, restless, can't concentrate, seems to be continually working under pressure, etc.)

*Behave most like this*          *Behave least like this*

_____          _____
_____          _____
_____          _____

Characteristic 7:
*Avoids dealing with problem situations.*

(For example, by physically avoiding or withdrawing, by wishful thinking or day-dreaming, by changing or avoiding certain types of conversation, by "gold-bricking," by concentrating almost exclusively on an activity in which he excels, etc.)

*Behave most like this*      *Behave least like this*

Characteristic 8:
*Unrealistic.*

(For example, sees his abilities as much better or poorer than they really are, makes plans which could not likely be carried out; tells tall stories about his past accomplishments, etc.)

*Behave most like this*      *Behave least like this*

Characteristic 9:
*Easily embarrassed.*

(For example, readily blushes, stammers, appears shy, etc.)

*Behave most like this*      *Behave least like this*

Characteristic 10:
*Blames his own mistakes or inadequacies on other persons, institutions or regulations.*

(For example, blames own failures on the other men, blames dating failures on the girls involved, attributes failure to take part in group activities as due to apathy or clannishness of other men, justifies own mistakes on the basis that others are just as much at fault, etc.)

*Behave most like this*      *Behave least like this*

Characteristic 11:
*Worries.*

(For example, frequently is apprehensive or fearful of what will happen from day to day. Lacks assurance that he will succeed in class, on his job, with girls, etc. Overly concerned about the impression he makes on others, etc.)

*Behave most like this*      *Behave least like this*

## SCHEDULE L. PERCEPTION OF COUNSELING INVENTORY

This inventory consists of numbered statements which have been made by persons prior to or during counseling.

Read each statement and decide whether you might make such a statement. You are to mark all your answers on the answer sheet. If you *strongly agree* (SA) with the statement, blacken between the lines of column 1, corresponding to the number of that statement. If you merely *agree* (A) with the statement but have no strong feelings about it, blacken between the lines of column 2. If you *disagree* (D) with the statement, mark column 3, and if you *disagree strongly* (SD) with the statement, mark column 4 corresponding to that numbered statement on the answer sheet. The code then, is this:

1. Strongly agree
2. Agree
3. Disagree
4. Strongly disagree

*Make a mark for each statement.*

Remember that these statements represent characteristic expressions of many individuals seeking counseling. Most of the statements are put in the present tense (e.g., "The counselor gives me reassurance"). Your job is to read over each of these statements and mark the degree to which you agree or disagree with the statement — that is, how well the statement describes how counseling looks to *you* as you mark these statements *now*.

Many thanks for your cooperation.

| Scoring Key | Scoring Weight | Item No. | Item |
|---|---|---|---|
| A | +3 | 1 | I describe my problem(s) to the counselor. |
| A | −4 | 2 | About all I do in getting counseling is take tests. |
| A | +2 | 3 | I'm here to gather information that will help me solve my problems. |
| A | +3 | 4 | I'm here to gather information about myself (tests, counselor's opinions, etc.) |
| A | +2 | 5 | I have to ask the counselor questions that will clarify my confusion. |
| A | +5 | 6 | Ultimately, I have to make my own decisions. |
| A | +3 | 7 | I have to tell the counselor what my desires are. |
| A | +3 | 8 | I tell the counselor about myself. |
| | NS* | 9 | I tell the counselor about what I would like to do. |
| A | −3 | 10 | I don't talk much myself — mostly listen. |
| A | +3 | 11 | I talk about anything I wish. |
| A | −3 | 12 | No one can really bring himself to express how he feels to a counselor. |
| A | −4 | 13 | I only need to answer the counselor's questions. |
| A | −4 | 14 | I am careful to avoid "giving myself away." |
| A | −3 | 15 | I try to make a good impression on the counselor. |
| A | +5 | 16 | I contribute as much as I can in terms of expressing my attitudes and feelings, discussing them and bringing in new ideas that occur to me in relation to my problem(s). |
| A | −4 | 17 | I keep most of my problems to myself, rather than expressing them to the counselor. |

* NS: These items have an item weight of +1 or −1 and were not scored in this experimental program.

| Scoring Key | Scoring Weight | Item No. | Item |
|---|---|---|---|
| | NS | 18 | I am very cautious about accepting suggestions the counselor makes. |
| | NS | 19 | There are things I have to do outside the interviews to help solve my problem(s). |
| A | −3 | 20 | I won't discuss those things that embarrass me. |
| A | −4 | 21 | What I do is up to the counselor. |
| A | +3 | 22 | I tell the counselor how I feel so that he is in a position to help me. |
| A | +4 | 23 | The counselor is interested in me as a person. |
| | NS | 24 | The counselor leads the interview with questions. |
| A | +2 | 25 | The counselor is more concerned with my personal characteristics, daily life, etc., than with test scores, grades, and the like. |
| A | −2 | 26 | The counselor mainly answers my questions. |
| A | +2 | 27 | The counselor describes how the counseling process works. |
| | NS | 28 | I don't understand how the counselor goes about helping people like myself. |
| A | +3 | 29 | The counselor inquires as to my idea of the problem. |
| A | +4 | 30 | The counselor helps me to solve my problems. |
| A | −4 | 31 | The counselor makes the decision as to the best course of action for me to follow. |
| A | +4 | 32 | The counselor leaves the ultimate decision as to a course of action up to me. |
| A | +2 | 33 | The counselor gives me suggestions as to possible solutions. |
| A | +2 | 34 | The counselor finds out what my personal characteristics are (like abilities, interests, courses, uncertainties, etc.) |
| A | +3 | 35 | The counselor tells me what the test scores mean. |
| A | +2 | 36 | The counselor may see the problem differently than I do. |
| A | +4 | 37 | The counselor tries to understand my problem as I see it. |
| | NS | 38 | The counselor mainly gives me information. |
| A | +4 | 39 | The counselor is interested in whatever I want to talk about. |
| A | +4 | 40 | The counselor tries to learn how I feel. |
| A | +4 | 41 | The counselor tries to learn why I feel as I do. |
| | NS | 42 | The counselor doesn't try to figure me out. |
| A | −3 | 43 | The counselor talks most of the time. |
| A | −3 | 44 | The counselor sticks to the test results. |
| A | +3 | 45 | The counselor is interested in my personality characteristics. |
| A | +4 | 46 | The counselor helps me think for myself. |
| A | −3 | 47 | The counselor does a lot of thinking for me. |
| A | +2 | 48 | The counselor is very frank in what he says. |
| A | −3 | 49 | The counselor is not completely frank with me. |
| A | −3 | 50 | The counselor's manner makes me feel ill at ease. |

| Scoring Key | Scoring Weight | Item No. | Item |
|---|---|---|---|
| A | +2 | 51 | The counselor presents a happy appearance. |
| A | −3 | 52 | The counselor presents a glum appearance. |
| A | +4 | 53 | The counselor is interested in me as a person. |
| A | −3 | 54 | The counselor is not particularly interested in me as a person. |
| A | +4 | 55 | The counselor is interested in aiding me in my situation. |
| A | −4 | 56 | The counselor is not interested in aiding me in my situation. |
| | NS | 57 | The counselor is quite talkative. |
| | NS | 58 | The counselor does not talk enough. |
| A | +3 | 59 | The counselor knows a lot about people and their problems. |
| A | +3 | 60 | The counselor is a likable person. |
| A | −3 | 61 | The counselor is a hard-to-like person. |
| A | +2 | 62 | The counselor is an easy person to get to know. |
| A | −2 | 63 | The counselor is a difficult person to get to know. |
| A | +4 | 64 | The counselor will accept *any* feelings or experiences I have had without surprise or displeasure. |
| A | −4 | 65 | The counselor acts somewhat surprised or shocked at embarrassing feelings or experiences I have had. |
| A | +4 | 66 | The counselor keeps my confidences. |
| A | +3 | 67 | The counselor presents a calm, relaxed manner. |
| A | −3 | 68 | The counselor presents a rather tense, uneasy appearance. |
| A | −2 | 69 | The counselor analyzes my personality. |
| A | +4 | 70 | The counselor is really interested in helping me. |
| A | −4 | 71 | The counselor is too busy to spend much time with me. |
| A | +4 | 72 | The counselor's job is to help me help myself. |
| A | +2 | 73 | The counselor is a real friend. |
| A | −3 | 74 | The counselor has a stereotyped opinion of me. |
| | NS | 75 | The counselor is here primarily for training and has little interest in me as a person. |
| A | −4 | 76 | The counselor's interest in me is primarily theoretical. |
| A | −4 | 77 | The counselor disapproves of beliefs of mine that are different from his own. |
| A | −3 | 78 | The test results are more important than my feelings when it comes to making decisions. |
| A | −3 | 79 | What to discuss will depend more on the test results than upon me. |
| A | −3 | 80 | The interviews won't last long enough to get at why I feel and/or act as I do. |
| A | −2 | 81 | If the discussion becomes very personal, I tend to hold something back. |
| A | −3 | 82 | The interviews are not concerned with getting at *why* I feel as I do. |

| Scoring Key | Scoring Weight | Item No. | Item |
|---|---|---|---|
| A | +2 | 83 | I get more help from the later interviews than I get from the first one or two. |
| | NS | 84 | I feel more secure once I have the counselor's opinion. |
| | NS | 85 | I feel more secure once I have the test results. |
| A | +2 | 86 | The interviews are more helpful once the counselor gets better acquainted with me. |
| A | −3 | 87 | I wouldn't seek counseling if I thought I would be ill at ease during the interview. |
| A | +3 | 88 | The interviews offer a great deal of help in resolving what concerns me. |
| A | +3 | 89 | The interviews give me a better knowledge of myself. |
| A | +3 | 90 | Much of the interviews are devoted to clarifying just what the problems are. |
| A | +2 | 91 | The interviews are informal and casual. |
| A | +4 | 92 | I do a lot of thinking about my situation and our discussions, between interviews. |
| A | +4 | 93 | My own opinions of myself are taken into consideration during the interview. |
| A | +3 | 94 | My confusions are clarified. |
| A | +4 | 95 | The interviews are kept confidential. |
| A | +4 | 96 | The atmosphere of the interviews is a friendly one. |
| | NS | 97 | Two or three interviews are necessary to handle what concerns me. |
| A | +2 | 98 | Maybe more than three interviews will be needed to handle what concerns me. |
| | NS | 99 | My taking tests consumes 1 or 2 hours. |
| | NS | 100 | My taking tests consumes more than 5 hours. |
| A | +3 | 101 | Taking tests may help in answering my questions. |
| A | +4 | 102 | The counseling process gives me some experience in a way of going at solving problems concerning me. |
| A | +2 | 103 | The interviews will narrow down the alternative courses of action I might follow. |
| | NS | 104 | The counseling process is the same for about everyone. |
| A | −3 | 105 | After I've "told my story," it shouldn't take more than one more interview to get some ideas as to what to do. |
| A | +2 | 106 | After I've "told my story," there is no way of knowing just how many interviews it will take to get some ideas as to what to do. |
| A | +2 | 107 | The interviews should give me some idea of my strong and weak characteristics. |
| A | +3 | 108 | During the interviews, the counselor puts a lot of weight on how I see things. |
| A | −4 | 109 | The interviews are not the place to bring up personal problems. |

194

| Scoring Key | Scoring Weight | Item No. | Item |
|---|---|---|---|
| A | +4 | 110 | Counseling is a process whereby I can define my problems better. |
| A | +4 | 111 | What I get out of counseling probably depends on the extent to which I am willing to work at it. |
| A | +4 | 112 | What I get out of counseling probably depends on my own desire to make some change in how I feel or in what I do. |
| A | +2 | 113 | It is easy for me to explain how I really feel. |
| A | +4 | 114 | The interviews help me learn how to look at my problem. |
| A | +4 | 115 | The interviews make me better able to solve future problems (over and beyond what concerns me now). |
| A | −2 | 116 | My problems should all be solved so I won't need any interviews again. |
| A | +4 | 117 | The interviews don't help me unless I try to help myself. |
| A | +4 | 118 | The interview time is my own — I can bring up whatever matters are of concern to me. |
| A | −2 | 119 | I don't want my family to know I am getting counseling. |
| A | −2 | 120 | I don't want my friends to know I am getting counseling. |
| A | −2 | 121 | I don't want my adviser to know I am getting counseling. |
| A | +3 | 122 | I have as many interviews as I need to resolve my problems. |
| A | +2 | 123 | Talking with the counselor is more helpful than taking tests. |
| A | −2 | 124 | Talking with the counselor is less helpful than taking tests. |
| A | −2 | 125 | Much of the interview time is devoted to advice, suggestions, recommendations. |
| A | +3 | 126 | The purpose of what goes on in the interviews is clear to me. |
| A | +2 | 127 | I don't know how many interviews I will need. |
| A | −2 | 128 | The tests will consume too much of my time. |
| A | +4 | 129 | It is a relief just to be able to talk fully about things that concern me. |
| A | +3 | 130 | The interviews help me to unburden myself. |
| | NS | 131 | I don't know what the interviews can do for me. |
| A | +3 | 132 | The interviews sharpen my sensitivity about myself. |
| A | −2 | 133 | I doubt if the interviews help me. |
| | NS | 134 | My problems are not important enough to me to take up more than 1 or 2 interviews. |
| A | −3 | 135 | My problems are not important enough to the counselor to take up more than 1 or 2 interviews. |
| A | −2 | 136 | I don't want to take up much of the counselor's time. |

| Scoring Key | Scoring Weight | Item No. | Item |
|---|---|---|---|
| A | −4 | 137 | In the interviews, all I want is the counselor to give me his opinions of what I should do. |
| A | −3 | 138 | I don't see why I need to see a counselor before taking tests. |
| A | −2 | 139 | The counselor wants to talk only about things that have gone wrong or are problems for me. |
| A | +2 | 140 | Counseling makes me less anxious. |
| A | +4 | 141 | Counseling results in improved ability to solve my problems. |
| A | +2 | 142 | The counselor makes some mistakes. |
| | NS | 143 | The counselor only deals with the specific problems that I bring to him. |
| | NS | 144 | The counselor only discusses the particular topic I come in to discuss. |
| A | +3 | 145 | The counselor is experienced in helping people with many kinds of personal problems. |
| | NS | 146 | The counselor is not an important influence in my life. |
| A | −3 | 147 | I keep the counselor at a distance. |
| A | −2 | 148 | I forget what the counselor says. |
| A | +3 | 149 | I respect the counselor. |
| A | −4 | 150 | I say what I think the counselor wants to hear. |
| A | −4 | 151 | I pretend one thing to the counselor but feel another. |
| A | +2 | 152 | I let the counselor know how I feel toward him. |
| A | −2 | 153 | I irritate the counselor. |
| A | −3 | 154 | I wait for the counselor to take the initiative. |
| A | −2 | 155 | I try to please the counselor. |
| A | −2 | 156 | I try to influence the counselor. |
| A | −2 | 157 | I misunderstand the counselor. |
| A | −3 | 158 | I bore the counselor. |
| | NS | 159 | With the counselor I behave the same way from one interview to the next. |
| A | −2 | 160 | I consider myself superior to the counselor. |
| A | −3 | 161 | The counselor considers himself superior to me. |
| A | −2 | 162 | I am easily influenced by the counselor. |
| A | +4 | 163 | I trust the counselor. |
| A | −2 | 164 | I am apologetic with the counselor. |
| A | −3 | 165 | I do what I think the counselor wants me to do. |
| A | −2 | 166 | I confide too much in the counselor, I feel. |
| A | −4 | 167 | I see no reason to trust the counselor with my very personal confidences. |

## SCHEDULE M. CLASSIFICATION INVENTORY: MOTIVATION TO CHANGE SELF THROUGH COUNSELING

This inventory consists of numbered statements. Read each statement and decide whether it is *true as applied to you*, or *false as applied to you*. You are to mark your answers on the answer sheet you have. If a statement is TRUE or MOSTLY TRUE, as applied to you, blacken between the lines in the column headed T. If a statement is FALSE or NOT USUALLY TRUE as applied to you, blacken between the lines in the column headed F.

Remember to give YOUR OWN opinion of yourself. *Do not leave any blank spaces if you can avoid it.*

In marking your answers on the answer sheet, be sure that the number of the statement agrees with the number on the answer sheet. *Make your marks heavy and black.* Erase completely any answer you wish to change. Do not make any marks on the booklet. Be sure you make your marks with the special pencil given you. Keep your pencil off the answer sheet except when marking your answers.

Remember, try to make some answer to every statement. *Work as fast as you can.* Turn over the page and go ahead.

| Key | Item No. | Item |
|---|---|---|
| T | 1 | A person should try to understand his dreams and be guided by or take warning from them. |
| T | 2 | I work under a great deal of tension. |
| T | 3 | I am sure I get a raw deal from life. |
| T | 4 | No one seems to understand me. |
| T | 5 | Evil spirits possess me at times. |
| T | 6 | I find it hard to keep my mind on a task or job. |
| F | 7 | I seldom worry about my health. |
| T | 8 | Much of the time my head seems to hurt all over. |
| F | 9 | I have had no difficulty in starting or holding my bowel movement. |
| T | 10 | I am an important person. |
| T | 11 | Most of the time I feel blue. |
| T | 12 | I enjoy reading love stories. |
| T | 13 | I like poetry. |
| T | 14 | I sometimes feel that I am about to go to pieces. |
| F | 15 | Any man who is able and willing to work hard has a good chance of succeeding. |
| F | 16 | I usually feel that life is worth while. |
| T | 17 | I have met problems so full of possibilities that I have been unable to make up my mind about them. |
| T | 18 | My hardest battles are with myself. |
| T | 19 | I don't seem to care what happens to me. |
| T | 20 | I like collecting flowers or growing house plants. |
| T | 21 | Criticism or scolding hurts me terribly. |
| T | 22 | Sometimes I feel as if I must injure either myself or someone else. |
| T | 23 | I have had periods in which I carried on activities without knowing later what I had been doing. |
| F | 24 | I have never felt better in my life than I do now. |
| T | 25 | I am afraid when I look down from a high place. |
| T | 26 | There is something wrong with my mind. |
| F | 27 | When I get bored I like to stir up some excitement. |
| F | 28 | I like to visit places where I have never been before. |
| F | 29 | I daydream very little. |
| T | 30 | I wish I were not so shy. |
| F | 31 | I believe my sins are unpardonable. |
| F | 32 | At times I feel that I can make up my mind with unusually great ease. |
| F | 33 | I should like to belong to several clubs or lodges. |
| F | 34 | I have been inspired to a program of life based on duty which I have since carefully followed. |
| T | 35 | I brood a great deal. |

197

| Key | Item No. | Item |
|-----|----------|------|
| F | 36 | I believe there is a God. |
| T | 37 | I have often felt that strangers were looking at me critically. |
| T | 38 | Life is a strain for me much of the time. |
| T | 39 | I am more sensitive than most other people. |
| F | 40 | My daily life is full of things that keep me interested. |
| T | 41 | I find it hard to keep my mind on a task or job. |
| T | 42 | If people had not had it in for me, I would have been much more successful. |
| T | 43 | I cannot keep my mind on one thing. |
| F | 44 | I am afraid of using a knife or anything very sharp or pointed. |
| T | 45 | Sometimes I enjoy hurting persons I love. |
| T | 46 | I am more sensitive than most other people. |
| T | 47 | Even when I am with people I feel lonely much of the time. |
| F | 48 | I am not unusually self-conscious. |
| F | 49 | I very seldom have spells of the blues. |
| F | 50 | A windstorm terrifies me. |
| T | 51 | Often, even though everything is going fine for me, I feel that I don't care about anything. |
| F | 52 | I am usually calm and not easily upset. |
| T | 53 | I am apt to take disappointments so keenly that I can't put them out of my mind. |
| F | 54 | I have felt embarrassed over the type of work that one or more members of my family have done. |
| T | 55 | I like to attend lectures on serious subjects. |
| T | 56 | I used to have imaginary companions. |
| F | 57 | I enjoy social gatherings just to be with people. |
| F | 58 | I enjoy the excitement of a crowd. |
| F | 59 | I believe that a person should never taste an alcoholic drink. |
| T | 60 | I have used alcohol moderately (or not at all). |
| F | 61 | I have had no difficulty starting or holding my urine. |
| F | 62 | Except by a doctor's orders I never take drugs or sleeping powders. |
| F | 63 | I do not mind meeting strangers. |
| T | 64 | I have no patience with people who believe there is only one true religion. |
| F | 65 | I am afraid of finding myself in a closet or small closed place. |
| F | 66 | I enjoy stories of adventure. |
| T | 67 | I sometimes find it hard to stick up for my rights because I am so reserved. |
| T | 68 | People can pretty easily change me even though I thought that my mind was already made up on a subject. |
| F | 69 | Sometimes I have the same dream over and over. |
| T | 70 | I shrink from facing a crisis or difficulty. |

198

# References

Allport, G. W., and H. S. Odbert. Traitnames: a psycho-lexical study. *Psychol. Monogr.*, 1936, *47*, No. 1 (Whole No. 211).

American Psychological Association. Technical recommendations for psychological tests and diagnostic techniques. *Psychol. Bull., Suppl.*, 1954, *51*, Part 2, 1–38.

Ashby, J. D., D. H. Ford, B. G. Guerney Jr., and Louise F. Guerney. Effects on clients of a reflective and a leading type of psychotherapy. *Psychol. Monogr.*, 1957, *71*, No. 24 (Whole No. 453).

Barron, F. An ego-strength scale which predicts response to psychotherapy. *J. consult. Psychol.*, 1953, *17*, 327–333.

Bendig, A. W. An analysis of the manifest anxiety scale. Univer. of Pittsburgh, 1953. Mimeo.

Berdie, R. F. Counseling — an educational technique. *Educ. psychol. Measmt.*, 1949, *9*, 89–94.

Berdie, R. F. Counseling. *Annu. Rev. Psychol.*, 1959, *10*, 345–370.

Bergman, P. A general theory of psychotherapy. Paper read at Amer. Psychol. Assoc., Cincinnati, September 1959.

Bergmann, G. Psychoanalysis and experimental psychology: a review from the standpoint of scientific empiricism. *Mind*, 1943, *52*, 122–140. Also reprinted in M. Marx (Ed.), *Psychological theory*. New York: Macmillan, 1951. Pp. 352–370.

Bordin, E. S. Ambiguity as a therapeutic variable. *J. consult. Psychol.*, 1955, *19*, 9–15. (a)

Bordin, E. S. *Psychological counseling*. New York: Appleton-Century-Crofts, 1955. (b)

Brayfield, A. H. Performance is the thing. *J. counsel. Psychol.*, 1962, *9*, 3.

Bridgman, P. W. *The logic of modern physics*. New York: Macmillan, 1927. Pp. 1–25. Also reprinted in H. Feigl and May Brodbeck (Eds.) *Readings in the philosophy of science*. New York: Appleton-Century-Crofts, 1953. Pp. 34–46.

Campbell, D. T., and D. W. Fiske. Convergent and discriminant validation by the multitrait-multimethod matrix. *Psychol. Bull.*, 1959, *56*, 81–105.

Carnap, R. Testability and meaning. *Phil. of Sci.*, 1936, *3*, 420–471, and 1937, *4*, 2–40. Parts reprinted in H. Feigl and May Brodbeck (Eds.) *Readings in the philosophy of science*. New York: Appleton-Century-Crofts, 1953. Pp. 47–92.

Carnap, R. *Foundations of logic and mathematics*. Vol. I, No. 3 of the *International encyclopedia of unified science*. Chicago: Univer. of Chicago Press, 1939.

199

Pp. 56–69. A part (the interpretation of physics) is reprinted in H. Feigl and May Brodbeck (Eds.) *Readings in the philosophy of science.* New York: Appleton-Century-Crofts, 1953. Pp. 309–318.

Carnap, R. The methodological character of theoretical concepts. In H. Feigl and M. Scriven (Eds.) *Minnesota studies in the philosophy of science. Vol. I: The foundations of science and the concepts of psychology and psychoanalysis.* Minneapolis: Univer. of Minnesota Press, 1956. Pp. 38–76.

Carnes, E. F., and F. P. Robinson. The role of client talk in the counseling interview. *Educ. psychol. Measmt.,* 1948, *8,* 635–644.

Cartwright, D. S. Self-consistency as a factor affecting immediate recall. *J. abnorm. soc. Psychol.,* 1956, *52,* 212–218.

Chodorkoff, B. Self-perception, perceptual defense, and adjustment. *J. abnorm. soc. Psychol.,* 1954, *49,* 508–512.

Clark, K. E., and Helen H. Gee. Selecting items for interest inventory keys. *J. appl. Psychol.,* 1954, *38,* 12–17.

Cochran, W. G., and Gertrude M. Cox. *Experimental designs.* (2nd Ed.) New York: Wiley, 1957.

Coleman, J. V. Patient-physician relationship in psychotherapy. *Am. J. Psychiat.,* 1948, *104,* 638–641.

Cowen, E. L. The influence of varying degrees of psychological stress on problem solving rigidity. *J. abnorm. soc. Psychol.,* 1952, *47,* 512–519.

Cowen, E. L., F. Heilizer, H. S. Axelrod, and S. Alexander. The correlates of manifest anxiety in perceptual reactivity, rigidity, and self concept. *J. consult. Psychol.,* 1957, *21,* 405–411.

Cronbach, L. J. Response sets and test validity. *Educ. psychol. Measmt.,* 1946, *6,* 475–494.

Cronbach, L. J. Further evidence on response sets and test design. *Educ. psychol. Measmt.,* 1950, *10,* 3–31.

Cronbach, L. J. Coefficient alpha and the internal structure of tests. *Psychometrika,* 1951, *16,* 297–334.

Cronbach, L. J. Assessment of individual differences. *Annu. Rev. Psychol.,* 1956, *7,* 173–196.

Cronbach, L. J., and P. E. Meehl. Construct validity in psychological tests. *Psychol. Bull.,* 1955, *52,* 281–302. Also reprinted with minor alterations in H. Feigl and M. Scriven (Eds.) *Minnesota studies in the philosophy of science. Vol. I: The foundations of science and the concepts of psychology and psychoanalysis.* Minneapolis: Univer. of Minnesota Press, 1956. Pp. 174–204.

Dahlstrom, W. G., and G. S. Welsh. *An MMPI handbook.* Minneapolis: Univer. of Minnesota Press, 1960.

Davis, A. Socialization and adolescent personality. In T. M. Newcomb and E. L. Hartley (Eds.) *Readings in social psychology.* New York: Holt, 1947. Pp. 139–150.

Dittmann, A. T., and H. L. Raush. The psychoanalytic theory of conflict: structure and methodology. *Psychol. Rev.,* 1954, *61,* 386–400.

Dressel, P. L. Evaluation of counseling. In R. F. Berdie (Ed.) *Concepts and programs of counseling.* Minneapolis: Univer. of Minnesota Press, 1951. Pp. 70–81.

Dressel, P. L. Some approaches to evaluation. *Personnel Guid. J.,* 1953, *31,* 284–287.

Dollard, J., and N. E. Miller. *Personality and psychotherapy.* New York: McGraw-Hill, 1950.

Duncker, K. On problem-solving. *Psychol. monogr.,* 1945, *58,* No. 5 (Whole No. 270).

Dymond, Rosalind F. Adjustment changes over therapy from self-sorts. In C. R.

Rogers and Rosalind F. Dymond (Eds.) *Psychotherapy and personality change.* Chicago: Univer. of Chicago Press, 1954. Pp. 76–84.

Edwards, A. L., and F. P. Kilpatrick. A technique for the construction of attitude scales. *J. appl. Psychol.*, 1948, *32*, 374–384.

Ellis, A. New approaches to psychotherapy techniques. *J. clin. Psychol.*, 1955, *11*, 208–260.

Eysenck, H. J. The effects of psychotherapy: an evaluation. *J. consult. Psychol.*, 1952, *16*, 319–324.

Fattu, N. A., E. Kapos, and E. V. Mech. Problem solving: a statistical description of some relationships between organismic factors and selected response measures. *Genet. Psychol. Monogr.*, 1954, *50*, 141–185.

Feigl, H. Operationism and scientific method. *Psychol. Rev.*, 1945, *52*, 250–259. Reprinted with some alterations in H. Feigl and W. Sellars (Eds.) *Readings in philosophical analysis.* New York: Appleton-Century-Crofts, 1949. Pp. 498–509.

Feigl, H., and M. Scriven. (Eds.) *The foundations of science and the concepts of psychology and psychoanalysis. Vol. I: Minnesota studies in the philosophy of science.* Minneapolis: Univer. of Minnesota Press, 1956.

Fenichel, O. *The psychoanalytic theory of neurosis.* New York: Norton, 1945.

Fisher, R. A. *Statistical methods for research workers.* Edinburgh: Oliver and Boyd, 1925.

Fisher, R. A. *The design of experiments.* Edinburgh: Oliver and Boyd, 1935.

Freeman, M. J. The development of a test for the measurement of anxiety: a study of its reliability and validity. *Psychol. Monogr.*, 1953, *67*, No. 3 (Whole No. 353).

Freud, Anna. *The ego and the mechanisms of defence.* New York: International Universities Press, 1946.

Gaier, E. L. Selected personality variables and the learning process. *Psychol. Monogr.*, 1952, *66*, No. 17 (Whole No. 349).

Grant, J. D., and Marguerite Q. Grant. "Therapy readiness" as a research variable. *J. consult. Psychol.*, 1950, *14*, 156–157.

Grayson, H. M., and Ruth S. Tolman. A semantic study of concepts of clinical psychologists and psychiatrists. *J. abnorm. soc. Psychol.*, 1950, *45*, 216–231.

Guilford, J. P. Factors in problem solving. Paper read at Western Psychol. Assoc., Long Beach, May 1954. (a)

Guilford, J. P. *Psychometric methods.* (2nd Ed.) New York: McGraw-Hill, 1954. (b)

Haigh, G. Defensive behavior in client-centered therapy. *J. consult. Psychol.*, 1949, *13*, 181–189.

Harlow, H. F. The formation of learning sets. *Psychol. Rev.*, 1949, *56*, 51–65.

Hathaway, S. R. Some considerations relative to nondirective counseling as therapy. *J. clin. Psychol.*, 1948, *4*, 226–231.

Hempel, C. G. Problems and changes in the empiricist criterion of meaning. *Revue internationale de philosophie*, 1950, *4*, 41–63. Reprinted in L. Linsky (Ed.) *Semantics and the philosophy of language.* Urbana: Univer. of Illinois Press, 1952. Pp. 163–185.

Hempel, C. G. *Fundamentals of concept formation in empirical science.* Vol. II, No. 7, of the *International encyclopedia of unified science.* Chicago: Univer. of Chicago Press, 1952.

Hempel, C. G. A logical appraisal of operationism. *Scientific Monthly*, 1954, *79*, 215–220.

Hilgard, E. R., L. V. Jones, and S. J. Kaplan. Conditional discrimination as related to anxiety. *J. exper. Psychol.*, 1951, *42*, 94–99.

Hillson, J. S., and P. Worchel. Self concept and defensive behavior in the maladjusted. *J. consult. Psychol.*, 1957, *21*, 83–88.

Hogan, R. A. The development of a measure of client defensiveness in a counseling relationship. Unpublished doctor's dissertation, Univer. of Chicago, 1948.

Hogan, R. A. A measure of client defensiveness. In W. Wolff and J. A. Precker (Eds.) *Success in psychotherapy*. New York: Grune and Stratton, 1952. Pp. 112–142. (a)

Hogan, R. A. A theory of threat and defense. *J. consult. Psychol.*, 1952, *16*, 417–424. (b)

Hoyt, C. J. Test reliability estimated by analysis of variance. *Psychometrika*, 1941, *6*, 153–160.

Hoyt, D. P. Differential outcomes of counseling with college men. Unpublished doctor's dissertation, Univer. of Minnesota, 1954.

Hoyt, D. P., and T. M. Magoon. A validation study of the Taylor Manifest Anxiety Scale. *J. clin. Psychol.*, 1954, *10*, 357–361.

Jahoda, Marie. *Current concepts of positive mental health*. New York: Basic Books, 1958.

Jesness, C. F. The effects of counseling on the self-perception of college men. Unpublished doctor's dissertation, Univer. of Minnesota, 1955.

Jewell, W. O. Differential judgments of manifest anxiety, defensiveness, and effective problem solving in counseling. Unpublished doctor's dissertation, Univer. of Minnesota, 1958.

Johnson, P. O. *Statistical methods in research*. New York: Prentice-Hall, 1949.

Johnson, W. *People in quandaries*. New York: Harper, 1946.

Kelly, G. A. The theory and technique of assessment. *Annu. Rev. Psychol.*, 1958, *9*, 323–352.

Kelman, H. C., and M. B. Parloff. Interrelations among three criteria of improvement in group therapy: comfort, effectiveness, and self-awareness. *J. abnorm. soc. Psychol.*, 1957, *54*, 281–288.

Lacey, J. I. Psychophysiological approaches to the evaluation of psychotherapeutic process and outcome. In E. A. Rubinstein and M. B. Parloff (Eds.) *Research in psychotherapy*. Washington, D.C.: American Psychological Association, 1959. Pp. 160–208.

Libo, L. M. The projective expression of patient-therapist attraction. *J. clin. Psychol.*, 1957, *13*, 33–36.

Lindquist, E. F. *Design and analysis of experiments in psychology and education*. Boston: Houghton Mifflin, 1953.

Lindsley, O. R. Free operant conditioning, persuasion and psychotherapy. Paper read at Amer. Psychiat. Assoc., Chicago, May 1961.

Luborsky, L. Psychotherapy. *Annu. Rev. Psychol.*, 1959, *10*, 317–344.

Luchins, A. S. Mechanization in problem solving: the effect of einstellung. *Psychol. Monogr.*, 1942, *54*, No. 6 (Whole No. 248).

MacCorquodale, K., and P. E. Meehl. On a distinction between hypothetical constructs and intervening variables. *Psychol. Rev.*, 1948, *55*, 95–107. Also reprinted in H. Feigl and May Brodbeck (Eds.) *Readings in the philosophy of science*. New York: Appleton-Century-Crofts, 1953. Pp. 596–611.

Magoon, T. M. Assessment of general and specific outcomes of counseling with college men. Unpublished doctor's dissertation, Univer. of Minnesota, 1954.

Maier, N. R. F. Reasoning in humans, I. on direction. *J. comp. Psychol.*, 1930, *10*, 115–143.

Marks, M. R. Problem solving as a function of the situation. *J. exper. Psychol.*, 1951, *41*, 74–80.

Maslow, A. H. A suggested improvement in semantic usage. *Psychol. Rev.*, 1945, *52*, 239–240.

May, R. *The meaning of anxiety*. New York: Ronald Press, 1950.

McGowan, J. F. Client anticipation and expectancies as related to initial interview performance and perception. Unpublished Ed. D. dissertation, Univer. of Missouri, 1954.

Meehl, P. E. *Clinical versus statistical prediction.* Minneapolis: Univer. of Minnesota Press, 1954.

Meehl, P. E. Psychotherapy. *Annu. Rev. Psychol.,* 1955, *6,* 357–378.

Mensh, I. N., and R. I. Watson. Psychiatric opinions on personality factors in psychotherapy. *J. clin. Psychol.,* 1950, *6,* 237–242.

Miller, J. G. Toward a general theory for the behavioral sciences. *Amer. Psychologist,* 1955, *10,* 513–531.

Mowrer, O. H. Anxiety theory as a basis for distinguishing between counseling and psychotherapy. In R. F. Berdie (Ed.) *Concepts and programs of counseling.* Minneapolis: Univer. of Minnesota Press, 1951. Pp. 7–26.

Mowrer, O. H. Neuroses and psychotherapy as interpersonal processes: a synopsis. In O. H. Mowrer (Ed.) *Psychotherapy: theory and research.* New York: Ronald Press, 1953. Pp. 69–94.

Mowrer, O. H. The unconscious, conscious, and repression: a reconsideration. Paper read at Amer. Personnel and Guidance Assoc., St. Louis, April 1958.

Mowrer, O. H., B. H. Light, Zella Luria, and Marjorie P. Zeleny. Tension changes during psychotherapy, with special reference to resistance. In O. H. Mowrer (Ed.) *Psychotherapy: theory and research.* New York: Ronald Press, 1953. Pp. 546–640.

Mowrer, O. H., and A. D. Ullman. Time as a determinant in integrative learning. *Psychol. Rev.,* 1945, *52,* 61–90.

Murray, E. J. A case study in a behavioral analysis of psychotherapy. *J. abnorm. soc. Psychol.,* 1954, *49,* 305–310.

Nakamura, C. Y. Measures of over-controlled and under-controlled behavior: their implications for assessment of psychotherapy. Paper read at Amer. Psychol. Assoc., Cincinnati, September 1959.

Norton, D. W. An empirical investigation of some effects of non-normality and heterogeneity on the F-distribution. Unpublished doctor's dissertation, State Univer. of Iowa, 1952. Also reported in E. F. Lindquist, *Design and analysis of experiments in psychology and education.* Boston: Houghton Mifflin, 1953. Pp. 78–90.

OSS Assessment Staff. *Assessment of men.* New York: Rinehart, 1948.

Parloff, M. B., H. C. Kelman, and J. D. Frank. Comfort, effectiveness and self-awareness as criteria of improvement in psychotherapy. *Amer. J. Psychiat.,* 1954, *111,* 343–352.

Pepinsky, H. B. Counseling methods: therapy. *Annu. Rev. Psychol.,* 1951, 2, 317–334.

Pepinsky, H. B. Some proposals for research. *Personnel Guid. J.,* 1953, *31,* 291–294.

Pepinsky, H. B., and Pauline N. Pepinsky. *Counseling: theory and practice.* New York: Ronald Press, 1954.

Perry, W. G. Jr., and S. G. Estes. The collaboration of client and counselor. In O. H. Mowrer (Ed.) *Psychotherapy: theory and research.* New York: Ronald Press, 1953. Pp. 95–119.

Phillips, E. L. *Psychotherapy; a modern theory and practice.* Englewood Cliffs, N. J.: Prentice-Hall, 1956.

Raimy, V. C. Self reference in counseling interviews. *J. consult. Psychol.,* 1948, *12,* 153–163.

Rao, C. R. *Advanced statistical methods in biometric research.* New York: Wiley, 1952.

Raskin, N. J. An analysis of six parallel studies of the therapeutic process. *J. consult. Psychol.,* 1949, *13,* 206–220.

Robinson, F. P. *Principles and procedures in student counseling.* New York: Harper, 1950.

Rogers, C. R. *Client-centered therapy.* Boston: Houghton Mifflin, 1951.

Rogers, C. R., and Rosalind F. Dymond (Eds.) *Psychotherapy and personality change.* Chicago: Univer. of Chicago Press, 1954.

Rosen, E. Self-appraisal and perceived desirability of MMPI personality traits. *J. counsel. Psychol.*, 1956, *3*, 44–51.

Rosenzweig, S. A transvaluation of psychotherapy — a reply to Hans Eysenck. *J. abnorm. soc. Psychol.*, 1954, *49*, 298–304.

Rozeboom, W. W. Mediation variables in scientific theory. *Psychol. Rev.*, 1956, *63*, 249–264.

Rubinstein, E. A., and M. B. Parloff (Eds.) *Research in psychotherapy.* Washington, D.C.: American Psychological Association, 1959.

Sanford, N. Clinical methods: psychotherapy. *Annu. Rev. Psychol.*, 1953, *4*, 317–342.

Sarason, I. G. The relationship of anxiety and "lack of defensiveness" to intellectual performance. *J. consult. Psychol.*, 1956, *20*, 220–222.

Sarason, S. B. *The clinical interaction.* New York: Harper, 1954.

Sarason, S. B., and E. M. Gordon. The relationship between 'test anxieties' and 'other anxieties.' Paper read at Eastern Psychol. Assoc., Boston, April 1953.

Scheffé, H. *The analysis of variance.* New York: Wiley, 1959.

Scriven, M. A study of radical behaviorism. In H. Feigl and M. Scriven (Eds.) *Minnesota studies in the philosophy of science. Vol. I: The foundations of science and the concepts of psychology and psychoanalysis.* Minneapolis: Univer. of Minnesota Press, 1956. Pp. 88–130.

Seeman, J. A study of the process of nondirective therapy. *J. consult. Psychol.*, 1949, *13*, 157–168.

Shaw, F. J. *Mutuality and up-ending expectancies in counseling. J. counsel. Psychol.*, 1955, *2*, 241–247.

Shaw, F. J. Counseling. *Annu. Rev. Psychol.*, 1957, *8*, 357–376.

Sheerer, Elizabeth T. An analysis of the relationship between acceptance of and respect for self and acceptance of and respect for others in ten counseling cases. *J. consult. Psychol.*, 1949, *13*, 169–175.

Shoben, E. J. Jr. A theoretical approach to psychotherapy as personality modification. *Harv. educ. Rev.*, 1953, *23*, 128–142. (a)

Shoben, E. J. Jr. Some problems in establishing criteria of effectiveness. *Personnel Guid. J.*, 1953, *31*, 287–291. (b)

Shoben, E. J. Jr. Some observations on psychotherapy and the learning process. In O. H. Mowrer (Ed.) *Psychotherapy: theory and research.* New York: Ronald Press, 1953. Pp. 120–139. (c)

Skinner, B. F. The behavior of organisms. New York: Appleton-Century, 1938.

Skinner, B. F. Are theories of learning necessary? *Psychol. Rev.*, 1950, *57*, 193–216.

Skinner, B. F. *Science and human behavior.* New York: Macmillan, 1953.

Smith, M. B. Optima of mental health. *Psychiat.*, 1950, *13*, 503–510.

Snyder, W. U. An investigation of the nature of non-directive psychotherapy. *J. gen. Psychol.*, 1945, *33*, 193–223.

Snyder, W. U. Psychotherapy. *Annu. Rev. Psychol.*, 1958, *9*, 353–374.

Snyder, W. U. Comment on changes in self and other perceptions following brief educational-vocational counseling. *J. counsel. Psychol.*, 1962, *9*, 29–30.

Spiker, C. C., and B. R. McCandless. The concept of intelligence and the philosophy of science. *Psychol. Rev.*, 1954, *61*, 255–266.

Stock, Dorothy. An investigation into the interrelations between the self concept and feelings directed toward other persons and groups. *J. consult. Psychol.*, 1949, *13*, 176–180.

Symonds, P. *The dynamics of human adjustment*. New York: Appleton-Century, 1946.

Taylor, Janet A. The relationship of anxiety to the conditioned eyelid response. *J. exp. Psychol.*, 1951, *41*, 81–92.

Taylor, Janet A. A personality scale of manifest anxiety. *J. abnorm. soc. Psychol.*, 1953, *48*, 285–290.

Taylor, Janet A. Drive theory and manifest anxiety. *Psychol. Bull.*, 1956, *53*, 303–320.

Thistlethwaite, D. Attitude and structure as factors in the distortion of reasoning. *J. abnorm. soc. Psychol.*, 1950, *45*, 442–458.

Thorne, F. C. Directive psychotherapy: VII. Imparting psychological information. *J. clin. Psychol.*, 1946, *2*, 179–190.

Thorne, F. C. Directive psychotherapy: theory, practice and social implications. *J. clin. Psychol.*, 1953, *9*, 267–280.

Travers, R. M. W. A critical review of techniques for evaluating guidance. *Educ. psychol. Measmt.*, 1949, *9*, 211–225.

Tyler, Leona E. Counseling. *Annu. Rev. Psychol.*, 1958, *9*, 375–390.

Vosbeck, Phyllis D. An exploratory study of the effects of counseling. Unpublished master's thesis, Univer. of Minnesota, 1959.

Walker, D. E., and H. C. Peiffer Jr. The goals of counseling. *J. counsel. Psychol.*, 1957, *4*, 204–209.

Weitz, H. Semantics in diagnosis. *J. counsel. Psychol.*, 1954, *1*, 70–73.

Weitz, H. Counseling as a function of the counselor's personality. *Personnel Guid. J.*, 1957, *35*, 276–280.

White, R. W. *Lives in progress*. New York: Dryden Press, 1952. (Now published by Holt, Rinehart and Winston.)

Whitehorn, J. C. Goals of psychotherapy. In E. A. Rubinstein and M. B. Parloff (Eds.) *Research in psychotherapy*. Washington, D.C.: American Psychological Association, 1959. Pp. 1–9.

Wiener, D. N. Subtle and obvious keys for the Minnesota Multiphasic Personality Inventory. *J. consult. Psychol.*, 1948, *12*, 164–170. (a)

Wiener, D. N. The subtle-obvious factor in vocational and educational success. *Amer. Psychologist*, 1948, *3*, 299. (b)

Williams, J. E. Changes in self and other perceptions following brief educational-vocational counseling. *J. counsel. Psychol.*, 1962, *9*, 18–28.

Williamson, E. G. A concept of counseling. *Occupations*, 1950, *29*, 182–189. (a)

Williamson, E. G. *Counseling adolescents*. New York: McGraw-Hill, 1950. (b)

Williamson, E. G., and E. S. Bordin. Evaluating counseling by means of a control-group experiment. *School and Soc.*, 1940, *52*, 434–440.

Williamson, E. G., and E. S. Bordin. The evaluation of vocational and educational counseling: a critique of the methodology of experiments. *Educ. psychol. Measmt.*, 1941, *1*, 5–24.

Winder, C. L. Psychotherapy. *Annu. Rev. Psychol.*, 1957, *8*, 309–330.

Winer, B. *Statistical principles in experimental design*. New York: McGraw-Hill, 1962.

Worchel, P. A critique of current trends in psychotherapy research. *J. counsel. Psychol.*, 1955, *2*, 297–303.

Wrenn, C. G. *Student personnel work in college*. New York: Ronald Press, 1951.

Wrenn, C. G., and C. A. Parker. Counseling theory. In C. W. Harris (Ed.) *Encyclopedia of educational research*. (3rd Ed.) New York: Macmillan, 1960. Pp. 341–350.

Zubin, J., and C. Windle. Psychological prognosis of outcome in the mental disorders. *J. abnorm. soc. Psychol.*, 1954, *49*, 272–281.

# Index

206